# Mademoiselle Libertine

## A Portrait of Ninon de Lanclos

NINON DE LANCLOS
After a painting attributed to Pierre Mignard.
(*Brussels Museum*)

# *Mademoiselle* ~ *Libertine* ~

### *A Portrait of Ninon de Lanclos*

*by*

### Edgar H. Cohen

### Houghton Mifflin Company
### 19 BOSTON 70

First Printing  w

Library of Congress Catalog Card Number: 71–120824
Printed in the United States of America

*To my wife Ruth*

The Frenchwoman whose independence seems . . . the most like that of a man is perhaps Ninon de Lanclos, seventeenth-century woman of wit and beauty. Paradoxically, those women who exploit their femininity to the limit create for themselves a situation almost equivalent to that of a man . . . Free in behavior and conversation, they can attain — like Ninon de Lanclos — to the rarest intellectual liberty. The most distinguished are often surrounded by writers and artists who are bored by "good" women.

Simone de Beauvoir
in *The Second Sex*

# Author's Note

To KNOW NINON DE LANCLOS, a byword in France for feminine fascination, we cannot go to her writings. Her known literary output comprises just a few, not particularly revealing, pages of satire and three or four deftly written poems consisting of one stanza each. She kept no diary. As to her letters, which *are* revealing, the extant ones number only about a score and a half, are mostly very short, and date almost exclusively from the evening of her long life. Her life resists a year-by-year approach. Delve as we may, scarcity of detail tends to make Ninon a somewhat elusive figure — at least in the first half of her life.

Apart from public records and notaries' files — which are scanty and seldom provide insights into character — it is only by her friends — the most distinguished and colorful people of the Splendid Century — that we can try to understand her. History has often been lamentably laconic in its frequent but brief recording of Ninon's encounters with the bright lights of the reigns of Louis XIII and Louis XIV. Sometimes a chronicler devotes but a paragraph or even a line to an incident. Sometimes it is only a flash of wit — with the context missing. Thus to get perspective on Ninon, we must have some knowledge of her circle and the moral, intellectual, and social climate which was its backdrop. Many of the names may be new. To aid in keeping straight the essential facts about possibly unfamiliar people, I have inserted in the front of the book a list of Principal Persons, arranged alphabetically. A few lines about each should serve to identify the particular person. There is also a Chronology.

In addition to presenting to the English reader a full-scale portrait of a great woman in a great century, the aim of this book is to point up Ninon's place as a significant figure in the progressive forces which assisted at the birth of modern man and modern woman. Ninon was of course superb in the boudoir, and neither this nor any other biography of her should fail to give la belle galanterie and her radiant femaleness their due. But concurrently this biography will highlight, instead of neglect, her role as a seventeenth-century link between the free inquiring spirit of the Renaissance and that of the Enlightenment.

For source material my thanks are due primarily to the Bibliothèque Nationale and other French libraries and to the McGill University library whose former librarian, Mr. Richard Pennington, and former assistant librarian, Miss Beatrice Simon, and their staff went beyond the call of duty in being helpful. I am deeply indebted to the late marquise de Villefranche, owner of the château of Villarceaux, who generously allowed me to inspect it. I am most grateful to M. Henri Koch, directeur des études, Banque de France, for aid in estimating the modern equivalent of seventeenth-century French currency, and to Professor Jean Fabre of the Sorbonne for guidance on French libertinism. My special thanks go to Professor Morton W. Bloomfield, chairman of the department of English at Harvard, whose keenness of mind and erudition were of inestimable value to me.

Translations, except when otherwise noted, are mine. In this connection I would thank Mrs. Edda Greenstein, who has checked some of the more difficult passages, particularly in poems. French poetry has presented somewhat of a problem. As much of the charm and all of the music is lost in an un-rhymed, unmetrical translation, I would like to have quoted the original in all cases for those who know French, followed by the English translation for those who do not. This would, however, have added considerably to the bulk of the text, and I have, therefore, had to omit the French in most cases, keeping — for flavor — only a few poems in the original.

A word about the modern equivalent of seventeenth-century currency. Economists agree that an accurate equivalent is not ascertainable, but an approximation *is* possible. When Cardinal Richelieu is alleged to have offered Ninon 150,000 livres to become his mistress — an offer she is said to have turned down — the reader legitimately wants to know whether this was a great deal of money or not. Research suggests that the seven-teenth-century livre was worth between $2.00 and $5.00 (U.S.) on the basis of today's prices. Thus the alleged offer had a modern equivalent of somewhere between $300,000 and $750,-000. The latitude is wide but we do get an answer — the offer represented a great deal of money. Throughout the book I have always quoted two figures — an upper and a lower limit.

This biographical portrait is drawn solely from the known facts of Ninon's life. No dialogue or incident is created nor liaisons imagined. When quotation marks are used, the words enclosed are actual quotations.

# Contents

# Principal Persons

*Aubigné, Françoise d':* See Maintenon, Madame de

*Aubijoux, comte de:* Ninon's second payeur. Elegant

*Boisrobert, abbé:* Founder of Académie française. Richelieu's literary factotum. Wit. Adored Ninon in asexual way.

*Bonrepaus:* Minister of Marine who befriended Ninon's son, La Boissière

*Bussy-Rabutin:* Author of *Histoire amoureuse des Gaules.* Cousin and and would-be lover of Madame de Sévigné

*Champmeslé, Mademoiselle de:* Leading actress, mistress of Racine and Charles de Sévigné. Ninon took Sévigné from her, though Champmeslé was nineteen years younger

*Chapelle:* Esteemed poet, great friend of Molière's whom Ninon banished because of his drunkenness

*Charleval:* Delicate poet who unsuccessfully wooed Ninon. A faithful, charming friend for most of her life. One of trio (with Miossens and d'Elbène) who made Ninon libertine

*Châteauneuf, abbé de:* Admirer and alleged lover of Ninon in her latter years. Brought Voltaire to see her. Wrote one of her epitaphs

*Christina, ex-Queen of Sweden:* One of most learned women of her time. Secured Ninon's release from convent at Lagny

*Coligny:* Descendant of great Huguenot, Admiral Coligny. Abjured Protestantism to win his way into Marion's bed. First man Ninon really loved. Did not reciprocate; disillusioned her and caused her to forswear marriage. Brother of Ninon's friend Henriette, comtesse de La Suze

*Condé, the Great:* While his father lived, known as duc d'Enghien. With marshal Turenne, shared top military honors of the century. Cousin of Louis XIII

*Coulon:* Ninon's first payeur. Unsavory

*Des Barreaux:* Marion de l'Orme's first and perhaps deepest love. Extremely handsome. One of the poets in Ninon's circle.

*Elbène, d':* Unselfish friend of Scarron. Squandered a great fortune, had to borrow from Saint-Evremond, and could not repay him. Ninon intervened and paid half of d'Elbène's debt to Saint-Evremond, but misunderstanding resulted in temporary, painful estrangement of Ninon from Saint-Evremond. See Charleval

*Emery, D':* Thieving superintendent of finance. Footed Marion de l'Orme's colossal bills

*Enghien, duc d':* See Condé

*Gassendi:* A liberal priest, scientist, and distinguished philosopher devoted to Montaigne and Epicurus. As teacher of several of Ninon's friends, had great influence on her. Great philosophical opponent of Descartes, though both believed in Reason and the scientific method. Along with Naudé and La Mothe Le Vayer, constituted the libertin trio sometimes called the "Three Wise Men"

*Gouges, Lucrèce de:* Wife of Riberolles. Was Henri de Lanclos's mistress

*Gourville:* Involved in fall of Fouquet. Fled leaving half his fortune with Ninon, the other half with a prelate

*Huygens, Christiaan:* Distinguished Dutch astronomer and mathematician. Composed poem in praise of Ninon's anatomy

*Lacger, Hercule de:* Unsuccessful wooer of Ninon who wrote a desperate but unavailing poem

*La Boissière, chevalier de:* Ninon's son by Villarceaux

*La Sablière, Madame de:* Ninon's protégée and friend whom Ninon tried unsuccessfully to help in her unhappy love for the marquis de La Fare

*La Sablière, Rambouillet de:* One of Ninon's three-month caprices. Unfaithful husband of Ninon's good friend Madame de La Sablière

*La Suze, Madame de:* Née Henriette de Coligny. Sister of Ninon's first love, Coligny. Wrote poem on Ninon's falling asleep at ball

*L'Orme, Marion de:* Exquisitely beautiful courtesan. Lovers included Des Barreaux, Cardinal Richelieu, Coligny, Miossens, D'Emery, probably Scarron, and perhaps Saint-Evremond and Condé. Died at thirty-nine in 1650. Introduced Ninon to society

*Maintenon, Madame de:* Née Françoise d'Aubigné, a Protestant. Forcibly converted to Catholicism. Met and admired Ninon at home of Scarron, whom she married; probably had affair with Villarceaux after Ninon and he were no longer lovers. Some twenty-three years after Scarron's death, married Louis XIV secretly. Unsuccessfully tried to get Ninon to come to Versailles to help her amuse the then morose Louis XIV

*Mazarin, duchesse:* Niece of Cardinal Mazarin. Fled from her crazed husband to Charles II of England in 1675. Intimate friend of Saint-Evremond in London

*Méré, chevalier de:* Quintessence of the honnête homme. Tutor of Françoise d'Aubigné, father of one of Ninon's children

*Miossens, comte de* (afterward maréchal d'Albret): cyclonic lover who overpowered, not persuaded, both Marion de l'Orme and Ninon. *See* Charleval

*Montespan, Madame de* (Athenaïs): Mistress of Louis XIV. Supplanted by Madame de Maintenon

*Navailles, comte de:* Blond officer who fell asleep in Ninon's bed and whom she rudely awoke next morning

*Raré:* Chronologically No. 2 on Ninon's list of lovers

*Riberolles:* Lucrèce de Gouges's brutal husband

*Saint-Etienne:* Handsome, slick boulevardier, who seduced the then virgin Ninon with fair but false words

*Saint-Evremond:* Classic honnête homme. Distinguished courtier, general, writer, wit, forced to flee France in 1661. The dominant influence in Ninon's life. His correspondence with Ninon from England in 1680–1700 constitutes the main primary source of information about Ninon. Died two years before Ninon, buried Westminster Abbey. Ninon's greatest friend and admirer

*Sandwich, Countess of:* Directed by Saint-Evremond to visit Ninon on her visit to Paris in 1699; the countess, less than one-third Ninon's age, charmed and was charmed by Ninon

*Scarron, abbé Paul:* Gifted writer and wit; crippled, brave. Married Françoise d'Aubigné, afterward Madame de Maintenon. One of Ninon's truest and most estimable friends. Died 1660

*Scarron, Madame: See* Maintenon, Madame de

*Sévigné, Charles de:* Son of comte de Sévigné. Perhaps Ninon's last lover. *See* Sévigné, comte de

*Sévigné, comte de:* Unfaithful husband of great letter writer, Madame de Sévigné. One of Ninon's caprices. Killed young in duel. Father of Charles de Sévigné with whom Ninon had affair twenty years later

*Tallemant des Réaux:* Seventeenth-century chronicler, author of *Historiettes,* one of most fertile (and tangy) sources on contemporary French society

*Vendôme, chevalier de:* Half brother of Louis XIII. Wrote disgruntled poem against Ninon who had refused his suit

*Villarceaux, marquis de:* Ninon's great physical love. Later probably the lover of Madame Scarron

*Yveteaux, Des:* Aged libertin, whom the young Ninon used to visit. Died 1649

# Chronology

1623: Probable year of Ninon's birth; alternative date, 1620. Apex of Flamboyant Libertinism
1630–1643: Approximate period of Erudite Libertinism
1632: Flight of Henri de Lanclos
1639: Ninon meets Saint-Evremond at Marion de l'Orme's
1640, 1641, or 1642: Ninon probably met Scarron in one of these years
1642: Ninon meets Coligny about this time
      Death of Madame de Lanclos
      Death of Cardinal Richelieu
1643: January 1, Accession of Louis XIV
      Scarron sends étrennes (New Year's gift) to Ninon
1643–1648: The Good Regency
1647: Henri de Lanclos returns to Paris
1648: End of Thirty Years' War
      Outbreak of Fronde
1649: Henri de Lanclos killed
1650: Marion de l'Orme dies
1652: Beginning of Ninon's affair with Villarceaux
1653: End of Fronde
      Birth of Ninon's son, the chevalier de La Boissière
1655: End of Ninon's affair with Villarceaux
1656: Ninon confined to Madelonnettes, visited by Queen Christina of Sweden at Lagny
1659: Probable date of Ninon's meeting Molière
      Ninon writes *La Coquette Vangée*

1660: Death of Scarron
      Banning of Society of Holy Sacrament
1661: Death of Mazarin
      Flight of Saint-Evremond
1662: Flight of Gourville
1668: Gourville returns and Ninon gives him back his gold crowns
1671: Liaison with Charles de Sévigné
      Ninon's active love life ends
1673: Death of Molière
1680: Beginning of Triumphant Libertinism
1680–1700: Main correspondence between Ninon and Saint-Evremond
1685: Revocation of Edict of Nantes
1689: Louis XIV pardons Saint-Evremond
1693: Death of Madame de La Sablière
1703: Death of Saint-Evremond
1705: Death of Ninon

# Mademoiselle Libertine

## A Portrait of Ninon de Lanclos

# ⁓ Chapter 1 ⁓

## No Time for Clods

LIKE MOST other distinguished visitors to the Paris of the last two-thirds of the seventeenth century, the famous Dutch scientist Christiaan Huygens found his way to the salon of Ninon de Lanclos, that extraordinary combination of physical attractiveness and intellect. Huygens, as had many before him, became so excited at the sight of Ninon, but particularly by her singing and skilled self-accompaniment on the lute, that he was moved to burst into rhyme. Poetry was not the good Dutchman's line — he was one of the great mathematicians and astronomers of the age — but nonetheless he managed to get his point across. Though he had come to France at the invitation of Louis XIV's first minister, Colbert, to do research on, among other things, celestial bodies, he seems to have at least temporarily forgotten about astronomy, so fascinated was he by an apparently equally heavenly though decidedly terrestrial body. Wrote he (in French, of course):

> She has five instruments which bring me to her feet,
> And four — her hands and eyes — first wrought my fall;
> As for the fifth — and of all of them most sweet —
> A man must fearless be, and venture all.* †

* This poetic bouquet may have been a bit of a seventeenth-century international cliché. About the same time in England, Andrew Marvell was writing:

More than eighty years later, in 1751, when the fever for Ninon, who had died long before, was mounting to a literary pitch, even Voltaire took quill in hand, remarking critically that the Dutch mathematician's verses were a little geometrical. For the prosaic twentieth century, however, the point worth remarking is that the Dutch scientist tried poetry at all. The answer is that he had to, if he wanted to win even a sigh from the most sought-after ladies of the Splendid Century (le Grand Siècle). Unfortunately, it is not known how successful Huygens's suit was, but there are strong grounds on the basis of literary canons for supposing that he remained an unsatisfied — but not dissatisfied — lover. Ninon could say no to a would-be lover and still keep him as a devoted, admiring friend. That and her retention of youthfulness were her great secrets. Ninon was probably in her fifties when Huygens, who had perfected a lens which enabled him to discover a satellite of Saturn, contentedly settled into orbit around her. If a man had distinction of one kind or another, Ninon would let him share her company, if not her couch. Huygens qualified. He never married.

There is little doubt that ladies of the upper class were difficult to please in those days. Of course money has never been an impediment, and women of that time could be influenced by the gift of a little château or an emerald pendant, but without wit and elegance, the swain of that day was likely to be de trop. This situation is notable, for then, in the century of

---

An hundred years should go to praise
Thine eyes and on thy forehead gaze:
Two hundred to adore each breast:
But thirty thousand to the rest.

† Translation taken from *The Red Ninon de L'Enclos,* by Helen Kendrick Hayes, London, 1908. Ninon's name is variously spelled: Lanclos, Lenclos, L'Enclos.

a bejeweled, privileged aristocracy, there was considerable democracy in the realms of love, perhaps at least as much as today, when sometimes a man finds himself lagging in the lists of love unless his corporation directorates are as interlocking as his embraces. This seventeenth-century requirement in the fine art of loving, this articulateness of mind as well as of body, was not confined to France. In Italy, not only must the lover find his way to the heart of his ladylove with a pretty poetic wit, but the cavalier who could set his verses to music was a triple-threat man and definitely had the edge over the tone-deaf clod, good soldier or huntsman though he might be. In England it was much the same. No lover worth his salt was incapable of rhyming a flattering or plaintive couplet to his beloved. Even clergymen were good at it. Wrote pastor Robert Herrick in an appropriately humble mood:

> I dare not ask a kiss,
> I dare not beg a smile,
> Lest having that, or this,
> I might grow proud the while.
> No, no, the utmost share
> Of my desire shall be
> Only to kiss that air
> That lately kissèd thee.

Modern man might well consider himself fortunate that he is not up against that sort of competition. But what of our women? Would not they too be under some strain if they were in the position in which Ninon found herself when the lofty chevalier de Vendôme,* Louis XIII's half brother, the

* Love child of Henri IV de Navarre (father of Louis XIII) and his mistress, Gabrielle d'Estrees.

Grand Prior of France, pushed his suit so vigorously, but unsuccessfully, that he was moved to fire off a testy quatrain:

> Unworthy of my passion, unworthy of my sighs
> Henceforth your poor beauty is naught in my eyes,
> 'Twas my love, Mademoiselle, your charms to you lent,
> For in truth I see none, now my ardour is spent.*

If one of our modern wooers, poetically gifted, were so to lose control of himself that he sent the object of his affection a verse or two, surely he would not be cad enough to expect an answer in kind. But Ninon rose to the occasion. Bidding her maid tell the chevalier's footman to wait, she dashed off a riposte in the same meter:

> Unmoved by your passion, unmoved by your sighs,
> What care I if my beauty is naught in your eyes!
> But if, as you say, love lends charms, I'd advise
> That you borrow a few for yourself — 'twould be wise.†

And it is recorded that the chevalier de Vendôme, put in his place so prettily and elegantly, was only too glad to be allowed to attend Ninon's soirées — in the capacity of esteemed friend and disesteemed lover. What manner of woman was this charmer, who had all Paris at her feet, who could duel with poems as effectively as her suitors with rapiers, who was inconstant as lover and constant as friend?

* Translation from Hayes, *The Real Ninon de L'Enclos*.
† Translation from Hayes, *The Real Ninon de L'Enclos*.

## ᴄᴏᴄᴏ Chapter 2 ᴄᴏᴄᴏ

### Pawn in Parental Struggle

NINON'S PARENTS were not well matched. Henri de Lanclos, of the lesser nobility of Touraine, was consciously an Epicurean — of whom there were many in the seventeenth century. The king under whom he served, that gay, swashbuckling Henri de Navarre, would give up the pursuit of the fleeing enemy to undertake that of a less fleet-footed damsel of the neighborhood. What was good enough for his liege lord was good enough for Henri de Lanclos, who was evidently not just a hard-riding, hard-drinking lady-chaser (note lady-*chaser* — Ninon's father seemed to draw the line at wenching), but a talented lutist and an amateur philosopher. He evidently was familiar with the *Essais* of that great liberal, Montaigne, and it is reasonable to suppose that Monsieur de Lanclos had read, and did not disapprove of, Rabelais. In short, Ninon's father was a charming, freethinking, and perhaps somewhat disreputable bon vivant.

Everything that Henri was, Madame de Lanclos was not, and vice versa. Whereas Henri was impious, his lady was most pious; he was loose-living, she extremely strait-laced; he merry, she somber; he fingered the lute with cheery abandon, she her beads with gray sobriety; he lived for this world, she for the next. Did opposites attract? Not at all. His wife, née Marie-

Barbe de La Marche, had a sister who had married into a family which had access to Cardinal Richelieu, Louis XIII's first minister. Henry de Lanclos may have thought in 1615 (or 1616) it would be good to have a relative at Court. Why Marie-Barbe married Lanclos is obscure. He was probably good-looking, and more than likely it was a mariage de convenance. Such marriages were very much the practice among the nobility and particularly among royalty. Louis XIII, the reigning monarch at Ninon's birth, had been married, age fourteen, for political reasons, to the king of Spain's daughter, also age fourteen; they lived unhappily ever after. Marie-Barbe had all the zeal of the crusader and fervently aspired to save the libertine Henri from what to her was sure hellfire. With this as her objective, and Henri no sheep, the battle was joined from the outset.

The chroniclers have dealt harshly with poor Marie-Barbe, picturing her as a one-track fanatic, with all the perceptiveness of a mule. This is probably true, but she seems to have been, though limited in her outlook, a good person of rocklike integrity. Whenever mention is made of Ninon's charm, gaiety, sex appeal, musical and dancing ability, the chroniclers have with one accord exclaimed, "Why, of course, she took after her father." Never a word of credit goes to Marie-Barbe, only mention of her narrow-mindedness and excessive piety. But notwithstanding Marie-Barbe's shortcomings, Ninon loved her church-absorbed mother. And since Ninon is known as much for her uncomprising integrity (Voltaire wrote a dull five-act play, Le Dépositaire, about it) as for her wit and evergreen attractiveness, it is perhaps time to assume that if she did not inherit her mother's religiosity, she did inherit the ethics of her religion.

What did Henri do for a living? Not much, but that put him on a par with most of the nobility, great and small. Henri's problem, however, was that he did not own large estates yielding fat revenues. Therefore he had to attach himself to the household of some great landed aristocrat who did. Lanclos entered the service of the jovial maréchal de Saint-Luc — as equerry and lieutenant in his regiment of infantry. Later he became captain. Two sons preceded Ninon; we know nothing of them but their names. Things were going better in Henri's military career than at home, for by the time his second son was born, Henri was spending more and more time away from home.

In 1620 or 1623 a girl was born to Henri and Marie-Barbe. Until the middle of the nineteenth century, the year of Ninon's birth was thought to be 1616, and her portraits show her dates as 1616–1705; but her baptismal certificate, discovered later, indicates 1620, and a legal document of her middle age shows 1623. It we accept 1623, it was only seven years after Shakespeare's death.

In France, in 1623, Louis XIII was twenty-two. He was pious, unhappy, sulky, ill at ease, and at times impulsively violent. Kings could still be brutal with impunity. But Louis was fanatically religious, and therefore the schoolbooks called him Louis the Just. Across the Channel, James I was reigning in an England becoming progressively less merrie with the rise of Puritan discontent. In France, too, the seeds of Puritanism were to fall, but Jansenism* never did nearly as well in the smiling, frivolous climate of France as Puritanism did in England or America. In America, just three years earlier, some pil-

---

* The Jansenists were the French Puritans, with a strong doctrinal belief in fate, as in Calvinism.

grims had landed near Plymouth Rock. It was three years before twenty-four dollars were paid for the purchase from a few
fast-talking Indians of some then dubious real estate now
known as Manhattan Island. It was the year when Mersenne,
an enemy of atheism, stated that there were 50,000 atheists in
Paris out of a population of approximately 500,000.

In Europe the Thirty Years' War was five years old. The red-
robed Cardinal Richelieu, still at the dawn of his career, was
charting the foreign policy of France, a policy that was to make
his beloved country the undisputed master of the Continent.
He may not have offered Ninon the alleged 150,000 livres
($300,000 to $750,000) to be his mistress, but he did, at the time
of his death, when Ninon was a girl of nineteen, present her
generation with a stage on which to play its part in an atmosphere of coruscating brilliance. It was the wily cardinal who
laid the political groundwork for, and ushered in, the Age of
Louis XIV — France's greatest period and, according to Voltaire, one of the world's four Great Ages.* It was of course the
Age of Louis XIV in which Ninon was to live out the mature
part of her life — the period which produced, among others:
the dramatists, Molière and Racine; the coiner of maxims, La
Rochefoucauld; one of the world's great letter writers, Madame
de Sévigné; the satirists, Boileau and La Bruyère; the creator of
ageless fables, La Fontaine; the philosophers, Saint-Evremond,
Bayle, and Fontenelle; the early novelists, Mademoiselle de
Scudéry and Madame de La Fayette — all of whom were
friends or admirers of Ninon.†

The seventeenth century was, like most centuries, a century

---

* Along with the Age of Pericles in Greece, of Augustus in Rome, and of the early
Medici in Florence.
† Even Madame de Sévigné, who had good reason to hate Ninon, came to admire her.

of contrasts. Reason lived alongside superstition. While Descartes was demanding in the name of Reason that one must prove everything, 100,000 human beings were being burned as witches in Germany. It was a time of great grossness — men urinated behind velvet curtains in the halls of Versailles — and of exquisite refinement in the salons of Madame de Rambouillet and Ninon de Lanclos. By our standards, by even those of the so-called permissive generation, it was an age of great sexual license; it also produced the précieuses, who disdained (or pretended to disdain) physical love in favor of poetic, platonic love. It was an age of extreme piety and sacrilegious impiety, when men baptized animals and charged the image of Christ in the churches, swords drawn, crying, "There is the enemy"; when the Great Condé, one of Ninon's admirers, tried to burn a piece of the True Cross. It was an age when it was heresy to question the orthodoxy of the pagan Aristotle, upon whose philosophy the Church had placed its imprimatur; heresy to believe the earth revolved around the sun. The Reformation in France, strengthened by Henri IV's liberal Edict of Nantes, promulgated just before the close of the sixteenth century, was struggling to keep its head above water against the harsh pressure of the Counter Reformation. At the time of Ninon's birth the Church, regrouping its forces lay and spiritual, had launched a vigorous Catholic renaissance and dealt the growing numbers of freethinkers heavy blows. Exhausted from the cruel, bloody, fratricidal wars between French Catholics and Protestants of the previous century, many thinking people cried, "A plague o' both your houses," and embarked on a flamboyant libertinism which reached its zenith the year Ninon was born. It was a chiaroscuro age, an age of official shadow cast by the monolithic image of Church and State, and of individual light, rayed forth by giants like Descartes, Galileo, Milton, and Molière. It saw the Enlightenment dawn. It witnessed the beginning of the scientific method, the attack on superstition and age-old fallacy, the questioning not only of whether Catholicism was better than Protestantism or vice versa, which had preoccupied the sixteenth century, but of organized religion itself.

It was an exciting time — bursting with an energy born not of the liberation of the forces of the atom but of the questing mind. Men may have trembled for their safety in the dark streets of Paris at night, but man's discoveries of the circulation of the blood in his body, of new lands on the earth and new galaxies in the sky, filled him with the joy of exhilaration and expectancy, not the fear of self-annihilation. The seventeenth century was still breathing the heady air wafted over from the Renaissance. It was adding fresh elements of its own: skepticism and burgeoning confidence in the promise of Reason. Behind the stately, seemingly uncracked facade of the absolute monarchy and the established Church, a courageous minority of independent intellectuals, dissenters, and freethinkers were to examine searchingly the hitherto almost universally accepted notions about matter, the divine right of kings, the nature of God. In brief, the seventeenth century was the midwife of modern man and, to a lesser extent, of modern woman — in the feminist sense — as well. Ninon de Lanclos was probably the most thoroughgoing feminist of her time.

It was into this diverse, pulsating, yeasty atmosphere, overlaid with piety and streaked with neo-Epicureanism that Ninon was born, and in which she was to live and love and leave her mark.

*

Her parents called her Anne. The choice of name was probably a victory for Madame de Lanclos's piety, as Anne recalled
the mother of Christ's mother, Mary. Henri de Lanclos did not
give up easily, though. Anne reminded him not of saintliness
but of mumbled prayers, of fidgeting with beads and close-
smelling chapels reeking with incense, and so he called the
fresh, pretty baby Annette; but that, too, did not catch the poetry, the renewal, the joyousness which the infant epitomized
for him. And being a man with a musical ear, he coined the
euphonious name Ninon, wherein — at least for him — larks
sang, springtime budded, and gaiety danced.

The baby grew to be a comely little girl, much doted on by
the neighborhood. What a beautiful, pure nun she will make!
thought the highly devout Madame de Lanclos. What a
charming, vivacious lady of the great world she will make!
thought the egregiously earthy Henri de Lanclos. "Ave
Maria," sang the mother to Anne at bedtime. "One and two
and three and," called the father to Ninon as he danced a saraband with her or taught her the elements of his beloved lute.
The mother took her to mass both early in the morning and
early in her lifetime. The churches were cold and drafty. The
father took her across the river to the Left Bank, to the fair in
the Faubourg Saint-Germain, where there still were green
meadows and great open spaces, where the air was fresh and
countrified, unlike the nauseating smells of Paris on the citified
Right Bank. The mother put a prayer book in the child's
hands, beads in her fingers, and gave her little crucifixes and
pictures of saints with halos. The father showed her dancing
bears at the fair, clowns on the recently built Pont Neuf, put
toys in her hands and hot pasties in her mouth. It was an

unequal struggle for the child's soul. Madame de Lanclos might have won if she had crusaded less and had Henri de Lanclos been passive. Even with all Henri's freethinking, Ninon was twice in her lifetime to retire voluntarily to a convent, both times flirting with the idea of taking the veil. Had her surging appetite for life not impelled her otherwise in the first instance, and the concupiscent archbishop of Lyons, elder brother of Cardinal Richelieu, not forced his physical attentions upon her in the second, the Church might have won an undistinguished convert and Paris society lost a distinguished leader.

The details of Ninon's education remain vague. What school, if any, she went to, or what tutor, if any, she had, is not known. Except for a rare few, girls of that day received little education. Instruction was mainly religious, with the domestic crafts such as sewing and cooking thrown in. We do know, however, that Ninon learned Spanish and Italian. Thanks to her father, she learned a good deal more. He encouraged her to read, and evidently widely, for Ninon knew her classical literature and history well. She was later to engage in Latin repartee in bed with the Great Condé. It is worth noting that she was able to mix Latin and Eros without prejudice to either, and Condé remained a powerful and faithful friend long after she had sent him packing as a lover. Tradition has it that Henri de Lanclos led Ninon, when still under ten, to read his skeptical, tolerant master, Montaigne, with relish. This suggests a wellnigh unbelievable precocity, for Montaigne is, of course, not exactly child's play. The tradition even goes further and claims that Ninon, when but a young girl, used to conceal either Montaigne or a romantic tale beneath her prayer book in church, thus satisfying simultaneously the desires of both parents.

More trustworthy than the claim that Ninon precociously read Montaigne is the account of the musical instruction which Henri gave to his young daughter. Henri was an accomplished lutist. We have as authority one of the principal social historians of Ninon's day, that chronicler of great attractiveness, Tallemant des Réaux. One day, he relates, Henri called on one of the leading lutists of the time, an old master, Gaultier. In those days musicians were not considered entirely respectable.

"You don't play the lute any longer, do you?" asked Lanclos. "As for me, I've given up the abomination."

"I wouldn't play it for all the world," replied the other, pretending to be horrified.

They dined, they talked, they went for a stroll. On returning, Henri noticed a number of lutes lying on a table. He tried to ignore them, but his fingers were itching to play. Guessing his thoughts, old Gaultier volunteered, "They are for the children. There isn't a sound cord among them."

Without saying anything, Lanclos took one of the instruments, tuned it, and began fondling it lovingly. Tentatively he began to play. "This little saraband, do you think it pretty?" he asked. By way of answer the old man picked up a lute and, completely forgetting his previously expressed contempt, strummed out a catchy air. "How do you like *this?*" he asked Lanclos, who was listening entranced. And then began what today we call a jam session. Tallemant says they did not stop for thirty-six hours, having forgotten in their ecstasy to eat or drink. Clearly the old man was in fine condition.

Three loves had Henri — Ninon, the lute, and Lucrèce de Gouges. The first two he combined by succeeding in making his daughter a first-class lutist. Many the long afternoon father and child spent tête-à-tête, playing sprightly duets, harmoniz-

ing sad Portuguese songs. They would dance jigs together, and
he would read to her — when Madame de Lanclos was not
around — medieval tales of high romance. For Ninon, these
periods with her father were always too short, but Monsieur de
Lanclos would plead that he must be off to attend on the
maréchal de Saint-Luc. That, however, was not the whole
story.

Years before, when Lanclos was about seventeen, he was half
in love with another little girl, aged eight — just a trifle older
than Ninon was at this time. Her name was Lucrèce de
Gouges. The young Henri was a frequent and welcome visitor
at her parents' home. He would play with Lucrèce and her
older sister in big-brotherly fashion. Some five or six years later
Henri married Marie-Barbe, much to Lucrèce's pain. The
young Lucrèce grew up to be a beauty. She did not marry, or
rather her parents did not marry her, until she was a ripe
twenty-five, and then not to somebody of her choice, of course,
but to a lawyer with connections, Jean de Riberolles, who was
secretary to the governor of the Périgord. Her husband sought
to turn his wife's beauty to account — to procure himself ad-
vancement. Lucrèce, a full-blooded, proud young lady, came to
hate him. Her thoughts turned to Lanclos, who was still an
occasional visitor at her parents' home. Lucrèce yearned to see
him and intimated to her husband that she missed seeing the
old friends of her family. Perhaps Riberolles may have reasoned that Lanclos, associated as he was with the influential
maréchal de Saint-Luc, might be useful. He invited Lanclos to
call.

Lanclos came, he saw, she conquered. The passage of time
and Lucréce's manifest unhappiness made Lanclos see her with

different eyes. He was captivated. To Lucrèce he was more charming than ever. For reasons unknown, Lanclos hesitated to take the next step. Then fate intervened and changed the course of Ninon's life.

In 1628 the governor of the Périgord had to return to his province. His secretary, Riberolles, was to go with him, but Riberolles not only did not take Lucrèce with him but left her without financial support. Lucrèce went to live with her married sister. Perhaps it was the brutality of the abandonment that caused Lanclos to abandon his scruples, if any. They became lovers — total, passionate, constant.

If we are to believe the testimony four years later at the trial for adultery (denied, of course, by Lucrèce and Henri), there were no holds barred. In the criminal suit brought against Lanclos, July 9, 1632, La Nauve, king's counsel, wanted to know whether Henri, present at the rising of Lucrèce, indulged in certain familiarities, such as when Lucrèce was dressing, "he had not fondled her breasts, she being completely nude?" Lucrèce, according to the court scribe, indignantly replied, "All was false and calumnious, saving the reverence of the court, and that if she had been so ill-starred as to have a bad thought, which was never, she would not have wanted to do anything unchaste at the house of her sister . . ."

But the interrogator, La Nauve, was persistent. He wanted to know "if it was not true that, several times, the said Lanclos, she in a standing position, had not put his hand under her slip and given her the whip on her naked thigh without her seeming to mind, even giving evidence of taking pleasure therein?" Lucrèce replied, "That was false . . ."

La Nauve made other stinging charges (all denied by Lucrèce), but one thing is clear — Henri and Lucrèce, in the rage of their passion, had not been cautious. Somebody informed Riberolles in the distant Périgord. Instead of getting violently jealous, all he did was to write home some nasty letters. Lucrèce paid the letters little heed. But after two years or so of absence, Riberolles returned. His mind was not on a cuckold's revenge — it was on money.

Riberolles complained to Lucrèce that he had not been able to collect a sou of wages for the last six years from his skinflint master, the governor of the Périgord. He needed her help — he would appreciate Lucrèce's handing over her dowry. Lucrèce declined. He decided to try another tack. He declared that his debtor and employer found her fair to look upon and suggested she act as collection agent for him by being accommodating to the governor. Lucrèce indignantly refused. Riberolles was not daunted; he waited for more propitious circumstances. After all, maybe his lord just did not appeal to her.

A number of times Riberolles brought home a councillor and expressed the wish that Lucrèce would not be cold to him. Lucrèce was adamant. Riberolles grew bolder. He brought the councillor into Lucrèce's bedroom. When the frightened girl fled to the stable, he followed, grabbed her by the throat, looked for his sword "which, by good chance, he did not find." He threatened "he would beat her well," making her incessantly "run the risk of her life." Whereupon she decided that "she wanted to put herself in safety" by petitioning for a legal separation and by living near her relatives.

No sooner had she fled her conjugal hell than she and Lanclos resumed their lovemaking. Danger seemed to add spice to their rendezvous, though now Lanclos felt it desirable to sleep with a candle always burning and a pistol handy. Meanwhile Riberolles's anger was rising; he ranted up and down Paris about the enormity of his wife's sin. He set about to collect evidence against the couple, and when he had what he thought was enough — he was a lawyer, it should be remembered — he entered a complaint of adultery around January 1631.

There are large lacunae in Ninon's life. They are even larger in that of her mother. Was not Marie-Barbe suffering great humiliation during these goings on which, in the small closed society of Parisian aristocracy, must have been public knowledge? Probably long ago she had ceased to care for Henri — if she ever had — but the fact that he was now named co-defendant in a court case undoubtedly distressed the pious lady keenly. She turned to the Church for support, prayed daily for Henri's salvation, and lost no opportunity to point out to Ninon that the wages of sin are perdition. Ninon was only eight at the time and was not likely to have understood the gravity of her mother's forebodings. But miss her father, with all the pain of a child in stark disappointment at being partially deserted, she most certainly did. Ninon probably hated Lucrèce de Gouges and moved closer to her mother.

It hurt Henri to be drawn away from the other love of his life, little Ninon, but he was now so caught up in his all-absorbing passion that he could scarcely think of anything but helping Lucrèce. Henri was a man of honor — according to his code — and determined to stand by Lucrèce at all costs. The costs were high.

The various suits and countersuits dragged on for two tormenting years. Riberolles stopped at nothing — paying witnesses to give fabricated and venomous testimony. A coward, who dared not face Lanclos alone, he enlisted others to fight his battle. One of them was a powerful adversary — Louis de Chabans — who helped Riberolles by procuring false witnesses and supplying assassins.

Returning one night to the hôtel * de Saint-Luc through the narrow streets of the Marais, the aristocratic quarter, Lanclos saw five armed men huddled near the Church of the Minimes. At the head was an ex-convict hired by Chabans; behind was Riberolles. When they spied Henri, they cried, "There he is!" Lanclos did not scare easily; on the contrary, he advanced toward them tauntingly. They retreated. He knew, however, that his life was in danger and held himself constantly on the qui vive.

What happened the last seven weeks before matters drew to a climax is unknown. There is little doubt that Chabans must have renewed his attempts to dispatch Lanclos, who was not a man to trifle with. Stationing himself outside the Venetian embassy, where Chabans had gone to confer with the ambassador, Lanclos waited for him. When Chabans came out, and as he was entering his carriage, Lanclos ran him through "in a manner," says Tallemant, "which could pass for an assassination." There has been speculation that Tallemant's use of "could" implies that it might have been a duel. Duel or not, Lanclos had to leave, for Cardinal Richelieu had made dueling a capital offense.

And so on December 26, 1632, the course of a nine-year-old's life was irrevocably changed. There is no definite record of the manner of Henri's hurried farewell. Much fiction has been written about the clop-clop of horses' hoofs on the cobblestones

---

* *Hôtel* in this sense means "town mansion," not "hotel."

of the Marais, Henri's heart-wrenching embracing of his terrified and stunned little girl, his words of advice, of courage, of tender, excruciating leave-taking. On July 23, 1633, the Criminal Court issued an order that "de Gouges and Lanclos be taken bodily and led as prisoners to the Conciergerie, if apprehended they can be . . . their goods seized . . ." We do not know what happened to Lucrèce, what the courts and Riberolles may have done to her. We do know that Henri reached the frontier without difficulty, leaving desolation behind him in three households.

## ⸓ Chapter 3 ⸓

### Love Is a Sometime Thing

HENRI DE LANCLOS's flight took place in December 1632. Madame de Lanclos felt that her erring husband had got what he deserved. To Ninon she carefully explained that it was a divine visitation, that God, though his mercy was infinite, could not continue to overlook that most heinous of sins, adultery, and that he was merciful in not having meted out sterner justice.

For Ninon, the world had crashed about her ears. Her playmate, her music teacher, her dancing master, her chief joy, were not only gone but were to be forgotten. Ninon had taken pride in her handsome, likeable father with his flair for charming and enlivening. Now she must be ashamed. Ninon would have liked to defend him. To her he was not a bad man — he was brave and kind and delightful. When she was older she concluded that her father had simply been unlucky, but at nine all she knew was that something had gone terribly wrong, that it was all grossly unfair, and that people were unspeakably mean to say what they did about her papa. Her childish inarticulateness, her inability to justify him, added to her heavy frustration which lasted several years. But Ninon's youthful spirit was resilient. By the time she was thirteen, Ninon was gay again, but the direction of her life — not that she knew it — had been unalterably changed.

Not long after Lanclos had spurred away from Paris into the void, Madame de Lanclos decided to move from their abode in the Parish of Saint-Jean-en-Grève to the rue des Trois-Pavillons (now the rue Elzévir) in the Marais. Presumably in straitened circumstances, they moved to a smaller dwelling. Furthermore, it was preferable not to stay in a place where old associations reminded her of a husband better forgotten. How they lived, and on what, we do not know. That they lived most modestly, we do know. Perhaps Lanclos was able to send home something from exile. Perhaps Marie-Barbe's sister, married to a man of some means, or Henri's sister, the baroness de Loches, may have helped.

Ninon loved the Marais. Except for a short interval she lived there all her life. She was a product of it. The Marais was a new section of Paris, its growth sparked by the building of Paris's great seventeenth-century square, the Place Royale, now the still handsome Place des Vosges. Situated on the Right Bank, the Marais had the shape of an almost isosceles triangle with its base on the Seine. It included among other landmarks the Château (and prison) of the Bastille, the famous Porte Saint-Antoine and rue Saint-Antoine, the huge hôtel of Madame de Sévigné with its red-bordered flower beds, now the Carnavalet Museum, the magnificent hôtel of the dukes of Rohan-Soubise, now the National Archives, and many other baronial mansions.

In the seventeenth century the Marais was the elegant sector of Paris, the aristocratic quarter, and the center of Paris's social and cultural life. The rue des Trois-Pavillons was near the Place Royale. As a young girl Ninon frolicked on the broad lawns of the Place, or played hide-and-seek in the columned loggias of the mansions surrounding the square. There, after supper, fascinated, she would watch young lovers meeting in the twilight, for the arcades afforded one of the best trysting places in town. She carefully took in the coquettish wiles of the young ladies, their artful manner of dressing, where they placed their beauty spots — on the cheek, on the forehead, on a semi-exposed bosom, for the position of the mouche or beauty spot indicated the mood of the wearer, signifying varying degrees of willingness.

Whether or not it was as an antidote to the education Ninon was receiving in the arcades of the Place Royale — Madame de Lanclos probably knew nothing of it — the harassed mother redoubled her efforts to get Ninon to attend church at the Minimes, just a step from the Place. Ninon showed herself unexpectedly pliable. God be praised, exulted the mother, the baleful influence of her father was lessening! Her dream of Ninon's becoming a nun seemed possible of realization. Nothing could have been further from the truth. The truth was that at the Minimes the show was better than in the Place Royale, perhaps because stolen fruits are sweeter. Church decorum had fallen to perhaps an all-time low. The ladies dressed not to worship but to be worshiped. Beneath flimsy scarves that were always slipping off their naked shoulders, they wore plunging décolletage. When they kneeled, the view was unobstructed. Jonathan Swift describes the scene:

> . . . Or on the Mat devoutly kneeling,
> Would lift her Eyes up to the Ceiling,
> And heave her Bosom unaware
> For neighb'ring Beaux to see it bare.

Billets doux circulated during the sermon. Nods and sign

language carried on a dialogue across the expanse of the nave. There was much joking and laughing, dogs wandered around, nobles trained their lorgnettes on any attractive woman, noble or otherwise. It was a place of rendezvous or to arrange rendezvous. The abbé Boileau found it necessary to deliver a sermon — "Concerning the nudity of bosoms":

> . . . Do you come into this sanctuary to make conquests there and to satisfy your sensuality? Do you come to take hold of God or of man? . . .

Perhaps Madame de Lanclos was so absorbed in her devotions that she did not notice that Ninon was all eyes, watching with wonderment the goings on at the Minimes. When the mischievous young girl did look down, it was not at her prayer book, but at a tale by Honoré d'Urfé or the like. Ninon was not alone in this pastime. It is told of the duc d'Orléans, regent of France, that he went to the trouble of having Rabelais bound in a prayer book. The lack of respect was the result of disillusionment, not so much with God, as with organized religion. The Religious Wars of the previous century between Catholics and Protestants had made many a man question what had hitherto been challenged only by the few — the essential goodness of religion. The clergy itself had all too often forfeited its claim to holiness. When the worldly Richelieu died, the pope hardly displayed profound faith when he allegedly said, "If there be a God, the cardinal de Richelieu will have much to answer for; if there be none, he lived a successful life." This was the day when popes and cardinals had mistresses — some openly, when hostesses relied on abbés to supply much of the gallantry at their parties.

In 1600, one-quarter of France belonged to the Church.
Young men often entered the Church not because of any spiritual calling, but because, like the civil service today, it provided
security. It offered more than the civil service in prestige, in
power over one's fellow. In the higher echelons, it offered the
fattest plums. For years cardinals were the prime ministers.
The Church disposed of great wealth and power and consequently attracted men who aspired to wealth and power, or —
in the lower echelons — to an easy life with ample time for
social activities. Of course not all churchmen were tainted.
Every age has its sincere, unselfish men, like Saint-Vincent de
Paul, but these were the days of a secular Church, with tempo-
ral mores informing the lives of its spiritual leaders. Such a
climate breeds disrespect. Men within the Church, such as the
highly esteemed Father Bourdaloue, strove for reform. "How
many mercenary priests do we see . . ." he asks, "priests vain
and presumptuous, priests lazy and sensual . . . ?"

As conformity was strong, the pews were generally well
filled, but particularly among the upper classes attendance was
often purely perfunctory and religious feeling absent. There
were magnificent ecclesiastical orators in the Grand Siècle —
like Bossuet with his famous funeral orations—but many the
preacher who had to strive exceedingly hard for dramatic effect
to capture the flagging interest of an audience all but fatally
disenchanted by a growing suspicion that what was assailing
their ears was hypocritical homily. The priest who was delivering one of the Lenten sermons at the Minimes when Ninon was
about thirteen, seems to have been straining to win the attention of his audience from the manifold distractions. It is not
easy to compete with glances from pretty eyes behind a fan that

promise untold delights, or to keep parishioners' minds on the lesson when low necklines suggested green pastures never contemplated by the Twenty-third Psalm.

The priest's voice was charged with dramatic content. His theme was the Passion, for it was Eastertide. But instead of dwelling on the redemptive value in the Passion, he described the suffering at Calvary in morbid detail. He had been working up to a climax, and when he graphically depicted Christ expiring on the cross, there was a babble of sobs. Ninon rebelled at what she considered deliberate whipping up of emotion. To what good end was he doing this? She suspected his sincerity. Before she knew it, she found herself singing in a clear, girlish soprano the words of a popular Spanish love song: *"Qu'importa que muero se ressuscitan?"* ("What matters it that he [it] be dead if he [it] rise again?") The priest's peroration was punctured; a stunned silence ensued. Then the priest, recovering, demanded furiously to know who the offender was. Ninon's mother, in shocked piety, indicated her offending daughter. What precisely happened is unknown. Some would have it that the preacher brought her before the curé for sentencing, painting a satanic picture of unspeakable impiety. No doubt the preacher fumed at the song's double entendre, with its erotic connotation. Men used this song to sing the praises of their ladylove. Ladies were said to sing the song to encourage their lovers.

We do know that the gravely concerned Madame de Lanclos took her daughter to a Jesuit and that all Ninon got was a scolding. The wise curé could not bring himself to believe that the young girl with the disarming manner was old enough to appreciate the double meaning of the song. The mild dressing down may have chastened her somewhat but it did not make her religious. The chronicler, Tallemant, adds, "She confessed to me that from that time on, she saw clearly that religions are nothing but inventions, and that there was no truth to all that."

Madame de Lanclos was alarmed. The incident of the Spanish song in church was not the only cause of her disquiet. She was concerned about Ninon's refusal to dress in the ultraconservative fashion that she, Madame de Lanclos, favored. Furthermore, Ninon transgressed in that she loved to dance — a sure sign of the devil's influence, according to the priest who advised Madame de Lanclos. Ninon probably matured early both physically and mentally. There is some evidence that she was precocious intellectually — her alleged reading of Montaigne at an early age. Certainly her father's exile had accelerated her mental development — she was forced to learn to rely on herself, particularly since she could not find an anchorage in her mother because of their basically different makeups. Ninon was endowed with voluptuous breasts and from early youth was very proud of her belle poitrine. The style at that time highlighted a low neckline. Décolletage, in those prebrassiere days, was often not only deep but unconfined, leading one contemporary writer to refer to the "bouncing breasts" of ladies of fashion.

Despite Madame de Lanclos's strictures, Ninon persisted in wearing clothes that at least suggested the promise that lay beneath. It was clear even to the unperceptive mother that she was losing the battle to make her daughter a nun. Showing unexpected elasticity, Madame de Lanclos decided that Ninon should marry early and thus be out of harm's way. Whether such an early marriage, with its greatly increased chance of failure, was not highly risky does not seem to have bothered her. She had done all she could — may God have mercy on her daughter's soul (and body). So Madame de Lanclos opened the doors of her house. The young men were not long in picking up the scent. Ninon's appearance, gaiety, charm had made her the darling of several princesses and duchesses who loved to show her off. It was in their mansions that she had heard the Spanish song that she had so aptly, fearlessly, and unwisely sung out in church. It was the current hit tune of society.

The sieur de Saint-Etienne soon ran into the lead in the race to win the latest debutante, aged about fifteen. This was not particularly young for those days. Saint-Etienne, very handsome and slick, was a good dancer, an unconscionable liar, a playboy. He loved to deflower. Trading on Ninon's inexperience and Madame de Lanclos's all but incredible connivance, he fed Ninon a line of patter that a few years later she would have laughed at. A good actor, he could swear undying love unblushingly. He talked vaguely of his inheritance in the far south, of his connection with the great Richelieu. He told Ninon what every young girl longs to hear and what anyone but Madame de Lanclos would have recognized as a package of lies. He was in fact a fortune hunter who had not the slightest intention of marrying a dowryless girl.

The fact that such an utterly useless rogue could have made headway with Ninon is eloquent testimony of her defenselessness. Madame de Lanclos, with her woman's sixth sense, might reasonably have been expected to smell a rat; instead she smiled, poured another glass of wine (tea was not yet introduced in France), and collaborated. In justice to Madame de Lanclos, it should be stated that her otherworldly way of life may have deprived her of knowledge of the ways of this world and that she was convinced, or at least had talked herself into it, that Saint-Etienne's intentions were honorable. On the other hand, Tallemant suspects that she was not as gullible as she seemed, alleging that she may have been venal, though he admits he is not sure.

Ninon evidently put up some resistance in defense of her virtue. Although her body thirsted, her spirit resisted. Saint-Etienne, always evasive when the subject of marriage came up, pulled his ace. If she loved him as he loved her, she would not make him suffer while he awaited permission from his father in the far south. Ninon was susceptible to this argument Nobody knows the details other than that the liaison was sweet and brief. Bursting with pride at having won the day (and the night) over his rivals, Saint-Etienne did not tarry long. There was no more talk of marriage.

When Madame de Lanclos became aware of the true state of affairs, she was frantic. For a long time Ninon was just numb, although Tallemant suggests there were stirrings in her womb, but he himself says he is not certain, and there is no evidence of Ninon's having given birth at this time. There is some evidence, though — far from conclusive — that Saint-Etienne may have reported favorably to Richelieu on Ninon, or boasted to him of his conquest. Voltaire who, as a boy, knew Ninon in her old age, and had listened to the tales that her contemporaries handed down, claims that "Cardinal Richelieu had the first favors of Ninon, which were probably the last of this great minister." If this alleged encounter with Richelieu did take place, it must have been before the end of 1642 — the date of the cardinal's death — when Ninon was nineteen. Another version is that Richelieu asked his mistress, the gorgeous Marion de l'Orme, to offer Ninon 150,000 livres ($300,000 to $750,-000) to be his mistress. The story goes that Ninon refused the offer, adding that it was too much from a lover and too little from one she did not love. Alas, although the reply shows a pretty wit, there is little evidence that Ninon was the author of it, and since she, all her life, had a horror of graybeards caressing her, she probably never slept with Richelieu. But that does not imply that Ninon had gone into cold storage. Saint-Etienne had awakened her, and her healthy young flesh hungered. He had thoroughly disillusioned her but not broken her heart. She had probably not really loved him but merely been infatuated, as well as having been pushed by her fatuous mother.

When the chevalier de Raré came along, perhaps having heard about Saint-Etienne's success, Ninon looked on him with different eyes. The criterion was not marriage but sex appeal. Scarron, a talented writer who was highly regarded in his day and by subsequent generations, called him "an amiable boy, well-made." Raré had won his degree in debauchery at an early age. He is said to have had, of all things, soulful eyes, which Ninon found irresistible. Madame de Lanclos, frightened by what had happened to her intended nun, was keeping as strict a watch on Ninon as her fast-failing health permitted. Ninon was rebellious and thought of leaving her but did not out of pity. But she was not going to deny herself indefinitely the pleasures of the flesh. She used to wait in the window for Raré to come, pretending to her mother she was knitting. One night she had slipped down when she saw him approaching. In the doorway they lost no time kissing. A beggar, no respecter of tender situations, importuned a handout. Raré evidently had no change so Ninon fished out an expensive lace handkerchief and gave it to the beggar, begging him to leave them in peace.

The affair continued until Madame de Lanclos's health took a turn for the worse, at which time Ninon shooed away Raré and the other hopefuls. She devoted herself to nursing her mother with single-minded zeal. She may not always have got along with her too well but she had a daughterly affection and, when needed, was at her bedside. So were black-robed nuns and priests. Their lugubrious chants and mournful mien irritated Ninon, who tried to cheer her mother up and let a little light into the darkened room rather than hold a dress rehearsal for the funeral. When Madame de Lanclos died in late 1642, Ninon managed to give her the expensive funeral with the full ritualistic pomp that she felt her mother would have wanted. Scarron refers to the "candles burning, censers swinging and priests chanting their funeral songs." (When Ninon herself died, some sixty-three years later, her will specified the simplest of burials.)

It is perhaps surprising that in her grief Ninon turned to the Church and not her friends for comfort. There is no mention anywhere of her brothers — the likelihood is they never reached maturity; thus Ninon at nineteen found herself completely alone except for a couple of aunts who do not seem to have been very close. It is true that Ninon had very little use for the Church and its often hypocritical clergy, but that does not mean she denied God. Throughout her life she tells us she had two daily prayers: "Every night I give thanks to God for my mind. Every morning I thank him for preserving me from the follies of my heart." The second prayer loses its piquancy unless given in the original: "Faites de moi un honnête homme et n'en fait jamais une honnête femme." ("Make of me an honnête homme* but never a chaste woman.")

Instinctively she seems to have known that the superficial pleasure-bent crowd she was moving in would be no use to her in her hour of sadness. She resolved to seek solace in a convent where the secluded life of piety would give her a chance to heal herself of her wound, a place where she could try to sort things out and determine a course of life. The nuns were kind and sympathetic. Always receptive to music, she found evensong a balm. The simple life agreed with her — Ninon was never to indulge in lavishness. For a time she considered taking the veil, as she evidently had found temporary peace. She would love to have pleased her mother. She seems to have experienced uplift from vespers and from her quiet meditative walks at eventide. But when the soul revives, very often the body perks up too. The pulses of life began to beckon; her active, bubbling mind could not long remain suppressed, her senses demanded fulfillment. Ninon quickly realized the difference between a cure and a lifelong vocation. Gratefully she kissed the nuns goodbye and went out into the world.

*

What a time it was in 1643 when Ninon left the convent! It was May in France after the long winter of Richelieu's constructive but stern rule. The strong cardinal had put down the haughty nobles with a mighty hand, determined to crush a

* Nobody has successfuly translated in two words *honnête homme* as used in the seventeenth century. It cannot be translated "honest man," though honesty was one of the constituents. An honnête homme was an honorable, cultivated, polished, gallant man — a perfect, or proper, or true, gentleman.

constant source of insurrection. The great fortified castles of the old feudal lords were leveled. Dueling, that passion of the French aristocracy, had been made punishable by death, and great seigneurs lost their heads by not heeding.

The nobility rejoiced at Richelieu's death in late 1642, close to the time of Madame de Lanclos's passing. About six months later Louis XIII followed his first minister to the grave. Louis had been a sour, dour monarch, and his court as a consequence was dull and lackluster. Uncomfortable with women, perhaps homosexual, he was anything but gallant. Annoyed one evening or frustrated by the deep cleavage in the décolletage of the lady next to him, Louis filled his mouth with wine and emptied it down her pectoral divide. When Louis died, the chief remaining restraint on the pleasure-loving nobility was removed.

The regent, Anne of Austria, decided to make up for lost time. For years she had been ignored by the king, who avoided her company as much as her bed. For five years, from Louis XIII's death in 1643 to the outbreak in 1648 of the Fronde — France's seriocomic rehearsal for the French Revolution — Anne and her court led the *dolce vita*. She teamed up with a protegé of Richelieu's, Cardinal Mazarin,* who sought out her company and bed in practically the same measure as her deceased husband had avoided them. Mazarin hoped to achieve by subtlety what Richelieu had by firmness. The nobles, mistaking the change of technique for a change in policy, started their intrigues again, both in politics and the bedroom. Their intrigues in government ended up in the Fronde, but their excursions in gallantry which, unlike Louis XIII, neither Anne nor Mazarin opposed, resulted in a period of great licentiousness albeit of an elegant nature.

---

* Mazarin, though a cardinal, had never been ordained a priest.

The time between Louis XIV's birth in 1638, and his father's death five years later, saw the star of the renowned salon of Madame de Rambouillet rise to its apogee. When Madame de Rambouillet, an Italian of noble birth, came to France as a bride shortly after the turn of the century, she found manners, morals, and language still smacking offensively of the crudities engendered by the terrible Religious Wars of the preceding century. She set about to refine the life of society. Thus, when libertinism of both manners and belief had its efflorescence during the regency, it took on an elegant character. The flamboyant libertinism of the year of Ninon's birth gave way to the elegant libertinism of twenty years after. Lovemaking was in style again, but it had to be done with style. Manners in bed became as de rigueur as manners in the drawing room. Not for nothing did Ninon's best friend, Saint-Evremond, nostalgically look back many years later, in a celebrated poem, to the "time of the Good Regency":

> There was no lover but served his king
> No warrior but served his lady.

It was this gay, sparkling climate that had beckoned to Ninon in the convent. She longed to bask in its sunshine — but how? Fall in love and marry a rich young lord? Perhaps she still harbored the thought, but it was not easy. The wretched matter of the dowry was in that hard century all but insurmountable. Marriage was a merger of moneybags, not a union of yearning bodies or souls. Furthermore, the scandal attendant upon her father's exile plus her lack of money had made her déclassée. True she did not lack for beaux, especially of the lupine variety, but Ninon wanted to satisfy more than just the sensual side of her nature. Undoubtedly at that juncture of her life, body came before mind, but not to the exclusion of mind. She was bent on living life fully, but the path was obscure. At the age of twenty, without family, without money, without advisers, without the possibility of a career, she was at a dangerous crossroads, having turned her back on the only alternative to marriage for a woman of quality — the veil.

Exactly when Ninon started to accept subsidies from Coulon, her first financial supporter, is a matter of some doubt. There is also disagreement* as to when Ninon met her first real love, Gaspard de Coligny, descendant of the great Huguenot, Admiral Coligny. Whether she began her seamy relationship with Coulon before or after falling helplessly and hopelessly in love with the highborn Coligny may hold the key to the explanation of why the fresh, flowerlike Ninon took up with the drink-addicted, dissolute Coulon. If her ill-fated liaison with Coligny preceded the relationship with Coulon, we can fairly safely infer that one of the principal reasons for Ninon's accepting in the person of Coulon what she termed a "payeur" (one who pays) is her acute disappointment in her love affair with Coligny. In the absence of definite knowledge on the point, but because it makes psychological sense, it will be assumed that Ninon had her bittersweet experience with Coligny prior to making her arrangement with Coulon.

Gaspard de Coligny, marquis d'Andelot and later the successor to his father's dukedom of Châtillon, was one of the entourage of the foremost captain of the day, the young duc d'Enghien, better known in history as the Great Condé. It was a glamorous set of the ranking young officers of France. The Thirty Years' War was still on, and the cream of French youth campaigned from the time when the ground hardened in the

* Tallemant says 1642; Magne, 1643.

spring until it froze in the late fall; winter they spent in Paris making love and frequenting the salons and cabarets. The long summer campaigns away from women led to considerable sexual perversion, and although most of the summer homosexuals were winter heterosexuals, their prowess in milady's boudoir, as a result of this dual allegiance, was often seriously attenuated, much to the chagrin of the ladies. It is a commonplace that it is difficult to serve two masters. It is even tougher to serve both a master and a mistress.

Gaspard de Coligny was a part-time sodomite. He engaged in homosexual relations with, among others, the duc d'Enghien, later one of Ninon's staunchest admirers. In all fairness, though, it does not seem to have dampened his ardor for the dazzling Marion de l'Orme, who was largely responsible for introducing Ninon to Parisian society. The comte de Chavagnac recounts in his *Memoirs* an incident involving Coligny and Chavagnac's brother. The latter's good looks had gained for him Marion's favor. Now handsome Chavagnac was far from a dog in the manger and could not think of keeping Marion all for himself, or from his good friend Coligny. Marion had a soul, too, and gallantly fell in with Chavagnac's suggestion that they make it a threesome. But battle called, and off went her two lovers true. Rushing back after the Piedmont campaign in 1639, they found a changed Marion. She had been gravely ill in their absence and had made a covenant with the Lord — in the future to use her body for the reclamation of the souls of Protestants. Chavagnac and Coligny, who were Protestants, thought the lovely Roman Catholic was fooling, but Marion was dead serious. Only when the two young soldiers converted to Catholicism did Marion take them to their reward. Remarks the comte de Chavagnac (brother of the convert), "The Lord uses all sorts of means to lead us back to him."

A man who puts his love of a woman before his love of the religion of his forebears sounds rather ardent. But fidelity to history demands mention that Gaspard was not making the sacrifice exclusively because of his passion for Marion. Evidently young Coligny had his mind set on making a good marriage as well as gaining an exciting prize. His choice for a wife was a certain Isabelle-Angélique of the great Montmorency family. She was Catholic and would not marry a Protestant, and Coligny evidently had in the back of his mind that he might as well kill two birds of paradise with one conversion. But history is seldom clear-cut. Just when the conclusion is reached that Coligny may not have been such an incandescent lover after all, contradictory evidence about his love life is encountered. Coligny died in battle early in the Fronde. What was he, the husband of Isabelle-Angélique de Montmorency, wearing under his armor? The blue garter of Mademoiselle de Guerchy, his mistress! It seems that the outstanding characteristic of Coligny's lovemaking was inexhaustible interest in women and a consistent inconstancy. In all probability enduring passion was not his forte or, if it was, he did not show that side of himself to Ninon.

Particularly in her early youth, Ninon was very susceptible to Coligny's brand of attractiveness. He was handsome, vivacious, a magnificent dresser, spent lavishly, and had won a reputation for great bravery on the field of battle. Ninon assumed he would be equally good on the proving grounds of love; she was, alas, to conclude differently. Ninon probably met him in the glittering salon of Marion de l'Orme where the duc d'En-

ghien and his lively band of warriors foregathered in the cold
months to warm their hearts and their bodies by gazing upon
their hostess — one of the most strikingly beautiful women in
Paris. At this particular moment rumor had it that Coligny
was beginning to tire of Marion. Ninon was not invited to the
*sanctum sanctorum* of society, the hôtel de Rambouillet, because of the scandal of her father's killing of Chabans, but her
popularity had come to Marion's attention, and she was welcomed at the latter's house. Ninon was ten years or more Marion's junior but was not as good-looking or half as experienced.
Marion, therefore, did not fear her as a rival. On the contrary,
her attractiveness, grace, unusual skill in lute-playing and dancing would make her a valuable and ornamental addition to
Marion's salon.

It must have been no mean tour de force for Marion to
handle and keep in line so large a group of playful officers,
many of whom frequented the famous Blue Room of the hôtel
de Rambouillet, where the ladies kept themselves on pedestals,
or at least pretended they did, and where exaggerated respect
for women made them all but untouchable. Alternating between the hôtel de Rambouillet where the ladies bloomed
under glass, and Marion's drawing room where good conversation, music, and dancing did not preclude lovemaking, the
young bloods could easily have got out of hand because Marion
was not promiscuous when she was in love. Each of the guests,
however, lived in the hope that his time would come. Marion
probably thought Ninon could help entertain and at the same
time maintain the elegant, decorous tone of her drawing room.
Marion was overconfident. Coligny was an inconstant lover.

When Ninon knew that Coligny had become aware of her,

she decided to precipitate matters. She wrote to him. This assumption of the offensive was not just a youthful tactical error. It was very basic in Ninon's character — directness and something more — the first sign of a determination on her part to adopt a man's technique. A student of mores from an early age, Ninon was already rebelling at what today we call the double standard. Why, she asked herself, should the world extol a man's prowess as an aggressive suitor but a woman's virtue? Why must a man always be the chooser, the woman the passive chosen? It was all convention and hypocrisy, for everyone knew that women have preferences, desire, and lust just as men. Let women, held Ninon, show their love, not retire behind a false modesty which too many men mistook for lack of interest. Furthermore, observed Ninon, a woman should contribute equally, not just sit back, look pretty, and let the man amuse her. The woman must be entertaining, too. Writing to her male alter ego, Saint-Evremond, many decades later, Ninon said, "It is not enough [for a woman] to be wise, one must be engaging." At an early age Ninon determined to live and act like a man.

And so she took the initiative and wrote Coligny of her love — openly, unashamedly. She probably felt she could offer the spoiled Coligny more than Marion: her first genuine love (she had not loved Saint-Etienne), her complete self — body, mind, and soul — a profounder, richer, more tender, and more subtle love than the superficial though ravishing Marion could possibly muster. Coligny was not the type to appreciate Ninon's candor and simplicity. Had he been deeper, he would have particularly valued this flouting of convention — all the more extraordinary because only the warmth of her feeling plus a valorous independence of mind could have brought her to break with custom at such an early age.

Coligny, of course, hurried to answer the call. But he brought only desire, not understanding; curiosity, not passion; half-heartedness, not abandon. Ninon's disappointment and shock the twentieth century would call traumatic. She had worn her heart on her sleeve — vulnerable, naked. Coligny was not an ardent lover, lacking stamina. Perhaps his masculinity had been weakened in those long summer evenings in camp with the duc d'Enghien. Ninon, at first not accepting defeat, is said to have tried to arouse the flagging Coligny by being even more prodigal of herself. This only made Coligny feel all the more inadequate, and he fled. But Ninon, who, as Tallemant says, "you will see later was especially the type that left and was not left, did not find this treatment bearable and complained of it to La Moussaye, who patched things up and brought back the fugitive." This time, however, Coligny convinced Ninon of his basic inadequacy. Having at least got him to come back, her pride a little mollified, she sadly let him go. Some say he went back to Marion. The contemporary vaudevillians said he returned to his "pretty boys."

The Coligny affair marks the end of Ninon's girlhood. Living in a classical, unsentimental age, Ninon probably never had too much of the hearts-and-flowers variety of love in her makeup anyway. Her tears seemed to have washed away any residual thoughts of marriage. Perhaps, until Coligny, Ninon had still dreamed of a knight on a white charger, who would not require a dowry. Now she became reconciled with reality. In addition, her growing spirit of independence was turning her against the whole idea of marriage — dowry or no dowry.

This was probably not just rationalization — to despise that which she could not have — it was part of her fight against the double standard. Marriage was an odious tyranny then, with the husband the tyrant and the wife not much better than a slave. To begin with, the *mariage de convenance* usually doomed itself from the start. Children were often affianced before their teens. A fifteen-year-old girl would be married to a sixty-year-old man. Infidelity under such circumstances was almost inevitable, but in that man's world, whereas infidelity on the part of the man was considered par, infidelity on the part of the woman was punishable by whipping, which in the upper classes was seldom invoked, or by imprisonment in a convent where corporal punishment could be added to enforced confinement for life. The threat of punishment did little to restrain the ladies, for obviously it takes two to make love, and if every faithless wife had been incarcerated, there would never have been enough convents to accommodate them; but the whole spiritual climate, even when duress was not used, was brutal and demeaning.

The seventeenth-century dramatist, the abbé de Pure, in his play, *La Précieuse,* has a young lady say:

> Evandre bought land in our province and sometime later bought a wife too . . . they spent three months in negotiating just the price . . . I was the innocent victim sacrificed to the obscure interests of my family, but sacrificed like a slave, bound, stifled, without having the liberty of speaking my desires, of choosing . . . [A wife is] obliged to love him whom she hates, respect an object of disdain . . . she is obliged to receive in her glacial bosom the ardors of her husband, to endure the caresses of a man she dislikes, who is the horror of her senses and her heart . . .

Childbearing was an inescapable duty, not a consummated wish. Pregnancies were frequent with a callous disregard for the woman's health. Madame de Sévigné returns to the same theme again and again in her letters to her daughter, Madame de Grignan, whose health and beauty she watched over carefully.

> Bear your pregnancy in a good manner and after that, if Monsieur de Grignan loves you, and does not want to kill you, I know what he will do, or rather what he will not do.

Another of Ninon's objections to marriage stems from her honesty, an honesty which later became proverbial. Ninon disliked the way married couples deceived each other. She had nothing against promiscuity, but she bridled at taking oaths of fidelity and then making a mockery of them. Lord Rochester, father of the countess of Sandwich, one of Ninon's greatest admirers in her (Ninon's) old age, wrote of the faithlessness at Whitehall in Charles II's time, a fairly good copy of what was going on at the French court:

> Then talk not of Inconstancy
> False hearts or broken vows,
> If I by miracle can be
> This live-long minute true to thee
> 'Tis all that Heaven allows.

Cuckolding was, more often than not, treated as a joke. There is probably nothing the French of the seventeenth century found funnier than a husband made ridiculous by a cheating wife. The story is told of the delectable duchesse de Montbazon that one night, while receiving a lover in her bedroom, her old husband, who used to sleep on the story below, came upstairs and opened her door. "I heard a noise," said he. "It wouldn't be a rat?"

"Quite so," replied his merry duchess. "But don't worry, I am holding it."

Ninon was part of her century in that she would have laughed as heartily at this incident as anybody else. Ninon was exceptional in that she did not want to be a party to it. If breaking one's vow was a necessary part of marriage, she'd have none of it. But Ninon needed financial support. Some not too reliable sources suggest she had an income, presumably from her father, of around seven or eight thousand livres a year ($14,000 to $40,000). This is unlikely. For when Monsieur de Lanclos left, his property was seized by court order. It may well have been lifted or partly so, as Madame de Lanclos and Ninon did get by somehow, and it is unlikely it was on the charity of relatives. But if Ninon had the equivalent of somewhere between $14,000 and $40,000 a year, she probably would never have accepted anything from Coulon, for, unlike Marion de l'Orme or the duchesse de Montbazon, her wants were modest all her life. "You know," she wrote to Saint-Evremond many years later, "the profit I could have made out of selling my body." What she did need was enough money to live nicely, to receive her widening circle of interesting people, otherwise there would have been no place for her in the society of that day. When she did get together enough money for that — she was a shrewd investor — she soon got rid of the Coulons.

## ᘓᔭ Chapter 4 ᔮᘗ

### Feeling Her Way

IF A MAN, as the saying goes, is known by the company he keeps, it might be argued that a woman is known by the men she is kept by. Tallemant states that Coulon paid 500 livres a month ($1000 to $2500) for the privilege of visiting Ninon once a month, starting probably in 1643. What do we know of Coulon?

He was a counselor in Parlement — a word not to be translated by "parliament." A closer rendering would be "court," a judicial body which also theoretically had the right to register or not register royal decrees. Coulon was such a drunk that the Parlement considered expelling him. Like many another playboy of the regency, he divided his time between drink and women. In a letter to the Great Condé in 1649 Lenet wrote; ". . . Last night debauchery held the stage . . . at Coulon's place, where they danced all night, completely naked, behind closed doors." Coulon's most unusual quality was his extraordinary relationship with the great financier, d'Emery — his wife's lover. Far from bearing d'Emery a grudge, Coulon publicly sang his praises. He evidently disliked his wife so much that he was grateful to d'Emery for taking her off his hands. Whether or not he got even with his wife for her many infidelities by being able to boast that the reigning toast of Paris,

Ninon de Lanclos, received him, he unconsciously got revenge by overplaying his role of admirer and leechlike friend of d'Emery. The latter finally got sick of Coulon's constant solicitations of favors for friends and took his leave of the Coulon ménage, abandoning Madame Coulon for Marion de-l'Orme. This must have hurt Madame Coulon greatly and undoubtedly had something to do with the bitter campaign of vilification which she now waged against Ninon.

Can Ninon be known by the men she was kept by? On the contrary, Tallemant states that Ninon divided her men into three classes: payeurs, martyrs, and favorites. The payeurs she had little to do with; the martyrs awaited her caprice; the favorites were those to whom she felt attracted at the time, and whom she took to bed but from whom she would not take a sou.

Ninon had five recorded payeurs: Coulon, the comte d'Aubijoux, Fourreau, Vassé, and young Moreau. Of the five, only Coulon was definitely off-color. Very little is known about Fourreau and Vassé other than that the former was very proficient with a knife and fork and that the latter had halitosis — neither of which qualities particularly qualified them as bedmates. The comte d'Aubijoux, who for years shared with Coulon the upkeep of Ninon, was a distinguished, well-educated, courteous gentleman of taste. In their joint support of Ninon and joint tenure of their limited privileges with her, Coulon and d'Aubijoux were not embarking on something entirely new. D'Aubijoux liked partnerships. He had shared the favors of the wife of Président * Tambonneau; her sister, d'Aubijoux thought, would be just right for Coulon. They made a

* *Président* means "judge."

merry foursome. The two cronies, having got along so well with two sisters, reasoned they might deepen their beautiful friendship by concentrating their attentions not on two sisters but just on one person — Ninon. This singular attitude evidently worked well, for there is no indication of any ructions. Coulon may well have had an attractive side to him. Otherwise the elegant d'Aubijoux, who is as good an example as any of the distinguished libertins of the regency, could not have stomached him.

Ninon's partisans, including the knowledgeable Emile Magne, show almost touching unanimity in claiming that the payeurs did not sleep with her. So sought after was she that they claim her drawing room became a kind of status symbol — an end sufficient unto itself and implying no physical intimacy. This theory might apply to Coulon, Fourreau, and Vassé, who seem to have needed acceptance rather badly and who would never have gained admittance to Ninon's house by dint of any consideration other than money. Moreau was simply star struck and would (and evidently did) have given anything to be in the presence of his goddess. But it hardly accounts for d'Aubijoux, who with his endowments and accomplishments rated admission on merit alone. Some say that he loved just talking with Ninon, intrigued by her wit and liveliness, and that perhaps he felt he secured this pleasure by being her protector. This assumption is not too convincing. D'Aubijoux was attractive. Their activities were probably not exclusively verbal. Tallemant is explicit about it: "Coulon and d'Aubijoux . . . did not touch her except when the fancy seized her." In other words, Tallemant is saying that their payments conferred no automatic rights, and that Ninon retained the power of veto. Magne, however, goes further. Evidently proceeding on the unarguable grounds that, though Tallemant was a contemporary, he was not an eyewitness, Magne says, "Coulon and d'Aubijoux, held waiting, did not assuage her joyful ardors which months of *chastity* intensified." [Italics mine.] Magne seems to be sure that the payeurs' admission to Ninon's couch was purely de jure, not de facto. Qui sait?

If Ninon did sleep with the payeurs, she had no qualms of conscience. For her the act of intercourse was nothing sacred, but just about on a level with having an exciting lunch with an acquaintance. Ever since her disillusionment with Coligny, Ninon regarded desire as a purely blind, mechanical or chemical force, aroused whimsically and presupposing no merit on the part of the arouser. Desire was a delicious gift of nature, but completely irrational, inexplicable, mysterious. Inasmuch as it presumed no depth of genuine feeling, nor implied any mutual obligations, Ninon saw no moral issue involved. Instead of marrying for money or security, or breaking the marital vow, Ninon preferred to sell her company rather than her integrity and independence. She felt that since love was unaccountably here today and gone tomorrow, fidelity was a foolish, restrictive convention that was both unnatural and unrealistic. On the other hand she considered that friendship, if soundly based, could be enduring. Thus she held friendship sacred, and to it she dedicated her constancy. Her contemporary, the duc de Saint-Simon, not noted for being saccharine, wrote in his *Memoirs:*

> . . . She was full of goodness and integrity. She often placed her purse and credit at the service of her friends and entered into important negotiations on their behalf, very honestly holding con-

siderable moneys and secrets which they entrusted to her. All of which caused her to be held in an esteem and respect altogether remarkable.

To Ninon this was morality, not sexual restraint. The usually tart-tongued Princesse Palatine, sister-in-law of Louis XIV, gave her the ultimate accolade. "There is nobody more of an honnête homme than Mademoiselle de Lanclos." It will be recalled that one of the indispensable attributes of an honnête homme is honor personified. Unlike other aristocratic ladies who accepted money, Ninon was never greedy, never hankered after great luxury. Though Ninon had many lovers, it was well known that she could not be bought. The Grand Prior, Louis XIII's half brother, could certainly have afforded to offer munificent inducements, as could many others who vainly sued for her favor, but Ninon was inaccessible unless the suitor was her physical (or less frequently, her mental) type. The memoirists refer frequently to her independence and pecuniary disinterestedness. Says Voltaire: "She went in for a life a little libertine, but was never a public courtesan. Never did self-interest cause her to make the slightest move." Well — hardly ever.

A few of Ninon's critics have called her a prostitute. For this ancient profession Ninon lacked two qualifications often attributed to it — venality and frigidity. Some reference has already been made to the first. Ninon would not or could not marry, and she had to live. Men in her day as in ours sold their ability for money, e.g., doctors, lawyers, the military. But a woman of the upper classes could not then earn a living, with the possible exception of the ill-favored Mademoiselle de Scudéry, whose books, fortunately, were the rage. There were no Eve Curies, Claire Luces, Eleanor Roosevelts, Helena Rubinsteins, Indira Gandhis. The stage was considered disreputable for women. Ninon had the courage of her convictions in refusing to submit to the bondage and deceptions of seventeenth-century marriage; she had to live, and to a limited number she sold the right to her company, but she was never available to anybody or everybody. That she considered the practice distasteful is shown by the fact that she never became rich but just accepted enough to maintain the minimum standard so that she would not lose caste. As soon as she achieved a modest financial independence, she dismissed the payeurs.

The other usual qualification of the prostitute — frigidity — Ninon did not have in the slightest. She reveled in nature's bounty without romanticizing or sentimentalizing sex, not distilling out its juice by allowing a sense of sin or remorse to creep in. She retained, longer than most, her ability to thrill to erotic sensation, though the stories of her driving men mad with desire when she was eighty-five are myths. With her impeccable manners and elegance of mind and heart, she is the antithesis of the prostitute. She engaged in what the French call "la belle galanterie," which elevated a relaxed and natural attitude toward sex to libertinism* — an elite philosophy whose seventeenth-century adherents had an ideological position to which they often clung more passionately and certainly more consistently than to their lovers.

Ninon's friend, Marion de l'Orme, also went in for la belle galanterie. Marion constantly weaves in and out of the first decade of Ninon's life in society, crisscrossing her path with

---

* As will be seen later, libertinism had two facets — that of manners and that of thought. La belle galanterie only embraced libertinism of manners.

common lovers or friends like Coligny, Miossens, Saint-Evremond, Scarron, and the duc d'Enghien. Ninon had probably
met all five at Marion's by the time she was twenty. Like
Ninon, Marion remained single. She was one of the great
beauties of the century. She "did not possess," says Emile
Magne, "Ninon's magnificent erudition, but she was more
beautiful . . . Painters have portrayed her playing the lute and
thus displaying her face and the delicacy of her hands but they
could not portray her proud carriage and deportment, which
were fit for a queen . . ."

The gallant French seem to keep a hold on themselves while
describing Marion's face and hair and shoulders and hands.
But when they attempt describing her body, they take right off.
"As to the rest," says her contemporary, de Corbeville, "bombs
and grenades explode."

Like Ninon, Marion came of the lesser nobility, but of a
much richer, country family. Chafing under the strict discipline of her father, she stealthily followed her lover, Des Barreaux, to Paris in 1636, some two or three years before Ninon
made her presence felt in society. Des Barreaux (later one of
Ninon's entourage) made a great mistake in introducing Marion, a splendid, luscious twenty-five, into Paris society. He
should have tried, if possible, to hide her light under a bushel.

She went to the top within three or four years, becoming
Cardinal Richelieu's mistress. But she was soon disenchanted.
He was stingy — or at least he was to her. "A cardinal, believe
me, he is nothing much when he no longer has on his red hat
and scarlet robe," she said.

Almost every man who was anybody in Paris flocked to Marion's salon. It was probably around 1642 that Ninon won Co-

ligny away from her. This turned out disastrously for Ninon, for not only did she know the bitterness of unrequited love when Coligny proved casual, but she earned Marion's understandable resentment for filching Coligny — short-lived though Ninon's triumph had been. Ninon became unwelcome at Marion's house and had to strike out on her own. But by this time she was well launched.

Marion did not have to pine over the loss of Coligny who may have gone back to her anyway. There was always a line-up waiting. Those who could not win her through love sought to win her by money. Great financiers like d'Emery vied to keep her. She kept high state. Her extravagance was in the grand manner. "She never," Tallemant tells us, "wore the same pair of gloves twice." Yet she did it all with such taste and decorum, that Tallemant reports that in any other such a life would have been held to be dishonorable, but not in Marion. The mighty not only flocked to her house but welcomed her to theirs. The Great Condé (later Ninon's lover), cousin to the king, invited Marion to his wedding.

Her beauty carried all before it. One day, wearing long gloves and a dress with the deep décolletage standard for the period, she visited a judge, the président de Mesme, to request the release of her brother who had been imprisoned for debt. After the interview the président escorted Marion to her carriage. "Is it possible, mademoiselle," said he trancelike, "that I have lived to this hour without having seen you?" What Marion replied is unrecorded, but it is recorded that that very day the brother was let out.

\*

Dreux du Radier, the eighteenth-century belletrist, wrote:

The nature of Ninon was firm, broad, elevated, noble — that of a true philosopher; Marion was only lively and amusing. The one formulated a system and thought deeply, even in the arms of pleasure, the other was all temperament. The mind in Ninon guided sentiment; sentiment in Marion guided the mind; one was seduced by the charms of Marion, but one could disengage himself when thinking things over; the more one reflected on the merit of Ninon, the less one was disposed to leave her. The infidelities of Marion annoyed her lovers and drove them away; Ninon was unfaithful with such judgment that one did himself an injury to blame her. One would never have been attracted to Marion if she had not been beautiful; it was her first merit. It was only the second of Ninon's, and without beauty she would have had a host of admirers; one almost forgot her physical attraction in favor of her mind, her character, and her conversation. But in Marion one saw only a charming creature, who had sprightliness and playfulness because of her beauty . . . The one was the way one would wish all women would be; . . . the other was the way they ordinarily are when they are agreeable and coquettish.

In the Hôtel Louvois in Paris, just opposite the Bibliothèque Nationale, there may be a modern comparison. As everybody knows, Frenchmen have two great loves — women and good food. In reverence and respect they commemorate great historical personages by naming dishes after them, e.g., Petite Marmite Henri IV (soup). At the Louvois, the menu would offer Ananas Ninon (pineapple) twice a week. And evidently with due consideration for Marion's star of lesser magnitude, the menu listed Gâteaux Marion de l'Orme (cakes) about once every two weeks. In other words, a ratio of four to one in

Ninon's favor. Evidently the French too, like the English, sometimes go in for understatement. It seemed ineffably Gallic and gracious of them to call the dish "Gâteaux Marion de l'Orme" instead of perhaps "Tarte Marion de l'Orme," as a less gallant Anglo-Saxon might have done.

Both Ninon and Marion exerted a strong gravitational pull on clergymen — high and low. Hobnobbing with a prince of the Church, Cardinal Richelieu, did not prevent the democratic Marion from being friendly with a simple abbé, Paul Scarron. Young Scarron, who was to become a powerful influence on Ninon, had no feeling whatsoever for the Church into which he had been thrust at nineteen by his stepmother to get him off her hands. Scarron came of a distinguished family. The usual pattern for sons of a good family was for the first son to become an officer; the second, instead of giving orders in the army, was usually expected to take orders and enter the Church. Even in an age when the Church took to its ample bosom hosts of young men and women who were anything but of the spiritually elect, Scarron was a worse misfit than most. He was a gay, frolicsome, witty bon vivant to the core, with authentic literary talent for high-class burlesque, picaresque fiction, and love songs. His writing eventually brought him fame and made him one of Paris's literary lions.

In 1637 or 1638 — shortly before Ninon made her debut — Scarron's life had taken a tragic turn in Le Mans, a small town some 120 miles southwest of Paris. According to La Baumelle,* considered by some an unreliable historian, the scene was carni-

---

* In *Memoires . . . de Madame de Maintenon*. Scarron was Madame de Maintenon's first husband.

val time — perhaps the Mardi Gras. Scarron, then a vigorous
twenty-seven or twenty-eight and presumably feeling intoler-
ably cooped up, had been watching the parade from his monastery. As the merriment and the carousing of the carnival
mounted to a peak, Scarron is said to have ripped open a mattress, smeared his naked body with honey, and dived into the
feathers. He emerged a bird with no recognizable Latin or
French name. The bird did somersaults and handsprings. At
first it terrified the women, chirping and capering. But then
some wench recognized the abbé and, summoning friends,
gave indignant pursuit to the feathered cleric who, they
thought, was a disgrace to the cloth he was not wearing. They
started plucking off the feathers. Scarron, who would have
given anything to be able to take to his wings, could only take
to his heels, and eventually eluded the panting pursuers by
plunging, half denuded of his feathers, into the freezing waters
of the river. He had to hide in the bulrushes until dark, shiver-
ing violently. The account may be apocryphal, but what is certain is that Scarron contracted paralytic fever which left him a
cripple for life. The only change in his condition was for the
worse. The progressive arthritis converted and twisted a once
lively, active fun-lover, bubbling with joie de vivre, into a de-
formed gnome, bound to his bed or chair by the iron grip of his
disease. Eventually he could only move his hands, using a stick
to scratch himself with. He had a chair rigged up with pulleys.
But his spirit and mind remained uncrushed.

Scarron moved to Paris, no doubt to be near doctors, then a
formidable menace. His literary ability soon attracted attention. He was given a small royal pension. The great and near-
great of Paris flocked to his dingy room to savor his conversa-

tion crackling with wit, his skillful thrusts at pomposity. He excelled in raillery, a much-prized gift among the French which might be termed a refined, rich relative of our word *kidding*. Raillery consisted mainly in exposing the ludicrous side of solemnity and stolidity. Ninon was a past mistress at it. A favorite of the ladies in the days of his health, Scarron had probably been admitted to Marion's bed. When he was seized by paralysis, Marion did not desert him but called on him regularly. Perhaps she brought Ninon with her. Scarron and Ninon liked each other immediately and became close friends for life. There is little doubt that Ninon honed the delicacy of her raillery on the sharpness of Scarron's brilliant mind. But hers was, as one might expect, feminine, less cutting, more good-natured. It is a miracle that Scarron retained any sense of humor at all, and natural that Ninon, who enjoyed resplendent health to a very old age, should have been more lighthearted and benign.

He was a man of great perception. He met Ninon when she was floundering around, unsure of her place in the world, heeding only one directive, that of the urgency of her senses. He soon saw that beyond her youthful wildness were depths that probably few others, except notably Saint-Evremond, suspected. The visitors to Scarron's drab flat used to bring their own meals and then sit around talking and laughing for hours. Ninon was not only attentive, but kind. To a cripple particularly, the tenderness of an attractive young woman was sunshine, warm and caressing, a reason for living, something to look forward to when his pain-wracked body could not even toss and turn through the hell of his sleepless nights. Ninon's tenderness Scarron repaid with great insight. He worried about her, but not about Marion, whom he knew to be a filly of a different color. Ninon, he saw, had a soul (though she always denied it) and could easily be hurt. Besides, she was a good deal younger than Marion and without protectors. It was the fashion to send New Year's gifts (étrennes). Scarron was poor and sent a poem instead.

> O beautiful and charming Ninon
> No one ever says nay
> To whatever you ask
> So great is the authority
> In all places of a young person
> When, along with a mind, she has beauty.
> Alas! This New Year
> I have nothing good enough or beautiful enough
> Out of which to fashion a present
> Therefore pray be pleased with my good wishes.
>
> Thus I wish for Ninon
> Not too surly a husband but one who is handsome and good
> Lots of game all through Lent,
> Good Spanish wine, fat chestnuts,
> Lots of money without which man is sad and wan
> And may every one esteem her as much as Scarron does.

This poem was written for New Year's 1643, soon after Ninon's mother died. It was after Ninon's love affair with Coligny, which had hurt her keenly and which was probably the last straw in causing her to give up the idea of marriage. Scarron evidently does not know of Ninon's decision and wishes that the highly nubile young woman of twenty will not get tied up with a brute of a husband. But it is the last line which is the

telling one — Scarron suspects that Ninon's unbridled life may
be ruining her reputation, fears not for her physical but for her
spiritual virginity, hopes that the world will not fail to appreciate and render its due to Ninon's essential goodness, high courage, and abundant talent. Thus in a bizarre, unlikely coupling,
the libertine Scarron joined the prim Madame de Lanclos in
worrying about Ninon, and strangely enough what both worried about, in their highly disparate ways, was Ninon's soul.
With one or perhaps two exceptions, they were probably the
only two people in all Paris, a city glittering brilliantly but
coldly like ice in the sunshine, who then cared a jot for her.

Forever pursing alleviation of his monstrous pain, Scarron
decided to move across the river from the Marais to the Left
Bank, hoping the baths of Saint-Germain might help. He sig-
nalized his departure in a poem — "Adieu au Marais et à la
Place Royale." A good deal of it, probably written in 1644, is
taken up with Ninon.

> . . . So true is it that a girl, too beautiful
> Starts nothing but quarrels.
> For fear that this happens
> Try not to wound so much
> And command your glances
> To cause fewer casualties.

Voltaire found this poem notable in that he thought it indicated that duels were being fought over Ninon. This seems to
be only conjecture; no contemporary mentions them. As a
matter of fact, Ninon had a singular talent for keeping the temper of her admirers below their ignition point and, even more
extraordinary, for keeping former lovers as faithful friends, not

disaffected sour gripers. What is perhaps more notable is Scarron's reference to Ninon as "too beautiful," which brings up the moot question of Ninon's appearance.

There is considerable evidence that Scarron engaged in exaggeration in terming Ninon "too beautiful." Even after allowing for poetic license and Gallic gallantry, "too beautiful" suggests exceptional beauty — something Ninon probably did not have. Tallemant reports, "As for beauty, Ninon never had much; but she always had great charm." Members of the cult which insist Ninon was a great beauty reply that Tallemant is a poor witness — he was one of those suspect Frenchmen who thought his wife wonderful.

Another contemporary, Segrais, author of *The Dictionary of the Précieuses,* has this to say:

> She is a very dreamy girl, who permits herself to indulge in a melancholy of which those who saw her only in company would scarcely believe her capable, for she appears agreeable there and shows a vivacity of spirit which makes her sought after by all those who know how to savor the pleasure of conversing with witty people. As for beauty, although she is well enough schooled in what it takes to inspire love, it must however be admitted that her mind is more attractive than her face and that many would escape her toils if they confined themselves just to looking at her.

Again, the members of the club devoted to proving Ninon was a Venus reply that Segrais was unfair to Ninon because she was not one of the précieuses that he so admired — the overrefined, affected, austere, platonic-lover type of précieuse that Molière ridiculed. Ninon was a précieuse galante and presumably not Segrais's cup of bouillon, they claim.

What is more, says the scholarly Emile Magne, none of the

contemporary writers on Ninon knew her before she was forty. It is all very well for the opposition to answer, say Ninon's adherents, that she was supposed to have retained her youth to a great age and therefore at forty her contemporaries did not have to read between the lines in her face, but still Ninon could not then by definition have been in what the French love to call the "full bloom of her beauty." By and large Ninon's portraits do not give much comfort to the proponents of her beauty. Most of her portraits or alleged portraits show a woman of fifty-plus, with a very plain face. An explanation might be that France, though bursting with talent in almost every other field of art, had mediocre portrait painters in the seventeenth century. They even succeeded in making Marion de l'Orme look almost like a scarecrow — that same Marion about whose marvelous beauty there was such unanimity.

Emile Magne contends, however, that one of Ninon's portraitists, Mignard, the official Court painter, produced a reasonable likeness, from which he draws the following:

> . . . Crowning with a halo the perfect oval of her face, her heavy golden chestnut hair . . . flows in silken ringlets toward her throat and shoulders. The head is small . . . mounted on a neck of deliciously molded suppleness . . . Her bodice, bordered with lace, veils . . . the harmonious bust of a goddess. Under a broad, bold forehead, radiating intelligence, black eyes, shadowed by the double arc of thick eyebrows . . . mingle gravity with sweetness. Slim, straight, delicate, the nose prepares us for the marvels of the mouth which lends to the face all its attractiveness, a dainty mouth, sparkling, where kisses and laughter still seem to flutter . . .

What a shame that the artist limited his work to a bust! But we know of what firm and coralline roundness the bosom of Ninon was made:

> Who fain would know the likeness in Nature
> Of Ninon's beautiful breasts?
> Let him imagine the bud
> Of a new rose;
> Sometimes, pushing back the corset
> This beautiful breast shows itself,
> And it is the rose bathed in milk
> Which alone is more beautiful.*

The admirers of Ninon praise her modest countenance, her timidity . . . her easy gait, her elegant figure, the happy proportions of her body. They attest to the enchantment of her voice and convey the charm of her gestures rendered beguiling by the delicacy of her well-manicured hands.

Ninon figures more than once in the contemporary fiction of the time. In Madeleine de Scudéry's novel *Clélie,* she appears as Clarice.

> Clarice . . . is capable of pleasing everybody by a certain natural way which gives her grace . . . She loves to conduct an innocent war against her friends . . . She has a tender and sensitive heart, she will cry with afflicted friends: she will cut short her pleasures when friendship requires it; . . . she is capable of keeping a secret and of discretion; she is generous and constant . . . and in sum so likable that she is loved by the most honorable people of the Court . . .

Equally complimentary is the picture of her as Pithie in Angélique Petit's *L'Amour eschapé:*

---

* Author unknown to me.

Nobody ever danced better than Pithie; she plays the lute in a
fashion which charms all who hear . . . When she has to be serious and to speak of lofty things, she does so admirably . . . In a
word, the capital . . . should consider itself fortunate to have such
an illustrious girl.

Consideration of the forgoing and much other evidence lead
to the conclusion that Ninon was not a great beauty. She evidently had that type of face which when passive was passable
but when animated was unsurpassable. She probably would
not have photographed well, having mobile features which the
still camera or painter cannot render. But she had something
which her contemporaries valued more than beauty — grace.
The arbiter of taste and elegance of that day was the chevalier
de Méré, who devoted a lifetime to the study of the art of living.
He wrote of the honnête homme with which polite society was
peopled. To Méré happiness lay in subscribing to the code of
the honnête homme, in moving urbanely, effortlessly, and elegantly in the paths of moderation with exquisite grace. There
must be no ostentation, nothing forced. He preferred half tones
to blatant colors in clothes, in conversation, in behavior. Naturalness, simplicity, subtlety, and ease were the desiderata. People wrote Méré — it was an epistolary age — on problems of
manners, expression, conduct, and propriety. "Beauty and
grace," he replied to Madame de Lesdiguières, "are the same
thing but appear diversely and under different names. If this
amiable quality shows itself with much glamour and is very
apparent, we call it beauty; and when it is a little somber and
one discovers it with some difficulty, we give it the name of
grace and charm; notice that this beauty, covered as if by a
cloud, is usually more perfect than that which is seen at once;

and from that it follows that a lady should consider herself happier that we find her charming rather than beautiful."

The princesse Palatine asserted that Ninon was one of the most honnêtes hommes she knew. The hat trick was not so much that Ninon, a woman, successfully lived the life of an honnête homme. It was that she simultaneously retained her incomparable feminine grace; with which Méré, though hard to satisfy, was well pleased. He became her lover, and Tallemant says she bore him a child.*

*

Ninon brought sunshine to more people than just the crippled poet Scarron, who perhaps out of gratitude had called her "a girl, too beautiful." When a charming, intelligent, young woman calls regularly on an invalid and shows him tenderness, it is not hard for the man to indulge in hyperbole. However, when Scarron called her "the most astonishing girl of the century," he possibly was a good deal more accurate than in his "too beautiful" description.

On one of those warm, sunny days in Paris when staying indoors is unthinkable, Ninon decided to go visiting — again to the Left Bank, but farther out than where poor Scarron lived. The object of this visit, which Ninon would never have considered an errand of mercy — for she delighted to enliven and make gay — was a septuagenarian. She evidently had not heard from him for some time and may have been concerned he might not be well. Ninon had brought along her lute, for he loved music passionately. It was probably through their common interest in music that they had come to know each other. Old Des Yveteaux had had the regard of the late king, Henri

* We know nothing of this child.

de Navarre, who appointed him as tutor to the duc de Vendôme, the sweet fruit of his liaison with the most beloved of his mistresses, Gabrielle d'Estrées. So well had Des Yveteaux discharged his duty that the king then made him tutor to the dauphin, afterward Louis XIII. The king's second wife, Marie de'Medici, did not like anyone even remotely connected with her rival, Gabrielle d'Estrées. When in 1610 Marie's husband was murdered and she became regent, she dismissed Des Yveteaux, allegedly because of his unorthodox position on religion.

The sieur des Yveteaux has been called the Epicurus of his time. The great Greek philosopher had been undergoing a striking rehabilitation. Like the tolerant Montaigne, like her father before her, Ninon and most of her friends — Scarron, Saint-Evremond, Des Barreaux, the chevalier de Méré — were practically all Epicurean skeptics. What did Epicureanism mean in the seventeenth century? It did not mean the philosophy of lecherous tosspots, living with irresponsible abandon, of the "eat, drink and be merry for tomorrow we die" type of pseudo-Epicureanism. The Epicureanism of the Grand Siècle was a philosophy of cautious, measured indulgence in the good things of life. Not to accept wholesomely, gratefully, and joyously the delights of this world such as good food, good wine, good talk, and good sex was unnatural and stupid, thought the bon vivant of the seventeenth century. "The abstinence from pleasure is a sin," said the world traveler and sunny philosopher, Bernier — one of Ninon's great admirers. But everything had to be in moderation; the golden mean was the desideratum. Don't deny yourself any sensible pleasure was the core of Epicurean thinking, with the emphasis on *sensible*. Never do anything that will cause regret — either in eating or in loving. Instead of the vulgarization of Epicureanism — "Eat, drink, and be merry, for tomorrow we die" — its motto might possibly have been "Eat, drink, but be wary or tomorrow we cry."

After his discharge as tutor, Des Yveteaux withdrew all the way — leaving Court and the Right Bank and going to live in what was then the country, the uttermost edge of Saint-Germain on the Left Bank. There at the age of fifty-two he built himself a fine house with a vast garden. He lived so far out that his friends called him "the last of men." There he read his beloved philosophers, listened to pastoral music, breathed in the solace of nature, sat upon a bank, and meditated about the fate of kings' tutors.

Just when it was that Ninon decided to call on Des Yveteaux after not having seen him for a long while is hard to pinpoint; it was probably when Des Yveteaux was in his seventies* and she about twenty. As she approached his parklike garden, she saw an old gentleman, dressed like a shepherd, complete with crook in hand and flowers in headband, chasing shapely young women garbed as shepherdesses but with a minimum of drapery to impede their running. The old man seemed in surprisingly good shape, having got his second wind, it appeared. At first Ninon might have feared he had taken leave of his senses, but when she learned the whole story she rejoiced in her aged friend's Indian summer.

One day a young girl, fainting from fatigue, had collapsed on his doorstep. She had been a cabaret entertainer and was pregnant. The good Des Yveteaux (Ninon always called him the

* There is some doubt as to when Des Yveteaux was born. Most biographers give 1559, others, 1567.

"bonhomme") had taken her in and revived her. To show her appreciation she played for him on the harp most enchantingly. Des Yveteaux invited the waif to stray no longer, but abide with him. She had the child and it died. The wishful thinkers say she even became Des Yveteaux's mistress, but whether or not the title was more honorary than accurate, Madame du Puy, for so she was called, undoubtedly warmed the declining years of what the French call a "vert galant."*

One of the most influential works of fiction of the century was Honoré d'Urfé's *Astrée,* in which the bucolic life is idealized and romanticized. The aristocracy loved to give masquerades where everybody came in rustic dress. Royal ballets presented shepherds and shepherdesses over and over again. Des Yveteaux staged his ballets in his park. He was always the male lead and Madame du Puy the female lead, though she was assisted by several other lithe young ladies. Sometimes Des Yveteaux impersonated a Greek god, other times a simple shepherd, still other times a satyr. It is not unlikely that the latter was his favorite role. There are those who feel that the bonhomme proved himself a good man after all and that he fathered a child to la du Puy. Whether he did not not, he seems to have lived out the last years of his life in a golden, mellow glow. When he was tired from pursuing his nymphs, Madame du Puy would play upon shepherds' pipes or the harp with such magic that she purportedly charmed the birds out of the trees.

There is no record of just how Ninon brought herself to interrupt this idyll and make her presence known. The old man, delighted to see her, begged her to partake of a picnic. Lunch over, each took up an instrument — Des Yveteaux his pipes, la

* An evergreen lover.

du Puy her harp, and Ninon her lute. It was a miniature pastoral symphony. They were so enraptured they played until the sun went down — a respectable stretch though not in the same bracket with Monsieur de Lanclos's musical marathon of thirty-six hours straight in company with old Gaultier.

Another time, on a religious holiday, when Ninon was visiting again, she teasingly asked Des Yveteaux whether he had been to church that morning. "It would be," he replied, "more shame at my age to lie than not to have been to mass. I have not been there today." Before leaving, she gave him a yellow ribbon which, according to Tallemant, "he wore I do not know how long in his hat." The prudes were sure that the ribbon came from Ninon's petticoat.

Tallemant des Réaux tells us that "Charleval, a Monsieur d'Elbène, and Miossens strongly contributed to making Ninon libertine." So had her father and the gentle Des Yveteaux and so did Saint-Evremond, the dominant influence in her life. It is important to understand what Tallemant meant by "libertine." He did not mean a licentious person though many libertines (but not all) were sexually uninhibited. He meant a freethinker, a person of independent mind. It is quite true that libertin had two meanings: that of a libre penseur,* and that of a free-liver. But by the time Ninon was born, the meaning of freethinker predominated and continued so for most of the century. When Tallemant termed Ninon libertine, he meant she was an esprit fort, literally a strong mind, a nonconformist. Actually Ninon would have qualified as a libertine in both senses of the word — freethinking and free-living, but debauch-

* Freethinker.

ery in the sense of vulgar orgiastic indulgence, she did not go in
for. Ninon was not only an honnête homme but a perfect lady.
What was a freethinker? Whence did he come? Why? To
understand Ninon we must understand libertinism, the philosophy or code by which she lived, the very kernel of her being.
There is no exact inception date, but when the bells of Saint-
Germain-l'Auxerrois sounded in the early morning blackness
of Saint-Bartholomew's Day 1572, calling the faithful to massacre, one of the main seeds of seventeenth-century libertinism
was planted. The great Protestant hero, Admiral Coligny, ancestor of Ninon's first love, Gaspard de Coligny, was murdered
while praying, his hands and genitals sold as trophies. Fetuses
were ripped from the bodies of mothers and smashed against
the ground. Estimates run from 5000 to 50,000 as the number of
Huguenots butchered in the name of religion.

The aftermath of Saint-Bartholomew was the fourth Religious War, which was followed by the fifth, sixth, seventh, and
eighth. The wars ended just about the time Ninon's father was
born — in 1593, when the tired Henri de Navarre abjured his
Protestantism, conceding realistically but without fervor that
Paris "is well worth a mass." The Age of Reason in France had
begun, also the Age of Skepticism. Who knew what was right
or wrong? How genuine were conversions that were pur-
chased? No wonder Montaigne, Henri de Lanclos's master, felt
that one should adopt the religion of one's prince,* as it made
for less trouble that way. Nothing, he felt, could be more irrational than to kill a man for his religious beliefs. Let there be
reason and peace.

Saint-Bartholomew's Day also ushered in the Age of Cyni-

* *Cujus regio, ejus religio.*

cism. No wonder La Rochefoucauld, who was to frequent Ninon's salon and try out some of his famous maxims there, saw self-interest as the basis of all human motivation. Or that much later on, near the end of the seventeenth century, when the philosopher Bayle used to attend the aged Ninon's little suppers, he was still of the opinion that "nothing is more common than to see orthodox Christians living evil lives and free-thinkers living good ones." Small wonder also that the seventeenth century was the Age of Classicism, of Absolutism, of Orthodoxy, of Order, when a strong government would have a better chance of keeping peace within the nation. The reverse side of the medal of authoritarianism is opposition thereto, and that is where libertinism comes in. Its field was mainly in matters of conscience, science, and philosophy; it was interested in politics only in a minor way. Naturally enough, libertinism started with skepticism. After the shambles of the sixteenth century, men of the seventeenth began to question everything which had previously been taken for granted.

In religion the Catholic Renaissance, part of the Counter Reformation, was in full swing. The Jesuits within the Church, the League among the laity, were indefatigable in promoting Catholic supremacy. Little escaped their interest or their interference. Soon the Society of the Holy Scarament, a vigilante lay group, was to prowl about, smell out heresy or irreverence, and denounce the alleged sinners for stiff punishments. So odious did the society become that it was eventually banned, but only after it had succeeded in getting Ninon incarcerated for about nine months. The skeptics, who challenged the Church's monopoly of the truth, resented the aggressive part of the Catholic Renaissance, not the positive part such as housecleaning or

the humanitarian work of many good Catholics whose unselfish achievements gave the period one of its well-known ap-
pellations — The Century of Saints. The opponents of the Catholic Renaissance were not for the most part against religion per
se, but against zealous bigots. They were thinking people who
did not like to have dogma shoved down their throats —
friends of laughter and good times, decent, reasonable folk.

There were also libertins who went much further — those
like Ninon who accepted God but refused to accept a religion
which, she charged, had been known to engage in bought conversions, forced conversions, and to countenance, all too often,
hypocritical, corrupt clergy. She felt this religion ungodly,
maintaining with the Protestant La Noue that "It is our wars of
religion that have made us forget religion." Not, be it noted,
that Ninon was attracted to the Protestants — she opposed all
sectarianism as inflammatory. Often in their spirited (and
risky) opposition to obscurantism, people like Ninon found
themselves in extreme positions of mockery of the excesses of
clericalism and finally of religion itself. At the end of the sixteenth century La Noue held that the Religious Wars had engendered "one million Epicureans and libertins" in France.
The bishop of Orléans flatly stated, "The majority of Christians are so only in name."

In philosophy the libertins felt a great attraction for Epicurus.
The libertins and Epicureans both adored nature. They loved
its harmonies, they submitted to its will with resignation, they
were grateful for its bounty. Nature plus the Golden Rule, they
implied, equals God. This did not sit well with the Church.

As in many movements, libertinism had its lunatic fringe —
the baptizers of animals, those who dressed up donkeys as

priests. Sex literature such as the *Priapists,* glorifying the phallus, flourished. The wave of honest protest, of sturdy independent thinking, of legitimate skepticism, was cresting into a froth of sometimes unbridled sensuality and sacrilege. It was the exposed fraction of the wave, not the great sane underpart, that gave rise to what H. Bremond calls "flamboyant libertinism." The state and its established religion felt a crisis had arisen — in the very year of Ninon's birth. They decided to make an example of a defenseless unfortunate called Vanini, who was accused of atheism. After his allegedly sacrilegious tongue was torn out with pincers, he was burned.

This ferocity was not an isolated case. Libertinism's wave prudently went underground, its sensational, blasphemous, topmost part lopped off. The Erudite Libertins met quietly behind closed doors, unobtrusively exchanging information on scientific experiments, reading aloud letters they had received from travelers in the Orient reporting on other cultures and other religions. Meanwhile Louis XIII was tightening the screws of repression. A little after the time that the thirteen-year-old Ninon deflated the histrionic preacher with her Spanish song in church, Louis renewed the mandatory punishment for blasphemy, including horrible torture. The libertins perforce lay low. But irreverence infected young and old.

The princesse Palatine tells the story of a young student at a Jesuit boarding school who was always getting into mischief. The reverend father warned him that the next time he misbehaved, he would be whipped. The boy went to a painter and got him to paint the head of St. Ignatius on one buttock, that of St. François Xavier on the other. He then went out on the town, returning long after curfew. The priest told him to lower his britches. The boy fell on his knees: "O St. Ignatius, O St. Xavier . . . do some miracle . . . to show I am innocent." The angry father, rod in hand, ordered the boy to stop the dramatics and strip. He did, revealing the faces of the two saints smiling benevolently from his backside. It was the priest's turn to fall on his knees, imprint kisses on the boy's posterior and beg forgiveness of him. Summoning the rest of the school, he recounted the miracle and bade them do honor to the boy so obviously, if a trifle oddly, favored of heaven.

With the death of the strict Richelieu in late 1642 and that of the pious and gloomy Louis XIII soon after, a new wave of libertinism joyously arose under the tolerant sun of the Good Regency. Refined by the influence of the charming and decorous Madame de Rambouillet, it was a far cry from the flamboyant libertinism of two decades before; it was a libertinism distingué. The principal actors in the cast were members of high society, rather than scholars with minds of their own, or bitter critics of the Church. Libertinism had become chic, even avant-garde. It was a smiling time. The twentieth-century literary critic, Monsieur Georges Mongrédien, gives a good picture of the elegant libertins.*

Those whom we shall call here libertins are simply Epicureans, people caring little about [conventional] morality or religion, addressing all their attention to what interests them and to their pleasures, likable and witty personages for whom the divertissements of love always had considerably more importance than the struggles between bigots and atheists, Jesuits and Jansenists, Catholics and Protestants.

In reality — independents. But so pleasant and amusing in their

* In *Libertins et amoureux.*

private life! In the same way . . . that the old bonhomme Des Yveteaux, former preceptor of the king, consoled himself for his disfavor in the arms of a harp player, they contrived, in the company of Scarron and Ninon de Lanclos, to apply as much as possible the *carpe diem* of Horace: to eat well and drink heartily, to chat easily without pedantry or prudery, to divert themselves with songs and epigrams, to jest at one's neighbor, and . . . to see nothing in love but a pleasure that passes, to give oneself to passion and to withdraw with prudence, to place happiness in the pleasures of *this* world, to be mistrustful of the other, to enliven life and love by grace, wit, prettiness and gaiety, this is the line of carefree and charming conduct of our libertins . . .

The debut of the new, elegant libertinism in 1643 almost coincides with the debut of Ninon, who was only twenty then. Gone were the flamboyant libertinism of the flaming twenties and the surreptitious, covert, erudite libertinism of the thirties. These were the halcyon days for the freethinkers and freelovers, soft, gentle lotuslike days, when it was always afternoon and the air smelled of attar of roses. It was the kind of time that fathers of today might wish they had lived in but would fear for their daughters. Scarron, who loved Ninon like a daughter — poor cripple he had Hobson's choice — feared that she might tread the primrose path of dalliance to her sorrow, to the prejudice and blighting of great qualities of mind and soul which he had the perspicacity to sense behind her front of wild abandon. A curious thing about Ninon's life — to a remarkable extent it parallels the curve of libertinism in the seventeenth century. Her birth, surely one of the great crises of life, coincided with the crisis of flamboyant libertinism in the early 1620s. In the thirties she was quietly growing up — the hushed but formative time of the erudite libertinism which was to have such an influence on emancipated thinkers of a later date such as Fontenelle and Bayle and indirectly Voltaire. Then came Ninon's emergence from modest girlhood into glamorous womanhood — just as libertinism pulled back the blackout curtains and danced in the streets of the Good Regency. Later in the fifties with absolutism in the saddle, libertinism suffered a decline; Ninon also knew the valley of the shadow in the fifties, thanks to the hounding of the prudes and bigots. But as the century wore on, the free in heart and spirit were to have an amazing comeback in what the perceptive Paul Hazard calls "triumphant libertinism." That coincides with Ninon's finest hour. But that is decades after her youthful days when "Charleval, a Monsieur d'Elbène, and Miossens strongly contributed to making Ninon libertine."

# Chapter 5

## The Making of a Libertine

THE SEIGNEUR DE CHARLEVAL would have liked to make Ninon, aged about twenty, libertine in both senses of the word. He would gladly have tutored her in both freethinking and free-loving. Unlike the dynamic comte de Miossens, one of his colleagues in making Ninon libertine, Charleval used an amorous technique which was low pressure and seemingly unaggressive. No doubt this was largely dictated by his physique, for he was frail and pale, as befits a poet with a romantically melancholy air. He brought out the maternal instinct in women, but no sooner had they let their guard down than he sprang to the attack with unsuspected vigor. His good friend Scarron, referring both to the delicacy of Charleval's build and his ethereal poetry, speculated that the Muses must have nourished him "on blanc-mange and chicken-broth." Not exclusively; somewhere and frequently, they must have slipped in some good red roast beef and maybe even oysters, for Charleval did exceptionally well with the ladies. Behind a disarming shyness was complete self-confidence. When he made up his mind to go after a woman, he conducted a veritable campaign. During its course he would report to his friends by letter, heading it: "From the camp before such and such a lady" — just as would a general laying siege to a strong point. His artillery consisted of words — launched either charmingly in conversation or in verse. Not many *cruelles* ("difficult ladies") remained cruel long. Perhaps they feared to subject this wan wisp of a sprite to prolonged strain. They could make a virtue of capitulation.

Much as Ninon admired Charleval's emancipated mind and prized him dearly as a friend, he remained in the class of martyrs. He did not give up easily though, continuing the siege, probing for a weakness in her armor, hoping to arrive "at the sweet moment of satyrizing her." But Ninon was firm: "You will have to await my caprice." The word *caprice* is significant. That is exactly what Ninon thought of love — a whim, founded on nothing explainable, a passing fancy, sweet while it lasted but to be abandoned before it loses its flavor. Love did not wither on the vine with Ninon. She ended an affair while it was in full bloom and thus was able to retain a pleasant memory of it at its best. Byron's "worm, the canker and the grief" were not for her. Poor Charleval awaited Ninon's caprice without success all his life. Yet they remained the best of friends. This was Ninon's prime secret; her alleged elixir of youth was secondary. Charleval's function was evidently to fill what Ninon called the "interludes between love affairs." He must have done it surpassingly well. Over half a century later, in 1697, Ninon would write Saint-Evremond that when she wanted to enliven the company in her salon, she would tell stories of the old times with Charleval and d'Elbène.

Charleval never graduated from Ninon's category of martyr to that of favorite or caprice, but on balance he got the better part of Ninon. She was a most desirable lover; indeed the tradition suggests that she was possessed of a prodigious erotic technique, but as a friend she seems to have been unique. And whereas her friendship was lifelong, her love had but the span of a day, a week, maximum three months.

D'Elbène, the second of the trio that was allegedly responsible for Ninon's libertinism, is usually known as "the friend of Scarron." A freethinker, an Epicurean, a lover of good conversation, poetry, and gourmet meals, d'Elbène fitted in well with Scarron's circle, where he would met Ninon, Marion, Charleval, Miossens, and Des Barreaux, once the great love of Marion. D'Elbène was probably never one of Ninon's lovers. He came to her for intellectual and social exercise. He separated his activities with women into compartments. He did not like mistresses who were either too smart or too intellectual. Keeping up with them was a strain, not a challenge. It ran counter to his indolence. Passion, embracing any depth of feeling, he avoided. Not for him the springtime, nor the sweet approach of even or morn. None of this soul mate nonsense for him. A deep-dyed Epicurean, he shied away from getting too involved in anything; pain could result. Incorrigibly lazy, he did not want to have to exert himself mentally or emotionally when his libido demanded satisfaction. He wanted his physical pleasures readily available. Subtle and often long drawn-out campaigns such as Charleval engaged in were not to his liking. Sex was a sometime thing, a toy, an exhilaration, the supreme dessert, not to be distilled of its natural juices by sentimentalizing, by jealousies born of taking it too seriously, by grief, by remorse.

Stripped of its grosser aspects, this was also Ninon's attitude toward love. Ninon drew the line at debauchery — hers was an elegant, refined eroticism. But the de-romanticizing of love, the de-idealizing of it, the clearing away of any halo of sacredness, the disbelief that it brought with it any moral commitment, the unconditional, healthy, sinless, joyous acceptance of it as nature's tastiest gift — all these were common to d'Elbène, to Charleval, to Miossens, and to all the neo-Epicureans. Then did not the three libertine gentlemen influence Ninon in the free-loving connotation of the word also? They probably did, though Ninon probably did not need too much of a push in that direction, being the daughter of Henri de Lanclos. But just after emerging from the peaceful convent in 1643, just after the death of her pious mother, Ninon needed an impulse to make her leave her vestigial religious moorings. It was simply *that* which Tallemant meant they supplied when he said they made her libertine.

D'Elbène had even some of Ninon's gift for steadfast friendship. He never ceased trying to bolster Scarron's spirits and sat by his bedside or chair by the hour, bringing friends like the poet Chapelle, one of Ninon's wooers, and the satirist Boileau to joke with Scarron when he was in the mood, or to have first-rate literary evenings, the whole to the accompaniment of the clink of glasses and the savoring of delicacies — for eating was the one physical pleasure left Scarron. Often, when the weather was damp, when the cripple's pain was worse than usual and his spirits were low, d'Elbène combined with Ninon to put on a show for Scarron which seldom failed to entertain and give him new courage. D'Elbène's fidelity to friends and his sophistication made a deep impression on the young Ninon. A quarter of a century later, when d'Elbène needed her, she did not forget him.

\*

Ninon's affair with Miossens, the third of the trio who contributed to her libertinism, may seem extraordinary, for he was not the type which generally attracted her. Ninon liked as bedmates men who could handle themselves well not only in the boudoir but in the drawing room too — men with grace and style. This is not to say that her lovers had to be intellectuals. Far from it, but usually she was attracted to men who could turn a phrase and who had charm. Miossens had none of these qualifications. He stuttered, tying himself up in knots; he did not write madrigals like the elegant Charleval, though he could write an effective letter. His amorous technique had all the subtlety of a bull, but he was evidently a tremendous lover and Ninon in her twenties was a rather vigorous young animal herself. Tallemant claims Ninon had a son by Miossens. If so, we know nothing of him.

His technique with the ladies was simple in the extreme. Not having words to waste, he moved directly to the attack, sometimes using his head not to charm but to batter down resistance. Women were divided in their reaction to his tactics. Some found him fatally lacking in the elaborate preliminaries: the verbal ballet, the battle of wits and wills, the sweet game of flattery, the mental titillation. Others looked for an excuse to yield, secretly admiring this latter-day cave man. Marcel Gobineau, in his novel about Ninon, writes, "When the woman pleases him, Miossens embraces her, bends her at the waist, seizes her in his muscular arms, caresses her, feels her, weakens her, excites her, stops with his voracious mouth the other mouth which would cry out and, while with one hand he holds her body which only defends itself for appearances, with the other he forages in her petticoats with a dexterity which surprises the happy victims and makes them desire a rapid conclusion, violent, virile," etc.

Even after taking a substantial discount on his formidable reputation, one can understand why Marion de l'Orme sent for Miossens after Arnauld de Corbeville, her incumbent lover, had had to rejoin his regiment. "It was," according to Tallemant, "because of a fantasy which seized her to sleep with him." He came over in a flash, but their affair was of short duration. With Ninon it was longer. To a full-blooded voluptuary of twenty or so, Miossens's overpowering masculinity had an imperious appeal. Years later, in the capacity of friend and former lover, Miossens was to come to Ninon's rescue with the aid of the queen of Sweden, just as Ninon was to help d'Elbène.

They were a loyal quartet — that trio of libertin preceptors and their receptive disciple.

"Let us have as much love as is necessary to enliven us, not enough to trouble our repose. The heart was given us for loving — a pleasant emotion, not for suffering . . ." The speaker is not Ninon. Nor is it Epicurus. It is Ninon's mentor, her male alter ego, her best and lifelong friend — the seigneur de Saint-Evremond. There is no question as to the validity of Tallemant's statement that Charleval, d'Elbène, and Miossens were influential in making Ninon a freethinker. Nor should her father's or old Des Yveteaux's part in her conversion be minimized. But incontestably the person who figured most prominently in forming Ninon in her late teens and early twenties was Saint-Evremond. Seldom has a more able teacher found a more willing, intelligent pupil. He was seven years her senior. Blessed with a keen, subtle mind, Saint-Evremond was

known in his youth as "the wit." He excelled at one of the
great social exercises of the time — polished raillery. He was
equally good in fencing with foils as with words, so much so
that the Saint-Evremond Pass, states his contemporary biographer, Des Maizeaux, "was famous among the skill'd in the science." His bravery and intelligence soon brought him to the
notice of the young duc d'Enghien, the close friend of two of
Ninon's close friends: Marion de l'Orme, and Ninon's first,
fine, careless rapture, Coligny. The duke, a highly cultivated
commander, well equipped to appreciate Saint-Evremond's
mind, courage, and breeding, loved to hear him talk, for Saint-
Evremond was one of the great conversationalists of an age
which raised good talk to a supreme art, a way of life all by
itself, a superprofession. Enghien made him a lieutenant in his
guards so as to have him close by. That was in 1642, the year
Ninon's mother died, and some years after Saint-Evremond
and Ninon had first met — probably in Marion's stylish drawing rooms.

France and Spain were still at each other's throats in 1642.
When the battle of Rocroi came a year later, when the duc
d'Enghien, with Saint-Evremond at his side, shattered the
flower of Spain's infantry, the victory coincided with the beginning of the Good Regency, which Saint-Evremond later celebrated in verse with such nostalgia. No historian of Queen
Anne's regency speaks of it without quoting Saint-Evremond,
who became its poet laureate. Brilliant victories in the summer
were followed by equally brilliant social seasons in the winter,
when lovely ladies rewarded with exquisite softness the
conquerors returned from hard, rude battlefields.

These were the salad days in Saint-Evremond's life, even

though he was seriously wounded at Nordlingen in 1645. He was riding a crest. In the summer he would distinguish himself with his sword and his rapierlike wit, delighting the gallant Enghien with his sallies both on the field and at mess. When the snow fell he warmed himself at Marion's hearth, or perhaps at that of the hot-blooded comtesse d'Olonne or at Ninon's. Saint-Evremond agreed with his and Ninon's friend Bernier that "abstinence from pleasure is a sin." He could not understand why most people put reason and passion at opposite poles. Passion, he argued, must be kept in bounds by reason and is thereby fortified. A fool lets passion rule him and often ruin him, but a wise man rationally takes his passion in moderation. The Epicurean in Saint-Evremond made him love nature and live life fully but that did not mean immoderately. He had a horror of mortification of the senses, equally a horror of excess. The golden mean was the reasoned indulgence of one's natural appetites, including passion. "I have never felt in myself this interior combat of passion and reason; passion does not conflict at all with what I have resolved to do out of duty; and reason consents readily to what I want to do following the dictates of pleasure." Like a good seventeenth-century Epicurean, Saint-Evremond did not marry.

Consistently enough, Saint-Evremond harbored a healthy regard for the pleasures of the table; he was a renowned gourmet, but never a gourmand — that would be un-Epicurean. There must be nothing to excess. He was a connoisseur of wine from early youth.

It is said that God fits the back to the burden. If Saint-Evremond in his youth had been nothing but a social dilettante in his Paris winter quarters away from war, he would have been ill-prepared for the slings and arrows of outrageous Louis XIV, launched at him twenty years or so later. Saint-Evremond was a facile poet. He might have settled down comfortably by the fire in Madame de Rambouillet's famous Blue Room and delighted that brilliant set with his mordant wit. Instead, Saint-Evremond preferred to sit at the feet of that extraordinary priest, Gassendi, that remarkable dualist who was able to keep in watertight compartments his religious conscience on the one hand, and his wide-ranging, independent, inquiring mind on the other. Like Montaigne, Gassendi and Saint-Evremond did not want to be heroes. They were not rebels in the activist sense of the word. All they asked was to be allowed to say to themselves, *sotto voce,* unprovocatively, "My mind to me a kingdom is." They only wanted freedom to think, to live an honest, rational, private life. Publicly they were quite prepared to conform. They remembered Saint-Bartholomew's Massacre, they had seen people in agony at the stake. They desired to live and let live.

So, essentially, did Ninon, but whereas most of the Epicureans dissembled their thoughts in public, Ninon's opposition, by virtue of the fact that she was a woman, took a different and more conspicuous form. Her pride did not allow her to live a lie, and hence she elected to live like an honnête homme, thereby contravening the sacred double standard. This in turn brought her into conflict with the bigots, religious and lay, before whom she refused to cower — to her peril and pain. But philosophically Ninon was no more of a revolutionary than Saint-Evremond. Neither acted the fiery proselytizer. Saint-Evremond's strongest action was a poetic protest against religion when vengeful or divisive.

Gassendi had brilliant pupils who were all friends of Ninon: Chapelle, a highly considered poet in his time; Bernier, a famous world traveler with a fine philosophic mind; and perhaps Molière. It was from the sweet-souled Gassendi that Saint-Evremond learned not only to enhance his enjoyment of life, but also to accept life, its reverses, and death.

What Saint-Evremond handed on to Ninon was not a frontal attack on God but on clericalism, ascetisim, assumed omniscience, mysteries, miracles. He was a skeptic and a humanist, devoted to man in the here and now, not a believer in the supernatural or the afterworld. He gives his own credo:

> I love virtue without harshness,
> I love pleasure without softness
> I love life and do not fear the end.

That was it — Saint-Evremond loved life passionately, more so in fact than he loved passion. His was not a torrid relationship with Ninon. They never scaled the heights nor plumbed the depths of desire. If passion, as distinct from lust, is a thing of the mind translated by the body, Ninon and Saint-Evremond should have been exceptionally passionate lovers. They were not. Writing to Ninon from England decades later, Saint-Evremond looked back at himself as having been neither "a mere friend, nor a veritable lover." The self-description permits of wide interpretation. Saint-Evremond was not a particularly passionate person, which may account for some of the ease with which he reconciled reason and passion so totally. He never got too excited about anything though he had a lively interest in almost everything — philosophy, the humanities, music, the theater, cooking, military but not natural science. (Unlike his master, Gassendi, he had little interest in astronomy or mathematics.) In the field of emotions or beliefs he cultivated indifference. He would discuss, but he never argued heatedly. Neither did Ninon. Again and again in his references to conversational style or deportment he uses the word *aisé* — easy, relaxed. Another of his favorite words was *modération*. One of his principal arguments against institutionalized religion was that it was divisive and inflammatory. Love could prove to be that too. He may not have been as sure of himself in love as Ninon was of herself — love might prove to be more than a genital matter. When in doubt, don't. The Classical Age had few truer sons than Saint-Evremond — disciplined, cool, rational.

There was another element. Saint-Evremond was not a woman-killer in looks, though his portrait shows a fascinatingly interesting face, full of depth, strength, nobility, and kindness. "Monsieur de Saint-Evremond," writes Des Maizeaux, "had blue eyes, keen and sparkling, a broad forehead, bushy eyebrows, a shapely mouth, a quizzical smile, a lively and engaging expression, an erect and well-proportioned figure and a general air of distinction and good breeding." It is not clear just when he developed a large growth or wen between his eyebrows; if in his youth, it undoubtedly would have intensified a native sensitivity. He first met Ninon when she was in her middle or late teens — her giddy period when good-looking playboys like Saint-Etienne and Raré appealed to her. Under the chandeliers in Marion's drawing room, he saw her make conquest after effortless conquest, always surrounded, always sought after. He could not or would not compete with the popinjays and the butterflies. And who could have been more different from him, the sensitive, suave, highly articulate honnête homme than Miossens, he who could hardly get a word out, who had the skin of an elephant, but whose stampeding brawn carried most women before him, including Ninon. So Saint-Evremond engaged Ninon on a different level, on his own terms — not just a mere friend, nor really a thoroughgoing lover. He became her master, even though she may not have become his mistress. And he probably concluded that time was on his side, that Ninon would eventually tire of the charm-boys, that the tumult and fever would pass and she would settle down — not to marriage but to a stable, enduring, lover-mistress relationship. Paradoxically the aristocracy at times seemed to show by their constancy to their mistresses that they were not necessarily promiscuous. Charles Hénault, president of the Parlement of Paris, had an affair with Madame du Deffand which lasted forty years.

It is a tribute to Ninon that so early in her wild youth she appreciated Saint-Evremond's type. She admired his erudition, which he never flaunted. She loved his openmindedness, his magnanimity, his tartness. Young though she was, she thrilled to the brilliance and sweep of his conversation which nonetheless was always aisé. "Never," comments the respected French critic, Sainte-Beuve, "was there language more beautiful, rich or subtle." His bons mots, his verbal darts, usually preceded by a mischievous smile, enraptured Ninon. Like hers, his wit was meant to amuse, not hurt. "Touché" would have been the comment, not "cruel."

Ninon, by all accounts, had a positive genius for friendship. In all probability its development and refinement were at least partly affected by Saint-Evremond who, in his concept and reasoned pursuit of pleasure, gave an all-important place to friend-ship. "I have always," he wrote, "admired the morality of Epicurus, and I esteem nothing so much in his morality as the preference which he gives to Friendship over all other virtues."

Ninon and Saint-Evremond brought out the best in each other. He would read his poetry to her, some of which she no doubt had inspired. When Saint-Evremond would occasionally throw off his classical mantle and wax lyrical and lay a poem before her as a gift, he touched a responsive chord in Ninon that no Saint-Etienne or Raré, those handsome fops, or muscu-lar Miossens, had suspected even existed. The way to Ninon's heart, which had nothing to do with her libido, was via her soul.

Saint-Evremond evidently continued her musical education, perfecting her technique on the lute. He was an excellent mu-sician, composer, arranger. Later in London his soirées often took the form of chamber music performances where he and his friends would play his own and others' compositions. He left his mark on her taste. Saint-Evremond could not stand opera. He found ridiculous the seventeenth-century attempts to sing conversations or make love at the top of one's voice. When Ninon became a grande dame, and her opinion was sought on matters of taste, she too poked fun at the Brunhildes of her century.

But above all Ninon loved him because he explained her to herself, gave her a philosophical *apologia pro sua vita*. Des Maizeaux said of Saint-Evremond, "Although he did not pre-tend to overrigid morals, yet he had all the qualities of a man of honor." The conflict generated in Ninon's psyche by the con-trary teachings of her parents persisted a long time. True, she had crossed her Rubicon, she had cast her die in her father's direction, but that does not mean she had no doubts as to the rightness of her decision. Ninon had not been able to accept the religion of her mother, and there was something needed to fill the vacuum. She could not be a party to the hypocrisy of seventeenth-century marriage, its betrayals, its dishonesty, its tyranny. She had decided to live like an honnête homme, not a chaste woman. Many married women in Paris society tried to ostracize her — particularly when Madame Coulon, who was sleeping with d'Emery, provoked an outcry about Ninon being kept by her husband. The ladies' point was not so much that she was sleeping with their husbands but that their husbands were spending money on her which they might have spent on them. What they particularly resented was her nonconformity. They did not mind so much that their husbands were straying, because the wives strayed too, but they were infuriated that the shameless hussy did not have the decency first to get married and then gallivant. Ninon, they complained, had it both ways, was taking unfair advantage of them, running around like married women but suffering none of the disabilities of marriage.

Did the malignancy of the scorned women weaken her self-confidence? Was she going to be able to retain her integrity, maintain her self-respect and the respect of people she valued, and yet be so unconventional? Saint-Evremond evidently thought so. Referring to Ninon he wrote some thirty years later: "One finds women who are as capable of keeping secrets and confidences as well as the most faithful of men-friends. I know of some who have no less wit and discretion than charm and beauty; but these are exceptions which nature, by design or caprice, is pleased to give us . . ." Then remembering it was a man's world he concluded, "These extraordinary women seem to have borrowed the merit of men; and perhaps they commit a kind of infidelity to their sex in passing from their natural condition to that of ours." In other words, Ninon had qualified as an honnête homme. Three hundred years before he had asked it, she was the answer to Professor Henry Higgins's ill-tempered question: "Why can't a woman be like a man?"

What Saint-Evremond did for the floundering Ninon in her twenties was to give her a rationalization of her behavior. He taught her an attitude, for philosophy may be too grandiose a term to apply to this early period of Ninon's life. This attitude was a compound of freethinking, skepticism, and reason. It was libertinism, a solid body of thought held by some of the most illustrious intellectuals of the day. It gave Ninon respectability in her own eyes, and she loved Saint-Evremond for making her whole again. He became her conscience, her superego. There may be some question as to whether Ninon and Saint-Evremond were bedmates. There is none that they were soul mates.

Saint-Evremond's habit of poking fun, which so amused France's foremost military commander, Louis de Bourbon, duc d'Enghien, eventually backfired when he started teasing the young duke himself. A haughty Bourbon of royal blood, cousin to the king, Enghien would roar when Saint-Evremond's gibes were directed at others, but roared his immediate discharge when the irrepressible Saint-Evremond leveled a barb or two at him. One just did not banter with Enghien. Ninon did, however, and got away with it.

At the time of their meeting — 1645 — Enghien was the national hero. Twice had he humbled the Hapsburgs — at Rocroi two years before in a brilliant victory and at Nordlingen more recently. History knows Enghien later as the Great Condé — the name by which he was called after the death of his father, the prince de Condé. The Grande Mademoiselle, cousin to both Louis XIV and Enghien, tells of what Queen Christina of Sweden, Ninon's great supporter, thought of him:

> She said that her dearest wish was to take part in a battle, and that . . . she envied the prince de Condé all his glorious feats of arms.
> "He is a good friend of yours?" she [Christina] asked.
> I answered, "Yes, and my very near relation."
> "He is the greatest man in the world," she said . . .

The women generally idolized him of course, even though he was not conventionally handsome with his large, aquiline nose, fierce, glinting eyes, careless dress. He did not bother much with women, Madame de Sévigné tells us, a trait which only seemed to pique their curiosity and embolden their wiles. Sandras de Courtilz,* not always the most reliable of witnesses, tells a credible story of what must have happened to Enghien not infrequently. This particular incident during the Fronde took place a few years after Ninon's encounter with him, just about the time when Turenne, his great adversary commanding the royalist troops, said of Enghien in connection with his magnificent defense of Paris, "I didn't see one Condé, I saw more than a dozen." Relates Courtilz:

> . . . But the ladies were those who exprest the most esteem for him, some of them being so forward as to prove† whether he

---

* In his *Mémoires de M(onsieur) le comte de R(ochefort)*. Courtilz, a seventeenth-century Frenchman, also wrote *Mémoires de Monsieur d'Artagnan* — the source of Dumas's *The Three Musketeers*.
† Test.

could acquit himself as well in an Amorous Engagement as he had in the late Battel. Madame Pie . . . writ to him, to tell him she had some affairs with him, of that importance that she durst not confide 'em to any . . . so he waited on her; when instead of some weighty matter in relation to the State . . . she made a Confession of her weakness, but begged him to make use of it like . . . a Man of Honour. The good Prince was touched with compassion, and prepar'd instantly to give her the most sensible* proof of it; but being at that time in her Closet,† where unfortunately there was no bed, he was put to his Shifts, yet by taking the Cushions and placing them one upon another, he did his best to oblige her . . .‡

Ninon did not write him any letters. Once bitten, twice shy. Two years before in 1643 she had made a fool of herself by writing Coligny, Enghien's friend and summertime lover. Ninon had learned much in the interim about handling men. This book will not attempt to list one by one the formidable roster of Ninon's lovers. Sainte-Beuve comments, "They have discussed and put in order the succession of her lovers almost as precisely as that of the kings of Assyria and Egypt." Her affairs, with one notable exception, never exceeded three months' duration and were usually much shorter. She called an affair a "caprice" and evidently kept score. At the time of the Enghien incident, she admitted she was "on my twentieth caprice." There had been no shame, no feelings of guilt, just fun, adventure, inquisitiveness; no involvement of the heart, just a joyous gratification of the senses. She had been living like a carefree honnête homme.

Ninon had met Enghien at Marion's and had been im-

* Tangible.
† A private room.
‡ From a contemporary translation.

pressed by his self-assurance, vitality, and mind. Enghien was
extremely well educated, was at home in both the classics and
philosophy. He was a friend of Gassendi's, the master of
Ninon's master, Saint-Evremond. He was a freethinker, at
times to the point of sacrilegious impiety. He had tried to burn
a piece of the True Cross. Madame de Motteville in her *Memoirs* writes; "On great occasions he would experience a return
to God, whose power he adored without submitting to His
commandments." He was a patron of the arts, later permitting
private showings of Molière's *Tartuffe* at his country seat at
Chantilly and at his city mansion when the Church had banned
it from public showing. Enghien was magnetic, eccentric,
enigmatic. There was a question mark as to his effectiveness as
a lover. Ninon, as did the rest of Paris society, knew of his
unhappy marriage to the niece of Richelieu, forced upon him
by the cardinal and Enghien's father. The Madame de
Champré incident was equally public knowledge. The young
duke had come across la Champré deep in the Bois de Bou-
logne, her coach disabled; Enghien had seized her (she not resisting in the least) and had carried her off like a prey into the
thicket. On the other hand, the alcoves buzzed with gossip
that in the long summer campaigns, far removed from women,
the duke had engaged in sodomy — with none other than
Ninon's former lover, Coligny — he who had proven so disappointing. Psychologists might ponder whether she may have
speculated for a moment on the vertiginous idea of how she
would fare in competition with Coligny for Enghien. The res-
ervations about Enghien's prowess as a lover no doubt piqued
Ninon. Where others might have failed in stimulating Enghien to realize his undoubted vigor, perhaps she with her sub-

tle blend of refined elegance and uninhibited eroticism would succeed. This was a challenge which aroused the conquering female in her.

The evidence of his questionable sexual power pointed both ways. Certainly he seemed to have been genuinely in love with Mademoiselle du Vigean, though perhaps he had got over it a little too quickly when he had had to depart, albeit reluctantly, for the German campaign. Rumor had it that Mademoiselle de Toussy knew. The ribald poet, the baron de Blot, one of Ninon's admirers, asked la Toussy as much:

> Tell us whether your heart's secret,
> And whether your prince has the vigor of Hercules
> To the same extent that he has glory and valor.

History does not record her answer, if any. On the other hand, Mademoiselle Senneterre had been explicit, at least according to the vaudevillians:

> *La petite Senneterre*
> *Met souvent le cul à terre*
> *S'écriant: "Louis de Bourbon*
> *Ha, que je le trouve bon!"*

> (The little Senneterre
> Supine on her derrière
> Would cry ecstaticly:
> "Oh Louis — you thrill me!")

It was inevitable that the national hero and the toast of Paris should rendezvous. The proud duke felt his victories entitled him to the prize. Ninon would have been the last to be lacking in patriotism in this respect. In due season a footman of the princely house of Condé presented young Louis de Bourbon's compliments, inquiring whether Mademoiselle de Lanclos would be gracious enough to permit him to call. Mademoiselle de Lanclos replied through her valet that it would be an honor to receive his master. The time was appointed. Ninon knew her distinguished visitor's tastes. Had he not, at the battle of Lerida, ordered twenty-four violins to counter the ugly sounds of war? She enchanted his soul with the caressing strains of her lute. Alas, she appealed more to his soul than to his body which, historians record, was hairily virile. But looks were misleading, for he lacked ardor and high passion. All the fire was in his eyes, or had been squandered on the battlefield or with Coligny. Enghien proved himself an ineffectual lover. Ninon was deeply disappointed and sadly acknowledged defeat. She was reminded, she told him, of a classical maxim: *"Vir pilosus, aut libidinosus aut fortis."* [A hairy man is either passionate or strong.] Then she added, "You must be very strong."

Enghien, however, evidently did not take offense for he continued as her devoted friend. Whenever he met her in town, he would descend from his carriage and greet her, even after he became the Great Condé. Years later, when Ninon's salon attracted the cream of Parisian intelligentsia, Condé was a frequent visitor, delighting to drink in the liberal and stimulating atmosphere which was nonexistent at the Court of the aging Louis XIV. One is tempted to wonder if Ninon was not a little hasty in her judgment of Enghien as a lover. After all, one swallow does not make a dinner. But she was very knowing in these matters and could probably tell right off. "It takes a hundred times more skill to make love," she observed, "than to command an army."

## ~∽ Chapter 6 ∽~

### No Holds Barred

There's not a budding boy or girl this day
But is got up and gone to bring in May.
. . . Wash, dress, be brief in praying;
Few beads are best when once we go a-Maying.
. . . Come, let us go, while we are in our prime,
And take the harmless folly of our time!
We shall grow old apace, or die
Before we know our liberty.
. . . Then while time serves and we are but decaying,
Come, my Corinna, come, let's go a-Maying.

SUBSTITUTE NINON for Corinna and Paris for London, and we have the psychological setting for that bright spring day when Ninon went adventuring in the Cours. She was then in what she used to call one of her "interludes" between love affairs. Her dalliances with the lusty Miossens and the unsatisfying Enghien were over and gone. The Thirty Years' War still dragged on, the ground was thawing in the spring sun, Saint-Evremond and other soldier friends had departed for the front. Doubtless she missed Saint-Evremond and worried about his safety, but Ninon was not one to mope. There was no immediate suitor on the horizon, but for Ninon there always seemed to be other good fish in the sea.

But at my back I always hear
Time's wingèd chariot hurrying near . . .
The grave's a fine and private place
But none, I think, do there embrace.

The seventeenth century, at least from the evidence of its poetry, seems to have been particularly preoccupied with the swift
passage of time. Ninon was very much a devotee of the *carpe
diem* school — live while the living is good. The incident in
which she forthrightly sought out adventure in the Cours (and
found Navailles) is the only one recorded in some detail, but it
was by no means the only one. Ninon went a-Maying throughout the spring, summer, and early autumn of her life.

The Cours-la-Reine,* or just Cours, as Ninon and her fellow
Parisians called it, was a majestic promenade about a mile long,
beginning at the Tuileries Gardens and going toward what is
now the Arc de Triomphe, paralleling the Right Bank of the
Seine, which formed one of its lateral boundaries. Four splendid avenues of elms extended the whole length of the Cours,
with a central alley about sixty feet wide flanked by two side-
walks of thirty feet in width. At the middle was a huge circular
area 300 feet in diameter, where more than a hundred vehicles
could turn easily. At either end was an imposing gate.

The Cours was the elegant gathering place of fashionable society. In the afternoon the great ladies would arrive in their
carriages, lesser ladies like Ninon in their sedan chairs. The
men trotted up on horseback, dismounted, and paid court bare-
headed to the ladies through the open doors or windows of the
coaches or sedan chairs. Privacy could be had by drawing silk
curtains. After exchanging compliments and gossip in the

* The Queen's Drive or Promenade.

huge rond-point,* lord and lady would pair off and promenade down the shady lanes of elms. It was a fashion show, a trysting place, a marriage mart. Vendors of sweets made as much money carrying billets doux back and forth as from the sale of their wares. "At the Cours," says Sauval, "people greet each other without knowing each other, and the men would . . . not dare not to greet the ladies, for fear of being thought incivil."

Then as now, before a young lady went out on display, she embarked on a ritual of preparation. Unorthodox as ever, Ninon took a daily bath — contrary to the advice of her mother who, like the vast majority of her century, did not think that cleanliness was next to godliness. A popular manual of the time expressed the general horror of water: "Washing with water injures the eyesight, causes toothache and catarrh, makes one pale and more susceptible to cold in winter and sunburn in summer." Ninon partly owed her clear complexion and un- usually long retention of youthful appearance to observing strict rules of hygiene. She must have owned her own bathtub, made of leather or wood, as there is no mention of her patroniz- ing a public steam bath. The Church often inveighed against the steam baths, not because it opposed the occasional cleansing but because of the sexual play which went on there. This of course was not Ninon's reason for not going — she wanted to bathe daily and insisted on her own tub. Another of her oddities.

As a result of her frequent bathing, Ninon had no need to per- fume her body with the strong scents which were then common. She did not like to reek of musk, preferred just a soupçon of light fragrance. That morning she probably did not affix a rib-

* Place (of round shape) where several roads meet.

bon to the first of the three skirts a young lady donned, known as the "secret" or the "faithful." If she had been in the midst of a liaison, she would have worn a ribbon in the colors of her lover on this the most intimate of garments, but she was now between affairs and owed no man allegiance. Next a lady of fashion pulled on another skirt called the "rascal," part of which showed — presumably saucily. On top of that came the "modest," the exterior skirt. It was modest only in the sense of not intimate, as the modest was often ornate — loaded with gold and lace, flounces and furbelows. A young miss was confronted with weighty sartorial and cosmetic decisions in those days. Not only did she have the usual problem of deciding which dress or skirt to wear, which scarf, shoes, hat, jewelry, and perfume, but there was a whole sign language to articulate — of which ribbons, bows, and beauty spots were the vocabulary. The mignon bow, placed over the heart, clearly did not apply to Ninon's unattached state; neither did the favorite which went in the hair. Ninon probably selected the bow that attached to the fan — it was called the "badin" and reflected playful fancy.

Where should she put the mouche or beauty spot? Next to her eye and signal passion? Next to the mouth which promised a kiss? On the lip to show a coquettish whim? In the middle of the cheek — for gallantry? On the nose to indicate boldness? She may have chosen the "assassin," placed high up on the exposed roundness of the right breast. "How big should a woman's breast be?" one of her admirers once asked her. "Big enough," she replied, "to fill the hand of an honnête homme." All her portraits, both of the pen and of the brush, attest that Ninon qualified in meeting the requirements of her own definition. She did not need to draw attention to her bust by choosing the "assassin." That day, however, Ninon may have been dressing to kill. She was twenty-two and in full bloom and not of a mind to deny the world at least a hint of nature's gifts. Much later she regretted a little her youthful daring. Answering a request from Philippe Emmanuel de Coulanges for a portrait, she wrote:

> I shall believe myself immortal if my face is at Ormesson* . . . Have a copyist cover a shoulder which I find one sees too much of and which in other times I used to find one did not see enough of. Time brings great changes in taste; mine are now modest unless the vanity which you give me, in asking for my portrait, spoils all my judgment.

If she followed custom, it would have been shortly after lunch that Ninon set out in her sedan chair with the gold-colored upholstery and gold silk curtains. Golds and yellows were among Ninon's favorite colors. Later she was to have a "yellow bedroom" which figures importantly in the debate still going on as to whether Madame Scarron was as virtuous as she claimed. Ninon's chair was carried by two stalwart fellows, one fore and one aft. The trip to the Cours probably took about an hour via the rue Saint-Antoine, one of seventeenth-century Paris's widest streets (not more than fifteen to twenty feet wide). Compared to most of Paris's other 600 streets, which varied from nine to fifteen feet in width, it was spacious. Nonetheless, it was habitually jammed by pedestrians, animals, coaches, and carts. Down the middle ran a little rivulet of stinking water into which householders poured their dirty washing water and the contents of their chamber pots. People walked

* Courlanges's estate.

on the high part of the street next to the buildings — as far away from the pestilent stream as possible. The origin of the custom of the man's walking on the outside of the sidewalk comes from his allowing the woman to occupy the higher and drier inner side next to the building. Not that the woman trod on clean pavement. Excrement from animals plus dirt formed a clinging, corrosive compound which had been ground into the pavement — the notorious "slime of Paris."

Thus Ninon could not have walked from the Marais to the Cours as she might have liked to on a bracing day. Her slippers would have been ruined, let alone rendered foul-smelling, her dress bespattered. Bourgeoises who had no coach or chair, carried their party slippers in a bag and changed into them before entering their hostess's dwelling. On a day when a fresh breeze had blown away most of the stench, the trip was enjoyable. The practice was to sit well back on the cushions of the chair, letting one's body sway with the rhythm of the bearers' strides. With the curtains drawn back, the sun could stream in. A popular way-stop, where the perspiring porters could rest and have a beer, was next to the Au Lion d'Or, a shabby place whose sign really meant *Au Lit On Dort* ("in bed one sleeps"). A man, following the practice of the times, might be relieving himself in full view against its facade. While the porters were in the pub, beggars solicited the waiting occupant of the sedan chair and street hawkers offered their merchandise: cake, warm pâtés, salads, Brie cheese, mushrooms, huge walnuts, rabbit skins, soles for shoes (frequently replaced by those who had to walk the filthy streets). In the fall they offered plums, peaches, and small red apples. They also sold water. When the men returned, the route left the crowded street and followed the riverbank of the Seine. Soon the bearers passed the Louvre on their right, entered the Cours and proceeded to the rond-point where they set the chair down.

The rond-point was full of carriages and chairs on the day of Ninon's visit. The ladies were sporting their new spring finery, as were the men who also spent fortunes on their elaborate clothes. Madame de Sévigné records that her son-in-law spent 800 to 1000 livres on a *justaucorps* ("jerkin or close-fitting garment"; 1000 livres would be between $2000 and $5000). Everybody was looking the other over, figuring out the cost of his or her outfit and grading accordingly. Ninon's outfit could not compete with that of most of the ladies, but her relatively simple clothes set off her freshness and vitality. Her friend, Saint-Evremond, had a theory that attractive women should not distract attention from their face or figure by overelaborate dress or trappings. Another of the opinions he and Ninon held in common. Ninon's chair had not come to a halt before several young men gathered round. On the way down the Cours to the rond-point, more than one, on seeing her, had ridden up on horseback and escorted her part of the way.

The talk, as would be expected on a day like this, was gay, superficial, lighthearted. Unfortunately, Tallemant made no record of the banter. Ninon was a good fencer. Then, after a while, across the rond-point she saw a brisk, handsome, blond young officer greet her friend, the maréchal de Grammont. When Ninon felt attracted, and the blood ran fast in her veins, her eyes grew brighter, a look which forty-two years later Saint-Evremond still remembered when he wrote of "those eyes by which I could always tell the new conquest of a lover, when they sparkled a little more than usual." Ninon, direct as always, asked who he was. The comte de Navailles, they advised, an intrepid hunter, a courageous officer in charge of an infantry regiment, one who had Cardinal Mazarin's favor. Ninon, according to the chronicler, suddenly felt the need for some confectionery. While the vendor was getting it ready, she hastily scribbled a note to the unknown Navailles, the exact wording of which Ninon's biographers would give much to know. She dispatched the note via the cake-man. Later that afternoon, when Ninon's bearers were carrying her home, she had a mounted escort riding beside her in the person of Navailles.

They dined by candlelight. Navailles was a very proper man, a little stiff, perhaps shy. Ninon probably did not find his conversation particularly stimulating, but the chemistry evidently was right. After dinner, Ninon led the unprotesting Navailles to a bedroom and told him she would join him before long. Navailles undressed and got into bed. Perhaps, as was his habit, he had been up early that morning to chase the wild boar. The meal had been plenteous, he had drunk a good deal of full-bodied red wine. Ninon was more than a few minutes in her dressing room; Navailles fell asleep.

If Ninon followed her usual routine that night, the maid sponged Ninon's body with a lightly scented preparation and combed her abundant hair. Then, having probably popped an aniseed lozenge into her mouth, Ninon went into the room where Navailles was.

Instead of being greeted by an impatient lover, she was greeted by a snore. Ninon was self-confident enough to take a joke on herself but was determined to get even. Gathering up his sword and clothes, she removed them to her own room, bidding the surprised maid to call her early next morning. Navailles was still sleeping soundly when he was startled by a figure bursting unceremoniously into his room, a figure of an infantry officer brandishing a naked sword. His mind still cobwebbed, Navailles thought the lady's husband or lover was about to dispatch him. "I am a man of honor," he pleaded. "I will give you satisfaction; no trickery in the name of God!" Ninon was not looking for satisfaction on the field of honor. Flinging off Navailles's uniform, she bounded into bed beside him with, says Tallemant, "a peal of laughter." Opinion is divided as to what happened. Some, the wishful thinkers, say they had a rollicking romp. Tallemant dissents, claiming Navailles "did not do well by her." In the absence of either an eyewitness account or a recorded statement by Ninon, Tallemant's position sounds likely, for Ninon never again went to bed with a blond man. Furthermore we do know that Navailles married a prude. Did prudes attract?*

Upon scanning the story of Ninon's seduction of Navailles, some twentieth-century readers may well wonder if she was not an egregiously brazen little minx, lacking in self-respect and dignity. But people must be judged against the customs current in their time. What were those customs?

Monsieur Georges Mongrédien observes in his authoritative *La Vie quotidienne sous Louis XIV:*

---

* Tallemant reports a variation on the incident described earlier wherein Ninon, disappointed at Enghien's lack of virility in bed, quotes a Latin maxim to the effect that hairy men are either libidinous or strong, and therefore she concluded Enghien must be strong. Tallemant claims Ninon's partner was Navailles, not Enghien. The tradition, however, has Ninon make the quip to Enghien. Is it possible that Ninon, pleased with the witticism, used it more than once — whenever she came up against a vigorous-looking man who proved disappointing as lover?

All these young ladies are devoured by ambition. Placed there [in the world of society] by ambitious and unscrupulous mothers, they know that it is not advisable . . . to demonstrate a fierce virtue. The mothers and daughters are ready to make any sacrifice to arrive at their goal.

That fertile source of information on the mores of the Court of Louis XIV, the princesse Palatine, sister-in-law of the Sun King, comments as the century was setting in 1699:

There are no longer any vices here of which they are ashamed; and if the king wanted to punish those who make themselves guilty of the greatest vices, he would see no longer around him either nobles, or princes, or servants, and there would not be a single house in France which would not be in mourning.

Actually there was less licentiousness in 1699 than during the languorous days of the Good Regency when Ninon sported with Navailles. The king was old by the turn of the century; his pious, morganatic wife, the black-garbed Madame de Maintenon, had successfully exhorted him to repent of his earlier loose living. Versailles was in deep shadow compared to the free and easy days of Louis's boyhood during the Good Regency or to his stallion years. Even in 1704, with Versailles growing blacker and bleaker, the Palatine writes:

The marquise de Richelieu is horribly debauched . . . One day she put herself in the bed of Monsieur le Dauphin [son of Louis XIV] without his having invited her to sleep with him. When he entered his apartment, the servant said to him: "Monseigneur, a lady awaits you in your bed; she has not cared to identify herself!" He approached the bed and when he saw it was the marquise de Richelieu, he slept with her, but on the morrow he related it to everybody.

The Palatine's censure was influenced by two factors: she was very unattractive and of necessity made a virtue out of virtue; her upbringing in Germany had been much stricter than she would have had in France.

Bussy-Rabutin, in his famous *Histoire amoureuse des Gaules,* writes of several decades earlier when Versailles and the Sun King were young:

> The princesse de Monaco, having thus lost her lover, and having only got a taste . . . of the monarch [Louis XIV], sought to console herself by the conquest of another but she was not very discriminating; she took so many chances that she succumbed in the end. A page, handsome and well-built . . . who was active all over Paris . . . having pleased her, she wanted to see if she would find him better than a number of men of quality whom she had already tried . . . But soon she died of the remedies [presumably against venereal disease] . . ."

The comte de Guiche, one of the handsomest men of the Court, had a sense of humor which we may find odd but, according to Primi Visconti, was not so considered by his fellow courtiers. In his *Memoirs of the Court of Louis XIV,* Visconti writes:

> To return to the . . . comte de Guiche . . . one night at the queen's game [of chance], where there was a circle, the princesses and duchesses being seated around the queen, while the other persons stood, the comte felt that the hand of a lady . . . was occupied in a place — concerning which modesty imposes silence — and which he covered with his hat; noticing that the lady was not looking, he maliciously raised his hat. All the spectators having started to laugh and whisper, I leave you to think how confused the poor little one became.

As the French themselves say, "other times, other manners." There is no intention here to suggest that by comparison with what many of her contemporaries were doing, Ninon was a nun. But the truth of the matter is that Ninon's age did not look askance at her promiscuity or aggressiveness or for that matter at Marion de l'Orme's. That the princely house of Condé invited Marion to their son's wedding is most significant. In every age, including our own, men of high society have had mistresses, but today there is nothing like the degree of public acceptance of the practice that there was then. Of course what better imprimatur could be put on the custom of publicly acknowledging mistresses than that of the head of French society, Louis XIV himself? The king, who set the style in everything, openly flaunted his mistresses, even giving them official status — maîtresse en titre (official mistress) — to distinguish them from the chambermaids and the partners in casual affairs. To be the official mistress of the king was a great distinction, and very profitable. That shrewd Italian, Primi Visconti, writes:

> I say once and for all that there is not a lady of quality who hasn't the ambition to become the mistress of the king. A number of ladies, married or not, have declared to me that it was no offense to her husband, nor her father, nor God to become beloved of her prince . . . But the worst is that the families, the fathers, the mothers and even certain husbands would draw vanity therefrom.

To be chosen by the king (or a great lord) as mistress implied a respect and admiration that marriage among the upper class seldom did. Consistently enough, the children of mistresses were usually much more loved and prized than legitimate issue, for the former were love children, not dynastic heirs procreated perfunctorily and dutifully.

Now the full flowering of the mistress system brings with it marked changes in attitudes on the part of both men and women. The mistress, particularly the single one, had to know how to please her man. She had no all-but-indissoluble marriage contract to assure her of at least financial security. She must be on her toes, put her best foot forward. And she took pride in being highly skilled in this amorous ballet, in being entertaining, charming, polished. She enjoyed and derived satisfaction from her finesse. A corollary of the mistress system was a greater degree of female independence. The mistress was not tied. If the man did not treat her well, she could take somebody else who did. Thus, men very often treated mistresses much better than their wives, for they could lose a mistress but not a wife — owing to the absence of divorce.

With the independence of single life went the necessity of the unmarried woman to fend for herself. Thus, quite naturally she might become more aggressive than a married woman, although not necessarily so, as in the cases of the marquise de Richelieu and the princesse de Monaco. Many others could be cited. Hence Ninon's conduct with Navailles would not per se have been considered especially notable in her time. Her notoriety, in certain circles, derived principally from the fact that she had not played the game according to the rules of her class — she had loved promiscuously and sometimes aggressively out of wedlock, whereas the game was to love promiscuously and sometimes aggressively in the married state. It just was not fair, complained her enemies, to take another woman's husband when she could not take yours back.

Of course there is one more fact to remember. Ninon was determined to live like an honnête homme, and what honnête homme worthy of the name did not drop everything when he saw a pretty girl and pursue her to possess her?

\*

Some fifteen years after that dark day in December 1632 when Ninon's father killed Chabans, Henri de Lanclos seems to have returned from his long exile. He probably never received an official pardon, but the furore had long ago died down; Madame de Chabans had followed her husband to the grave in 1634 and was therefore not around to bother Henri. Whether Riberolles, the husband of Henri's beloved, Lucrèce de Gouges, was still among the living we do not know, but certainly we do not hear of him again. The death in 1642 of Richelieu, stern dispenser of justice, and the advent of the easygoing days of the Good Regency no doubt helped to facilitate Henri's return. It is perhaps strange he did not turn up till 1647.

Wonder as we may about the fate of the vital, ill-starred Lucrèce, history is tantalizingly silent. There has of course grown up an extensive apocrypha on Ninon and, in some of the fiction associated with her, Henri comes back to his ever-faithful Lucrèce, knows some hours of sweetness but not for long — he is murdered, presumably at Riberolles's instigation. In fact, history gives us but the briefest glimpses of Henri after his flight. We do not even know the country of his exile or how he existed. Perhaps his lute served him in good stead. He undoubtedly kept in practice and may have composed during his exile — perhaps poignant lays for his faraway little daughter and embattled mistress — for there is definite evidence of his musical activity when he returned. Even more tantalizing is the silence of the record regarding his relations with Ninon. The tradition is that he had kept in touch with his family by secret correspondence. We have only one fragmentary quotation of any speech between Henri and Ninon — a deathbed utterance. Where he lived in Paris we do not know, but probably not with his daughter. Emile Magne speculates that Henri did not want to cramp her style. Perhaps he feared to expose her to embarrassment or worse if the old charge was raked up again. Of all the lacunae in Ninon's life, the lack of information about the long-awaited reunion between father and daughter is the most exasperating.

We do know he resumed his friendship with those masters of the lute, Gaultier the Old, and Gaultier the Young, whose fame had meanwhile spread throughout Europe. The older Gaultier, now in his seventies and well off, had retired to his estate near Vienne. Henri went all the long way south to do homage to the maestro and to indulge his passion for making music with the old gentleman.

In Paris, Gaultier the Young presided over a cult of artists — musicians, painters, engravers — all devoted to music in general, the lute in particular. Henri was a respected performer and composer and was welcomed there. He was evidently distinguished enough to be included by the contemporary musicologist, Father Mersenne, in his *Universal Harmony,* which lists Henri as a composer of suites for flute, violin, and bass. Henri was probably extremely happy in the gentle society of which Gaultier the Young was the center. It is pleasant to think that notwithstanding Madame de Lanclos's strictures to the contrary, a good Providence saw fit to accord Henri one or

two good years before he died. In 1648 the Thirty Years' War
ended but the Fronde began. Henri, though fifty-six or fifty-
seven, once again answered the sound of the trumpet. He must
have been a fairly young cinquegenarian to have taken the
field. Perhaps Ninon inherited some of her propensity for abid-
ing youthfulness from him. Be that as it may, Henri never
knew longevity. He seems to have joined the forces in opposition to Mazarin. At the beginning of 1649 he is said to have
been killed near Rouen without a goodbye to Ninon. Another
version is that though mortally wounded, he was able to give
some parting advice to Ninon who had rushed to his bedside.
"Be," said the dyed-in-the-wool Epicurean, "less particular
about the number than the quality of your pleasures." This
suggests that father and daughter may have become close again
after their long separation, that he had seen the way Ninon was
flitting from one man to another, and that he did not entirely
approve of the multiplicity. After all, even *he* had been faithful
to Lucrèce for years.

Ninon was now twenty-six. She had no parents, her brothers
seem to have disappeared, she had few relatives. Though popular, she was all but alone. Though most of Paris's eligible men
yearned to be her lover, she probably had not more than three
close friends at this time: old Des Yveteaux, Scarron, and Saint-
Evremond. Des Yveteaux was soon to die; Scarron was a piti-
ful though courageous cripple, more in need of help than able
to help; Saint-Evremond cared, but Ninon was such a gadabout
that his sensitivities and pride must have been occasionally hurt
and the closeness of their relationship interrupted from time to
time. Besides, the Fronde had taken him away from Paris, as it
had many others of Ninon's world.

The Fronde, that costly civil war, bereft Ninon of her father, tore friends and lovers away from her, and ravaged France. Some writers tend to treat it as a musical comedy squabble, instigated by intriguing beauties. They romanticize it, seeing the whole affair as but a dangerous sport in which lovers gladly charged redoubts and sacked cities to win a smile from their ladies. But the Fronde was no joke. At least the early part of it, the Fronde of the Parlement, was a genuine revolt, not against the abuse of the royal power but against the abdication of it — to regencies foreign* in composition. It was also a protest against the pillaging of France by unscrupulous ministers of finance like d'Emery, who kept Marion de l'Orme in jewels and the taxpayer in rags.

D'Emery eventually tired of Marion's spendthrift magnificence and shifted his attentions elsewhere. After d'Emery left Marion in 1648, her star began to decline; she went into debt. Unlike Ninon, who steered clear of politics, Marion got herself mixed up in the Fronde, taking sides against Mazarin. She also got herself pregnant. Her end came tragically and suddenly, in June 1650, at the early age of thirty-nine, when, according to Tallemant, "she was as beautiful as ever," her frequent pregnancies not having impaired her stunning beauty. Unlike our neurotic age, when glamorous women die of overdoses of sleeping pills, Marion succumbed to an overdose of antimony which she had taken to make her abort.

Her final sickness lasted but two or three days, during which

---

* Since Henri de Navarre's assassination in 1610, France had lived through two regencies, that of the Italian Marie de Medici (when Louis XIII was a boy) with the Italian Concini as her first minister and lover, and that of the Spanish Anne of Austria (when Louis XIV was a boy) with the Italian Mazarin as her first minister and lover.

Marion, ever devout, confessed ten times. "She seemed always to have something new to say," explained Tallemant. For twenty-four hours she lay in state on her bed crowned with, of all things, a "virgin's coronal" until the curé, who had given her absolution, bridled at the virgin's coronal and proceeded to bury her, "for all Paris was coming to see her, as if she had been a saint."

Whether Ninon and Marion had ever made up again after the coolness which resulted seven years earlier from Ninon's having temporarily stolen Coligny away from Marion is unknown.

The Fronde saw the death of Ninon's father, of her first love, Coligny, of Marion, of Marion's estranged supporter, d'Emery, of the bonhomme Des Yveteaux. It split her friends down the middle. Scarron wrote diatribes against the Mazarin faction. Saint-Evremond threw in his lot on the side of Mazarin and the royal family, distinguished himself militarily, was made a brigadier general, and given a handsome pension. Miossens gained a marshal's baton. Ninon tried to keep clear of the struggle which, except in the very early part (the Fronde of the Parlement), degenerated rapidly into a sordid, unprincipled grappling of selfish aristocrats — the Fronde of the Princes. Paris was frequently under siege with its attendant horror — hunger. Lawlessness and ribaldry were rampant. Ninon would have liked to get out. She found herself an excuse in her passion for Villars — a romantically handsome cavalier.

The best seller of those days was a romance by La Calprenède called *Cassandre,* whose hero was Oroondate, a mighty man in both battle and boudoir. In traditionally romantic fashion, for which Ninon had no taste, Oroondate spent a good part of ten volumes chasing Cassandre over wild terrain. Society identified Villars with Oroondate and nicknamed him Villars-Oroondate. It appears that while the torrent of Ninon's and Villars's passion was in full flood, Villars was called to military duty in the vicinity of Lyons. Ninon, sick of the unpalatable mess that was Paris during the Fronde, as well as lovesick, entreated Villars to take her with him — something he of course could not do. He left. Impetuously, Ninon, in the manner of Oroondate pursuing Cassandre, set out to rejoin him. Disguising herself as a man, she donned sword and pistols. As she was going to live like an honnête homme, she might as well dress like one. The journey was a dangerous one — even for a man. The countryside was full of marauding soldiers and bandits become aggressive in times of anarchy. In her haste to overtake Villars, she did not wait for a passenger coach but went by post chaise with the mailbags. Faint heart may never win fair lady, but there is no guarantee that the bold heart wins a man. In this case, anyway, it did not.

We do not know the details — whether Ninon ever made contact with Villars or, if so, what occurred. All we do know is that Ninon was so disconsolate in Lyons that once again, for a second time in her life, she entered a convent. But she was not to find peace there, thanks to Cardinal Richelieu — not the great cardinal-minister of Louis XIII's reign who had died six years before, but his older brother, Alphonse du Plessis, bishop of Lyons. While making his rounds, Monsieur de Lyon cast a covetous eye upon the attractive penitent from Paris. She was talking about becoming a nun. The cardinal took it upon himself to dissuade her.

Ninon recoiled from this Cardinal Richelieu with much greater distaste than Marion had from his younger and more famous brother years before. The bishop of Lyons was a little crazy and more than a little mediocre. He had been a problem to his father who had hoped his son would become a chevalier of Malta. He did not make the grade. By some curious process of reasoning the father came to a queer conclusion. "Go," he ordered. "You are good for nothing — except the Church." Monsieur de Lyon took his post of pastor so seriously that, like Des Yveteaux, he dressed in pastoral garb, exchanging his miter for a crown of poppies, his cross for a shepherd's crook. Fashionably rustic, the cardinal loved to cavort in the beribboned costume of a shepherd with the ladies of the diocese who were flimsily dressed as bergères ("shepherdesses"). Tallemant says the cardinal committed "a thousand follies" — folies bergères, no doubt.

In one of his sermons Father Lejeune inveighed against parents' dumping on the Church the rejects of humanity:

> If you have a child ill-favored by nature, homely, heavy . . . hunchbacked or lame, it is worthless in the world; it must be given to the Church. If you have a daughter, ugly, misshapen, deformed, and brainless, you might . . . shut her up in a convent.
>
> And why make him a priest? In order that in this job he can make a living, in order that he may earn a few sous in saying mass just as his brother does in making a pair of shoes? . . .

Generally the elder Richelieu agreed with Father Lejeune — the Church was not a trash can for human dregs. But consistency does not seem to have been his strong point. Instead of welcoming a splendid specimen like Ninon into the Church, he tried to seduce her. Horrified, Ninon fled the sacred precincts which she refused to defile. Sacrilege was not in her nature.

A wealthy bourgeois of Lyons, a Monsieur Pérachon, "smitten through and through" by Ninon according to Tallemant, came forward to help the homeless young woman — ostensibly with no strings attached. He offered her the use of a mansion worth 24,000 livres ($48,000 to $120,000). Ninon was not naive, and the fact that she accepted his suspiciously generous offer may provide confirmation for the thesis of those who claim that Coulon got nothing in return for his subsidy (which was still going on, by the way) except the right to her company, but not her bed, once a month. In other words Ninon may have thought that if it worked with Coulon, it might with Pérachon, too. But when Pérachon eventually made it clear that he expected to take out the rent in kind, Ninon gave him back the key. Little as she wanted to return to Paris in the grip of the Fronde, she evidently liked less the oppressive atmosphere of a muddy, provincial city. In low spirits and hating herself for having run after Villars in the first place, she made her perilous way back to Paris — probably in early 1649.

There she heard, with much sorrow, grievous news about the bonhomme Des Yveteaux, whom she had continued to visit up to the outbreak of the Fronde in 1648. While Ninon's youth had danced along trippingly till the Fronde, old Des Yveteaux's years had been advancing with heavy tread. "The days pass," sighed Des Yveteaux, "in ignorance and indolence, and these days destroy us and make us lose the things to which we are attached." But his chatelaine, the lovely Madame du Puy, had stayed ever with him, soothing and caressing him with her soft melodies, though the tempo was somewhat slower than before. The old man had remained in excellent health except for his bladder, which a surgeon had to sound daily. He was said to be in his late eighties, and people were sure he would go on indefinitely, strolling in his vast garden with the always attentive Madame du Puy, reading his Greek authors, delighting his soul with music. But the Fronde came and with it the blockade of Paris. Des Yveteaux had fled to a country hamlet where a strange doctor, sounding his bladder, fatally infected him. When the end was near, he asked Madame du Puy to play him a saraband to ease his passage into the other world. She did and he died peacefully, clutching in his gnarled hand the yellow ribbon which Ninon had given him years before.

Before long Ninon resumed her old round of pleasure at an accelerated pace — probably to drown out the humiliation of the Villars affair and the bad taste of the experience with the lecherous Cardinal Richelieu and the wolfish Pérachon. Besides, during the Fronde, as is usual in times of crisis, sexual license was even more widespread than before.

It was probably at this time that the incident with the Grand Prior, the chevalier de Vendôme, Louis XIII's half brother, occurred. The chevalier had accepted with ill grace Ninon's refusal to take him as a lover. After all, he was Henri IV's son, with a bar sinister, by the beloved Gabrielle d'Estrées. He was no doubt proud of his bar sinister, showing that he was a true love child. In the case of the chevalier, though, his illegitimacy does not seem to have conferred special distinction, for Ninon spurned him, thus provoking his protest in poetry which Ninon answered in the same meter. Perhaps the unfortunate chevalier was wooing at a bad time, when Ninon may have been salving

her feelings hurt by Villars with the balm produced by reject-
ing a suitor of royal blood. He may have thought it wise to bide
his time, for he pocketed his pride and joined the ranks of
Ninon's admiring circle, hoping against hope she would relent,
but content, if she would not, with just her company.

The chevalier de Vendôme, once his indignation at Ninon's
refusal to sleep with him had cooled off, must have been a
rather good sport, for Emile Magne claims, "He even had a
share in the comedy with which the Sévigné household was
regaling the town" — a comedy in which the ubiquitous Ninon, not unexpectedly, played a principal part.

Henri, marquis de Sévigné, was not, says Tallemant, by any
means an honnête homme. Of course Sévigné's infidelity to his
famous wife was not, in the seventeenth century of all centuries,
the reason he was not accounted an honnête homme. The reason was that the marquis was using his wife's funds to support
his mistresses, well-nigh ruining her.

The French are very proud of their history. Several times a
week Parisians, or visitors to Paris, may attend conférences —
walking tours in various sections of the city. They are generally led by charming French ladies of indeterminate age. The
tour of the Marais of course takes in the Carnavalet Museum,
once the magnificent home of Madame de Sévigné. In telling
the story of the Sévignés, the tour leader is wont to state that the
marquis died in a duel over Ninon instead of over Madame de
Gondran. In France, as is well known, when something is
amiss and there are no clues, they say "cherchez la femme."
When they speak of the seventeenth-century femme, people

seem to assume that the lady was always Ninon. Such is the legend that has grown up around her.

But although Sévigné did not fight a duel over Ninon, he did fall in love with her, much to the distress of his young wife. Her cousin, Bussy-Rabutin, sprang to give her comfort with an alacrity not entirely disinterested. The opportunity came when one day Bussy met Sévigné who confided perhaps a bit boastfully that "he had passed the previous night in the most agreeable fashion in the world, not only for him, but for the lady with whom he had been. 'You can believe' [he told Bussy], 'that it was not with your cousin: it was with Ninon.' "

"So much the worse for you," Bussy replied, "my cousin is a thousand times better, and I'm certain that if she were not your wife, she'd be your mistress."

"That could well be," the marquis conceded dryly.

Bussy lost no time in relating the conversation to Madame de Sévigné, particularly the part where he stood up for her and claimed she outpointed Ninon. Madame de Sévigné fought scorn with scorn when told of her husband's latest conquest. "He has not so much to boast of in that," said she. Madame de Sévigné, contemporaries record, had a beautiful complexion which flamed scarlet when she was angry. Bussy cautioned her not to underrate Ninon — she would do so at her peril. He also counseled retaliation — via an affair with him.

"You must be mad to give me such advice, or perhaps you think I am mad," said Madame de Sévigné.

Bussy saw his opening. "You certainly will be, madame, if you do not give him tit for tat. Avenge yourself, my beautiful cousin; I shall be a party to your vengeance, for after all your interests are as dear to me as my very own."

Madame de Sévigné, whom Bussy a little suspectly calls cold, was not that easily persuaded. "Softly, my dear Count; I am not so worked up as you think."

When Sévigné got home, his wife evidently read him the riot act, for next day in the Cours-la-Reine, Sévigné jumped into Bussy's carriage. "I gather," said Sévigné with understandable heat, "that you told your cousin what I related to you about Ninon, for she gave me quite a going over."

"Me?" replied Bussy, feigning hurt. "I told her nothing, my dear sir, but, as she is no fool, and as she talks so much on the subject of jealousy, she cannot help hitting upon the truth sometimes."

Sévigné evidently thought it was too nice a day in the fragrant Cours to spoil by arguing, for he readily accepted Bussy's rather lame explanation and got back to a happier subject — "and then, having told me the thousand advantages there are to being in love, he concludes by saying that he would like to be in love all his life, and that at that very moment he was as much in love with Ninon as it is possible to be; that he was going to spend the night at Saint-Cloud with her . . ."

Bussy gave Sévigné some friendly and free advice. He warned him that he might drive his wife to despair and that if some cavalier came along just at the time that Sévigné was "doing her a dirty trick," she might seek "sweetness in love and vengeance" — something which she would not have otherwise considered. Whereupon Sévigné took his leave for Ninon.

There is no record of Madame de Sévigné's having taken a lover either during her marriage or long widowhood. But she had a great capacity for fun. Speaking of her bubbling joyousness, the dean of French literary critics, Sainte-Beuve, writes,

"She was a living proof of the truth of the words of Ninon de Lanclos: 'The joy of the spirit is the measure of its power.'" Ninon too loved laughter, but she does not appear to have been so thoroughgoing about it as Madame de Sévigné. There was a darker, deeper side to Ninon's nature, which constituted a shadowy counterpoint to her gaiety. It seems a shame that Ninon and Madame de Sévigné, both dispensers of merriment, were on the outs for so long. One certainly cannot blame Madame de Sévigné. Not unexpectedly her animosity toward Ninon continued into the second generation when Madame de Sévigné's son became Ninon's lover. Unlike retribution in the Pentateuch, however, it stopped in the third generation, with Madame de Sévigné's insisting on her grandson's, the marquis de Grignan, attending Ninon's school for grooming young gentlemen.

Ninon was consistent in her inconstancy. Her affair with Sévigné lasted about three months, without its costing Sévigné, except for the bitter resentment of his wife, anything more than "a ring of little value" — with which Ninon apparently was quite content. After Sévigné came Rambouillet de La Sablière. The delicate Charleval, one of Ninon's "martyrs," doomed to wait endlessly for her favors, had spotted Rambouillet for her. It may have been good sportsmanship on his part to bring the two together — if it was fated that he should not be one of the elect. Or possibly he felt that he might advance his own cause and put Ninon in his debt, by introducing her to a handsome chap like Rambouillet, known as "le grand Madrigalier," for the frail Charleval was wily. Pointing out Rambouillet to her he whispered, "My dear, *there* is one who has the looks to be one of your caprices." Tallemant says, "She wrote him [Rambouillet] jokingly: 'I believe I shall love you three months; for me it is an infinity.' During her passion, no one saw her but this one [the reigning lover]; many others visited her, but it was only for conversation or sometimes for supper."

Ninon set a rather good table. To this day, says *Vogue* magazine in its December 1963 issue, gourmets serve Crème de Ninon de Lanclos — a soup which is a "blend of purée of peas with consommé, a hint of lemon, a tot of dry sherry — then, added at the last minute, a froth of whipped cream, a quart of champagne." Speaking of the easy flow of Ninon's conversation, her contemporaries said that though she never took so much as a nip, she was as if intoxicated from the soup on. Perhaps it was that tot of sherry and quart of champagne in the crème, although in fairness to the contemporary testimony, Ninon, like the natural hostess she was, became so exhilarated by the thrill of entertaining and was so responsive to the stimulating talk that poured out of guests like Scarron, d'Elbène, Saint-Evremond, the Great Condé, La Rochefoucauld, and later Molière, Boileau, and Racine, that intoxication without alcohol was for her easy.

When Rambouillet's allotted time was up, Ninon asked his opinion in selecting a successor. She had heard of someone who sounded interesting. "Tell me," she said, "is so and so handsome, for I have a craving for something spicy?" Tallemant does not record Rambouillet's answer but adds a cryptic sentence: "She asked this tolerably chastely, for she never overdid anything and but rarely took chances on getting pregnant." One thing is clear — Tallemant did not find remarkable the great number of Ninon's lovers, almost as if it were the norm at that time. This merely reinforces the conviction that it was later ages that added the scarlet hue to Ninon's reputation and that had she not been unorthodox in not marrying and in not conforming religiously, she would have incurred the wrath of next to nobody. Note "she never overdid." Ninon was around twenty-seven. Saint-Evremond's Epicurean teaching of avoiding excess must have already sunk in.

But trouble was brewing for Ninon. In 1650 Aubijoux who, with Coulon had been subsidizing her for about nine years,* persuaded her to move from the Marais on the Right Bank across the Seine to Saint-Germain on the Left Bank; there she would be closer to him, be able to breathe pure air and enjoy the spacious gardens. Coulon and Aubijoux's beautiful friendship, so touching in the way one always found a girl for the other, had foundered — probably because Aubijoux could no longer stomach Coulon's grossness. Coulon objected to the move, but Ninon welcomed the opportunity of getting rid of the chronic drunkard, for she ignored his protests. It was then that the rich, sensitive youngster, Moreau, jumped at the opportunity to replace Coulon as financial supporter. Tallemant, on one page, says he does not know whether Moreau slept with Ninon or not but states that he rendered her the homage due a queen, perhaps content just to be admitted to her presence and adore her from a decent distance. But on an earlier page he was categorical, saying Moreau "died without having received any favor." He was only about eighteen when he first stood in awe of Ninon and but twenty-two when he died. Scarron's obituary poem speaks highly of Moreau, indicating he was im-

---

* Nine years according to Tallemant, but if Magne is right in saying that Ninon did not start up with Coulon until after her mother died, i.e., 1643, then it would be seven years.

patient of mediocrity and richly endowed as to both mind and body. With these qualifications it is strange that Tallemant had to record that Moreau in all probability was excluded from Ninon's couch. Perhaps Ninon refused him *because* he contributed to her upkeep, although that restriction does not seem to have applied to other payeurs, like Vassi and Aubijoux, who were admitted "when the fancy seized her." But then it would be a little ungallant to expect that kind of consistency from Ninon, even if she was an honnête homme.

Trouble was brewing for Ninon among the prudes at Court who usually were religious bigots as well. They were jealous of Ninon's many easy conquests, of her single blessedness; they resented her philosophical and religious freethinking. Ninon made no bones about her rejection of organized religion. During a recent and all but fatal illness, she did not, Tallemant tells us, retreat from her position, "only receiving the sacraments out of a sense of propriety." Whether she had read Montaigne or not as a girl, she was certainly reading him now. To Montaigne, skepticism created the climate for tolerance, from which led the road to the Epicurean ideal of serenity. Along with Saint-Evremond, she abhorred fanaticism of any kind. Many clerics were fanatics. Ninon, never lacking in courage, and far less circumspect than the Erudite Libertins who cursed the Church in the privacy of their studies but genuflected in public, could not be hypocritical. She did not mount barricades in the streets, but neither did she refrain from making highly nonconformist remarks like: "He is to be pitied who needs religion to find his way through life, for it is a certain sign of either a limited mind or a corrupt heart."

Ninon no doubt believed that religion came between man

and God, that it was divisive, causing bloodletting schisms among people, and on balance did more harm than good. But she continued to pray to God all her life. According to her lights, she was an ethical deist, feeling strongly that she served him better by being honest, kind, steadfast, and generous than by being chaste and observant of the forms of religion. This was dangerous heterodoxy in those days, and the harpies around Anne of Austria were just waiting for the opportunity to jump. They duly noted reports of Ninon's jibes. "On Ash Wednesday," their spies told them Ninon had said, "instead of the words the officiating priest uses while lightly touching the forehead of the penitent, he would do better to say: 'You must give up love, you must give up love.'" They heard that Ninon had taken a priest to a dying friend to administer extreme unction and said, "Monsieur, do your duty toward my friend. I assure you that notwithstanding all his reasoning he knows no more about it than you." They never failed to keep posted the pious queen who did not like the impiety at all — not at all.

Their chance came not long after Ninon moved to the Left Bank where her house became the scene of many a lively party. Among those who flocked to her apartments was the eminent président Tambonneau, who seemed to have been well mated. His wife, the présidente, philandered to just about the same degree as he. They seemed to have worked out a mutually satisfactory *modus operandi,* which included even a little concern for each other. Monsieur Tambonneau so admired Ninon's lute-playing that he could not bear to think that his wife should be deprived of the pleasure of hearing her. The trouble was that Madame Tambonneau belonged to that clique of which the venal Madame Coulon was the ringleader and which was applying social sanctions against Ninon by not receiving her. But Madame Tambonneau was ingenious. She suggested that Ninon and she be separated by a tapestry, and thus she could enjoy the music without letting down the social barriers. The président was indignant. "In good sooth, my little lady," he told his wife, "seriously I assure you that she is as modest as the next person; and then she has, don't you know, an attendant, Anne, altogether as prudish as yours." Tallemant adds that Ninon would almost die laughing in telling the story, "for Madame Anne was the procurer for the président's wife."

Tallemant makes mention of the "little Charpentier," a young lady who evidently was a regular visitor to Ninon's house about this time. She was apparently beautiful but a little stupid. Ninon was besieged by callers and perhaps the little Charpentier hoped to pick up pointers on how to handle men, or maybe to help with the overflow. The conversation was on historians and the little Charpentier, who "had not said a word for three months," decided to express an opinion: "As for me, I am crazy about Rodote," she said, meaning to say Herodote (Herodotus). The président Tambonneau, evidently charmed by the gaffe, sent her some cider and then proceeded on his next visit to make "sweet eyes" at her. The little Charpentier opened her mouth and did it again: "Président, send me lots of cider but don't come near, for you stink too much." Since the rest is silence, it is not improbable that the horrified Ninon dispensed thereafter with the company of the little Charpentier.

Ninon made a mistake in going to Saint-Germain, which was unlike the unconstrained atmosphere of the Marais. It was in the parish of Saint-Sulpice, over which presided the joy-killing priest, Jean Jacques Olier. His right arm was the dreaded Society of the Holy Sacrament, a group of lay vigilantes who went around denouncing people for alleged religious and moral laxity. Report had it that Ninon ate meat during Lent. In those days of totalitarian religion, flouting of prohibitions was regarded seriously.

During Lent in 1651, Ninon gave a dinner party. The menu included poulet and possibly a fair amount of some heady white wine, for the company got rather boisterous. In good Henri VIII fashion, one of the guests tossed a wishbone out the window. As luck would have it, one of curé Olier's spies was directly beneath the window, and the chicken bone caromed off his bald pate. Gleefully clutching the evidence he rushed back to his superior, who in turn swore out a complaint to the bailiff of Saint-Germain-des-Prés. By the time the bailiff got the story, not only had Ninon's party been gorging on meat, but two men had been killed there. The bailiff was a merry rogue and warned Ninon of her danger. Shortly after, two noblemen clattered up to the bailiff's door. By dint of a little suave talk and even more suave palm-greasing, the bailiff was convinced that the complaint should be quashed. But busy tongues did not cease to wag at Court. One of the great wits of the day, Madame Cornuel, quipped that the abbé Boisrobert's chasubles were made out of Ninon's discarded skirts.

The religious party, which had Queen Anne's ear, stepped up the pressure. They dinned in over and over again that the impious Ninon was perverting the religious and sexual morals of many a fine, God-fearing youth. Anne said she might send her to a convent for wayward girls — Les Filles Repenties. Ninon, however, was not without her defenders. That would be unjust, protested a courtier, Bautru, "for, madame, elle n'est ni fille, ni repentie" (she is neither a fille, nor repentant). *Fille* is a word with a number of meanings: girl, maiden (in virginal sense), spinster, servant girl, nun, prostitute. Bautru was punning, of course, but probably, since he was championing Ninon, his primary meaning was that Ninon was neither a prostitute nor repentant. Curiously enough all the other meanings of *fille* except "spinster" would apply, for Ninon at twenty-eight was not a girl, nor a virgin, nor a servant girl, nor a nun. The play on words with its multiple meanings so pleased the good-natured queen that she forgot about punishing Ninon. But when Ninon's masculine supporters were not around, the indefatigable Court vixens again started their clawing and this time wore Anne down. She dispatched an officer with a lettre de cachet * requiring Ninon to withdraw to a convent of her choice.

Fortunately, Ninon kept both her wits and her wit about her. "Since the queen," she replied gaily, "has the great goodness to leave to me the choice of *couvent* to which she wishes me to retire, I pray you tell her that I choose the Grands Cordeliers." The lettre de cachet used the word *couvent* which means either convent or monastery. The Grands Cordeliers were an order of monks. Originally highly ascetic, by the seventeenth century they were a byword for lechery. In the eighteenth century a rich lady who belonged to the Aphrodites, an exclusive and expensive club devoted, as the name implies, to lovemaking, kept a detailed list of her paramours over a span of twenty years. Very systematic, she broke down her 4959 lovers into categories: the largest class was officers — 929, but in second place were monks — 439, nearly all Cordeliers. Anne's officer, put off

* Arbitrary warrant.

balance by Ninon's attractiveness, was dumbfounded by the boldness of her reply and meekly returned to the queen to whom he repeated the answer word for word. Anne was charmed to the tips of her fingers — said to be the prettiest part of her, by the way.

"Fie, the villain," she laughed. "Let her go where she wants," and she called off the dogs.

Ninon may seem to have handled this dangerous situation with lighthearted bravado, but actually she realized she was skating on thin ice. Though she felt strongly about religious freedom and the right to live one's private life as one pleases without interference from public censors like the Society of the Holy Sacrament, she had not the slightest desire to be a martyr. Like Saint-Evremond, she had seen people burned at the stake and the horror had burned itself into her memory. She would try hard to follow his dictum: "Think as you like, but behave like the others." Discretion would be the better part of valor. She knew that the religious party would not easily give up persecuting her and wisely took steps to placate their fanaticism. She planted the rumor that she was going to America. Through the window she could be seen praying.

In church, where Ninon had gone to show what a good girl she was, a certain Madame Paget found herself seated next to a young woman whose appearance and deportment she liked. Bored with the sermon, Madame Paget engaged Ninon in conversation and was much taken with her. Wanting to know who she was, she asked a certain Jean Dupin her name. Dupin was in a playful mood. "She is Madame d'Argencour of Brittany who has a lawsuit here." (Dupin was, of course, punning on the word *argencour,* meaning "short of money.") Madame

Paget, whose husband was a Master of Petitions, offered Ninon her assistance. "Madame, you have an action? I shall help you; I would have the greatest pleasure in the world in soliciting for such an amiable person." Just then the abbé Boisrobert went by and bowed to Ninon. "How do you happen to know that man?" asked Madame Paget. "Madame, I am his neighbor." Madame Paget, who incidentally was no more chaste than she had to be, replied, "I shall never forgive him for having left us for a Ninon, for a villain." "Ah! Madame," said Ninon, holding in the laughter, "one shouldn't believe everything that is said, she is perhaps a chaste girl. Perhaps they can say the same of you and me; slander spares nobody." As Madame Paget was going out, Boisrobert came up to her. "You've had a nice little talk with Ninon." At first Madame Paget was in a rage at both Boisrobert and Ninon, but later when they met again at a mutual friend's, she sought her out to converse with her. Boisrobert used the incident in a comedy, *La Belle Plaideuse,* wherein Ninon appears as Corinne. Molière, who was to avail himself of Ninon's critical judgment vis-à-vis his plays, may indirectly have another literary debt to her inasmuch as his *L'Avare* may derive, in part, from *La Belle Plaideuse.*

The abbé Boisrobert was one of a group of poets whom Ninon considered it wise to welcome to her home while the heat generated by the hounding Society of the Holy Sacrament was on. She reasoned that poets would be looked upon as more suitable company than the suspect freethinkers. Actually the rest of the group of poets — Saint-Pavin, Des Barreaux, and Chapelle, were all freethinkers too, but apparently poets were considered a better security risk than the philosophes. Certainly this group — writers of light, witty verse and sensual love poems — was not considered dangerous. Thus Ninon with one stroke accomplished two objectives — she used her association with the poets as a smoke screen to conceal her continuing interest in libertinism while at the same time keeping in touch through the relatively innocuous poets with the libertins whose cause she was resolved not to abandon.

The abbé Boisrobert was a likable, extremely human, and humane person. Like many another cleric, like the warmly earthy abbé Scarron, like Boisrobert's former master, the unethereal Cardinal Richelieu, he had no business being in the Church except for business — it gave him a comfortable living. He had been Richelieu's factotum — literary adviser, entertainer, procurer. A great raconteur, he could make the cardinal laugh as could no one else. A poet and playwright of more than average ability, he had founded the great Académie française in 1635 and was always soliciting handouts from Richelieu for needy writers and intellectuals. Like so many others, including Saint-Pavin and Des Barreaux in the little group of poets Ninon was currently cultivating in order to put the Society of the Holy Sacrament off the scent, he engaged in homosexuality, though probably not to the exclusion of mundane, prosaic heterosexuality. He had all the vices and most of the graces.

Boisrobert probably had met Ninon at Marion's. He was old enough to have been her father — having been born in 1592, the same year as Henri de Lanclos. Nonetheless he used to call Ninon his "goddess" and loved to pay her court. One day, Tallemant tells us, Boisrobert visited Ninon accompanied by a "pretty, young boy."

"But," objected Ninon, "this little villain *always* accompanies you."

"Yes," he replied, "I've tried putting him to work but he always turns up again."

"That's because," said Ninon, "they don't do for him what you do."

# Chapter 7

## Of Poetry and Passion

IF WE ARE TO BELIEVE the poetry written to Ninon at this time, we might have to conclude that she indeed was close to being a public menace, but not for the reasons advanced by the bigots. On the contrary, the charge would have been inaccessibility, unkindness to desperate suitors, exciting (though not deliberately) without satisfying, driving men mad or to the brink of suicide. "Shall I never see Ninon?" The anguished cry comes from Hercule de Lacger, a friend of Rambouillet de La Sablière. Evidently feeling that a lover emeritus, now graduated to the status of friend, might put in a good word for him, Lacger brought Rambouillet a long poem he addressed to him but which he intended that Rambouillet show Ninon.

> For mercy's sake, take me to her.
> I yearn to see this beauty.
>
> Perhaps for my suffering,
> Amid the weighty sighs
> Of so many dukes and marquises
> Which such beautiful eyes have conquered,
> My sighs will be treated
> By this cruel one as trifles.
> But perhaps not,

For when one speaks of Ninon
She is either contrary or willing
According to whether it pleases her caprice,
And her caprice, they say,
Often counts more than reason.

I want to see those adorable eyes
From sunset to dawn.
I shall see their scintillation
And all her other beauties,
Her good humor, her great genius,
I shall hear the lovely harmony
Of her lute, whose sweetness
Surpasses the concert of the nine sisters.

No longer disappoint my hope,
I'm already dying of impatience
And if I don't see her Tuesday
You will see me dead Wednesday.

Rambouillet, fearing Lacger was *in extremis,* rushed over with the poem. But Ninon was not to be stampeded. She had received too many of these supplicatory poems not to be suspicious of poetic license, let alone licentiousness. Often the composers were grubby little men given to inflated talk. In bed they were apt to be gauche. Still, the poem amused her, and she made inquiries about the sender. Lacger, she was told, was "roly-poly and not in the slightest an honnête homme." Furthermore, he was a boaster whose harsh Midi accent spoiled the cadence of his verses when he recited. In all probability his first name, Hercule (Hercules), would prove a misnomer. The answer was no. He tried again, pleading bottomless despair. The answer was again no. A search of the records of the morgue of the time will reveal no suicide by the name of Hercule de Lacger.

Saint-Pavin, who along with Boisrobert, Des Barreaux, and Chapelle, comprised the quartet of poets to which Ninon turned when the Society of the Holy Sacrament was baying at her trim heels, was also moved to express in poetry his feelings about the "cruel" Ninon. His tone, however, is sour rather than adulatory like Lacger's. He complains:

> I begin to disown you,
> You run away from me, ungrateful one!
> Your heart, so tender [to others]
> Why alone for me cannot it be the same?

Then he chides her for her inconstancy. But Saint-Pavin grumbled in vain. He was a little hunchback of nearly sixty when Ninon was a statuesque twenty-eight.

Chapelle, the only one of the group of four poets who was not at least a part-time sodomite, was probably the hardest hit by Ninon's obduracy, although none of them was half as badly stricken as he claimed. Like Boisrobert, Chapelle had great weaknesses but also much that was redeeming. He was highly regarded as a poet by his own and the succeeding century. Voltaire termed him a genius. He had a good deal in common with Ninon — lively wit, admiration for Gassendi's Epicureanism, disdain for the golden calf, love of liberty, peace and sweet, soft pleasure. Neither needed champagne to become stimulated — sparkling conversation was intoxicant enough, but there the similarity ended. Ninon never drank anything except water, but Chapelle was a pathological drunkard.

Like Saint-Evremond, Chapelle had ease and charm in his light verse, but like Saint-Evremond, it was in conversation that he probably shone most brilliantly. Obviously he had all the necessary qualifications to be admitted to Ninon's salon, but alas for him, not to her bed. Physically he was unattractive — thin, dissipated-looking, a peasant face surmounted by an unruly crop of hair.

Chapelle was the illegitimate son of François Luillier, a bachelor, a rich Epicurean, and a good friend of Gassendi's for two decades. Tallemant tells that Luillier would take his son Chapelle with him to his brothel. But he entrusted his education (other than in sex) to a priest — the broad-minded Gassendi, who stayed at Luillier's house when he was in Paris. When Gassendi returned to his native Provence, Luillier sent Chapelle to him to continue his studies. Each year, his sisters, who were evidently chippies off the old block, forwarded Chapelle jams by the hand of a pretty serving girl. If Chapelle liked her, she would stay on.

There is some doubt whether Molière actually studied under Gassendi, but if he did not, he was certainly a disciple. It is not unlikely that Chapelle, a lifelong friend of Molière, introduced him to Gassendi while Gassendi was staying at his (Chapelle's) father's house. Some claim that it was Chapelle who introduced Molière to Ninon in 1651. If so, Ninon's friendship with Moliére did not ripen until later.

Chapelle wrote several poems to Ninon. A verse from one will suffice to give the facile flavor.

> *Ton entretien attire à soi;*
> *Je n'en trouve point qui la vaille,*
> *Il pourrait consoler un roi*
> *De la perte d'une bataille.*

> (Your conversation is magnetic
> I find nothing to equal it,
> It could console a king
> For the loss of a battle.)

Poor Chapelle, he not only failed to become Ninon's lover, but the tradition has it that Ninon eventually declined to see him because of his terrible drunkenness. To get even, he is supposed to have replied,

> Don't be astonished
> If frequently she discourses
> Upon the sublime virtue
> With which Plato was clothed;
> For if her age is taken into account,
> She could have slept
> With this great personage.

Ninon, probably in her thirties at the time and not needing to be the least bit sensitive about her age, is said not to have taken offense and to have retorted that she would have preferred sleeping with Plato to Chapelle. Emile Magne denies the whole thing, saying the poem was not by Chapelle and is addressed to an unknown.

Ninon was not alone in not being able to put up with Chapelle's addiction to the bottle. The critic and satirist, Boileau, also became fed up with it, and only fear of Molière's anger prevented him from breaking with Chapelle. Molière was extremely attached to Chapelle. Bernier tells us, "the illustrious Molière could not live without his Chapelle," who evidently was very amiable and good-hearted. Coming events, it is said, cast their shadow before. We do not know the whole story as to what precipitated Ninon's expelling Chapelle. Perhaps he

made himself unbearably obnoxious when drunk, but he seems
to have been such a good fellow that Ninon's action appears a
little harsh. Voltaire, who only knew Ninon when she was
over eighty, wrote, "She had in her mind maxims of an austere
philosophy." Perhaps there were signs of this fifty years earlier.

\*

Instead of going to America, Ninon fell in love. She stayed
in love with Louis de Mornay, marquis de Villarceaux, for
thirty-six months — twelve times as long as with anybody else.
Villarceaux was her grand passion. Ninon is constant — she
must be getting old, people said. She was twenty-nine.

It is a commonplace that looks are deceiving, but the saying
applies with particular force to portraits of a bygone age. Many
a celebrated beauty, whose face could have launched a thousand
ships, appears to us in her portraits, all too often done by second-
rate artists, unattractive and stolid. Since physical attraction
was the main pull between Ninon and Villarceaux, curiosity
about Villarceaux's looks is of course automatic, notwithstanding the knowledge that his portrait may not yield the answer.
Certainly the one in the Louvre is unrewarding. It shows a
pouting, rodentlike face enclosed in heavy locks hanging below
the shoulders. The viewer cannot but wonder what Ninon saw
in him — body or soul — with his long nose, dry shapeless
mouth, and general air of sulkiness. Then one mutters that
standards were different then, or speculates that the likeness is
poor, and gives up. It so happens, however, that at the château
of Villarceaux, some fifty miles northwest of Paris, is a portrait
in the entrance hall which shows an entirely different Villarceaux. He is the picture of gallantry in his breastplate, white

neckerchief, blue scarf, and brown silk doublet — a strong mustachioed face looking out from a frame of lustrous, brown hair. There is also a slight hint of cruelty in the face — often fascinating to women. The artist is obviously superior to that of the Louvre portrait. It is unfortunate the château portrait cannot be reproduced in this book because it explains a great deal. It emits a high charge of masculinity.

Louis de Mornay was born in 1619, or four years before Ninon if we accept 1623 as her birth date. He came of a very wealthy, proud family. Tallemant says Louis's mother had wit but not judgment. Her son seems to have taken after her. Though no intellectual, he dabbled in poetry and painting. He had a lively, quick mind and an independent nature. His great forte was hunting. When Louis XIV was still but a boy of ten, Villarceaux caught his eye with his equestrian skill, and the young king made him, four years before he met Ninon, captain of the royal pack of seventy hounds. When Louis grew up, he chased the stag with Villarceaux. Tallemant tells us Villarceaux also hunted "game that was neither feathery nor shaggy." He seems to have pursued women with as much success as animals. He is often referred to as "a slim-hipped wolf."

Villarceaux does not appear to have been a very estimable person, but he had a way with him. He easily stole the heart and maidenhead of Marie de Girard, whom he was supposed to marry but did not. Instead he married money. Ninon probably knew very little about Villarceaux when she first met him. Before she had time to look him up, it was too late — she was in love and there was no going back. Too long had her hungry, healthy body been lying fallow with her physically unappealing poet friends or but inadequately satisfied by the casual encounters of recent days. She immediately felt a deep attraction for the athletic Villarceaux who strongly reciprocated the feeling.

Intent on having her to himself with no competition, Villarceaux suggested that they go to the countryside, near his family seat, and there, close to the rich fecund earth, celebrate an idyll of love in the tangy spring weather. He could not very well take her to the château of Villarceaux, as his wife and children were in residence, but he accepted the hospitality of a nearby friend, Valliquierville. Ninon was glad to leave Paris, still torn by the Fronde, but she probably would have gone anyway, for she was hard hit. She recklessly gave up everything — her friends and, of course, Aubijoux and young Moreau, her financial supporters.

Valliquierville considered it a privilege to shelter such lovers as Ninon and Villarceaux, obviously intended by a benign nature to explore uninhibitedly and unashamedly the delights of a towering passion. Valliquierville's estate was near Ruel, in the Vexin, that lush region west of Paris of rolling hills, sounding streams, loamy earth, fat cattle, abundant crops, romantic castles. Their host, a man of fifty-two, was considered eccentric. One of his oddities was that he refused "to eat anything which had had life." But as to his guests, their vigor must be fed, and Valliquierville denied them neither fish, flesh, nor fowl, treating them with the solicitude usually reserved for pregnant women. He seemed to stand in almost reverent wonder at their mighty love; he paid it homage, nourishing and sustaining it. He did this not only with his fine victuals and by supplying every comfort and privacy; he himself was a very necessary factor in keeping Ninon happy.

It has been noted that Villarceaux, though no fool and not

untalented, was far from an intellectual, lacking depth and subtlety. On the other hand, Valliquierville was a rather rare combination — a man of action and a philosopher too. So while Villarceaux was spurring his horse after the fleet boar or softly cantering along shady, sylvan trails, Valliquierville and Ninon would range over the fields of the mind, exploring the stoicism of the Roman Republicans, Montaigne's skepticism, and ethics. He himself practiced a strict morality and engaged in an unflinching resistance to tyranny. They would take long walks in the country lanes; they read to each other from their favorite authors. The days evidently flew for them every bit as quickly as did Villarceaux fly in full career on his froth-specked stallion. For Valliquierville it was infinitely piquant just to be in the company of a gracious, attractive young woman who paid him the consummate tribute of listening respectfully and appreciatively. For Ninon it was a slaking of her thirst for knowledge, enlightenment, and good conversation. Thus, Valliquierville ministered unto her mind by day and Villarceaux unto her body by night. She had never known such bliss.

Valliquierville would tell her of his conspiratorial days. Rightly or wrongly he had considered Richelieu an expendable despot. With fanatical zeal he had strained to overthrow this upstart cardinal who was arrogating unto himself power which Valliquierville considered unrighteous. Unlike many of his co-conspirators, who were base self-seekers, Valliquierville passionately felt it incumbent upon him to oppose Richelieu because voices within told him it was right to do so. Before Amiens he had sworn a fierce oath to humble the haughty cardinal into the dust; the plot had failed, and he had fled to England to escape the vengeance of Richelieu. Though politically nonpartisan herself, Ninon was endlessly fascinated by this austere revolutionary, this contemplative activist. All Paris knew of his reputation for high physical courage, how a dozen years before in a night action at Huytaert, he had had his horse shot from under him. Cool in action, self-disciplined, organized, incorruptible, he had the boundless confidence of his comrades. "To my way of thinking," said Scarron's friend, the revolutionary cardinal de Retz, of Valliquierville, "the truest gentleman of his century." Consistent in his unswerving opposition to those he considered usurpers, Valliquierville had joined the Frondeurs against Mazarin. He was lucky still to have his head upon his shoulders. He had withdrawn from the revolution, was now lying low, a disillusioned, disappointed man, reading Roman and Hebrew literature.

Valliquierville was a freethinker but an exceptional one in the sense that instead of following, as did most libertins, Epicurus, advocate of sensible pleasure, his model was Cato, that stern Roman of rigorous virtue and disinterestedness. Valliquierville's austerity had a powerful attraction for Ninon. We have noted earlier the grave or sober side of Ninon's nature — her dismissal of the amiable Chapelle for drunkenness, Voltaire's remark about the austerity of her philosophy. Ninon, herself, in a letter to Saint-Evremond thirty-five years later, referring to the fact that she then wore spectacles, says, "But they don't suit me badly; I have always had a grave look." Segrais refers to the melancholy side of Ninon, which those who only knew her superficially would never suspect. Ninon's gaiety was not just a cover-up for her sense of the tragedy of life. She had a genuine love of life, and she sparkled naturally and as effortlessly as a bird sings, but she was far from the one-dimensional playgirl that to some she may have seemed. It is this intermingling in Ninon, this blending of light and shadow, that constitutes her depth. Saint-Evremond, with his usual keen understanding, summed her up neatly:

> With wise yet indulgent concern,
> Did Nature conceive Ninon's heart.
> Epicurus did teach it to burn,
> But Cato did virtue impart.*

Valliquierville's eccentricity did not stop at incorruptibility or vegetarianism — he had a rabbi living with him. Ninon's curiosity was, of course, aroused. Valliquierville related how when he had been to Venice, he had frequented the ghetto there and become friendly with two long-bearded rabbis who instructed him in Hebrew and the Torah. He became so deeply interested in the Torah that he learned to speak Hebrew, accumulated a considerable Hebrew library, and brought back to his château a rabbi so that he might have someone to converse with in Hebrew. Valliquierville came to the conclusion that "in Genesis are contained all the Sciences and Philosophies," that in the Pentateuch he would "find all the truths of Physics." He delved into the occult and the mystical Cabbala. All this was Valliquierville's way of being a libertin, a man who thinks freely.

On the days when the weather was not inviting, although still not bad enough to keep Villarceaux from exercising his dogs, Ninon and Valliquierville would closet themselves in the library and, according to Tallemant, "reason." Some visitors interrupted them and inquired what they were doing. "We are attempting," replied Ninon with probably a perfectly straight

---

* Presumably translated by W. Dutton Burrard.

face, "to reduce to articles our belief; we have already made some progress; another time we hope to get even more work done." They must have accomplished a good deal, for Ninon, when she emerged from her course of instruction under Valliquierville, which probably went on for two summers, seemed more sure of herself in her intellectual and moral orientation to the world. Ninon had for years been gradually progressing, under the intermittent tutelage of Saint-Evremond and other like-minded men, toward the definition of standards by which she could live at peace with herself. This is not to say that she consciously wished to join formally any particular school of philosophy. That would probably be overintellectualizing her thought processes at this time. But she was a rational person and could not feel comfortable with herself until she had evolved a rational basis for her way of life. Valliquierville seems to have put the finishing touches on her skepticism and libertinism, reinforced her sturdy sense of right and wrong, and sprinkled a little slow-acting fertilizer on a tiny seed of stoicism, the existence of which he may have detected, but which in any event was not to sprout until her old age. It was not very long after Ninon's experience with Valliquierville that she came to be referred to as Mademoiselle de Lanclos instead of Ninon — presumably in recognition of her growing dignity and the respect which an increasing number of people were paying her. Valliquierville was unquestionably a factor in this graduation from the period when emphasis was on satisfying her physical appetites to the period when emphasis was on acquiring stature, on being accepted on her own terms without in any way lowering the flag on her principles of independence, opposition to bigotry, and loyalty to friends.

*

The romantic high point of Ninon's life was her summer so-
journs with Villarceaux at Valliquierville's country château.
The novelists and dramatists not improbably have pictured the
lovers strolling hand in hand after supper in the ebbing Normandy twilight, Villarceaux stuffing his pockets with shiny
chestnuts gathered for Ninon on the bridle paths. Fall has
come and the leaves drift into Ninon's bedroom during the
night through the unshuttered windows (glass panes were still
a rarity). They are reluctant to go, wanting to prolong the
spell. Particularly Villarceaux is pictured as fearing to return to
Paris, afraid that the notoriously inconstant Ninon will stray.
But Ninon, deeply happy, feels no such urge. Valliquierville
suggests they wait for Indian summer. He will miss the exhilaration of Ninon's presence; he had permitted himself the indulgence of luxuriating in her radiant femininity, in inhaling the
fragrant emanation of her body as, tête-à-tête, they had pored
over dusty tomes which Valliquierville had not taken down for
years. Valliquierville never so much as tries to take any liberties
with her, alone though they are for hours on end. Villarceaux
is his friend, he is Villarceaux's host; it would not have fitted
into his code. Besides, when Ninon is in the midst of an affair,
she is as inaccessible as a virgin.

The day of departure arrives. Dry-eyed, always in command
of himself, the steel-gray old rebel, depicted as looking older
than his years, stands stiffly at his château entrance, bidding the
lovers farewell. Ninon kisses the worn cheek fondly, begs him
to write her so she can continue under his intellectual guidance.
Then they are off. A little piece of Valliquierville accompanies
the young lovers in the receding coach, already absorbed in
themselves, unmindful of his grieving.

Perhaps in the mysticism of his Cabbala Valliquierville derived some comfort.

> For Summer and his pleasures wait on thee,
> And, thou away, the very birds are mute:
> Or if they sing, 'tis with so dull a cheer,
> That leaves look pale, dreading the Winter's near.

In Paris Ninon had no intention of returning to the Left Bank parish of Saint-Sulpice where the spies of the fanatical Jean Jacques Olier eavesdropped beneath one's windows. Besides, Villarceaux wanted her near him. He therefore installed her on the rue de Richelieu on the Right Bank, and, to be in a position to watch her every moment, he bought his friend Boisrobert's house, opposite where Ninon lived. A condition of the sale was that Boisrobert be permitted to live on in the house, a provision which must have pleased Ninon greatly, as she was very fond of the good-hearted abbé and his impromptu wit.

One night Villarceaux noticed that the lights in Ninon's bedroom were ablaze, though the hour was late. Worried that she might be sick, the marquis sent a lackey to inquire. He brought back the answer that Ninon was in the best of health. Right away Villarceaux suspected that Ninon was up late writing to a lover. In a rage he decided to confront her. Hastily getting dressed, he grabbed a silver ewer on the hall stand instead of his hat and clapped it onto his head so hard that it took both Ninon and a valet to pry it off. He then demanded to know what Ninon was doing up so late. Ninon let him understand that it was none of his business, resenting the intrusion on her privacy. In a tantrum the furious Villarceaux rushed back to his house where he fell seriously ill, with a high fever. Poor

Boisrobert was in despair. When Ninon learned from him of Villarceaux's fever, she cut off her beautiful chestnut locks and sent them to the delirious marquis, as evidence she was not planning to deceive him. Villarceaux's temperature returned to normal forthwith. Relieved, Ninon came to visit him. He must have recovered his strength fast. When he saw her, looking fresh and delightful as a flower, even though she was minus much of her hair, he pulled her into bed where, according to Tallemant, they remained eight entire days.

There is no record that Ninon caught his ailment — a tribute to Ninon's resistance to bacteria, if not to Villarceaux. But when she arose her residual hair was a mess. She is said to have summoned the famous hairdresser Champagne, one of whose tricks was to lay down his scissors and comb in the middle of a haircut and refuse to go on till his fair client had given him a kiss. Queens of foreign lands had bid for him. He had been inveigled for a time to the Polish court, and thence to Stockholm where he coiffed the renowned Queen Christina. Champagne, making a virtue out of necessity, created a new hair style for Ninon which became popular and was called "coiffure à la Ninon." Perhaps this was the origin of the bob. To this day, Harrap's Dictionary lists *cheveux à la Ninon* as meaning "bobbed hair."

So as not to be without Ninon for a moment, even when she only lived across the road, Villarceaux had her painted — resplendently nude. It is said that Madame de Villarceaux had knowledge of this portrait, as presumably did others, for the abbé Boisrobert seemed to love to show it, not wanting, in his generosity, to keep such wealth just to himself and Villarceaux. This knowledge is not likely to have lessened Madame de Villarceaux's chagrin. Naturally she hated Ninon. One day the abbé decided to pay a call on the marchioness at the château of Villarceaux where she was supervising the education of her children. The tutor, in wishing to show to advantage the learning of one of the children, picked an unfortunate subject.

"Quis fuit primus monarcha?" he asked, referring to Genesis 10: 8–9.*
"Nembrot," replied the child.
"Quem virum habuit Semiramis?" asked the tutor, referring to the legendary Queen of Assyria.†
"Ninum," the child said.

Madame de Villarceaux, evidently no student of ancient history and allergic to anything sounding like Ninon, was hotly indignant. "Really," she expostulated, "you do well to teach my children such filthy rubbish. You show me contempt in pronouncing this name in front of me." Ninon, who heard it from Boisrobert, may have related the story to Molière, for it appears somewhat altered in his *La Comtesse d'Escarbagnas,* scene 19.

The coiffure à la Ninon was not the only fruit of Ninon's neighborly eight-day visit to Villarceaux when he lay sick just across the street. Nine months later, probably in the summer of 1653, and perhaps at Valliquierville's, Ninon gave birth to a son. He was a welcome baby to both parents. Following the practice of the times, Ninon entrusted the baby to a nurse for a time but later took him back to rear according to the principles of Montaigne. There is no doubt that she took her motherhood seriously. The National Archives conserves a document of

* Who was the first king?
† Who was Semiramis married to?

July 10, 1655, in which she settled on Louis-François de Mornay 6000 livres ($12,000 to $30,000), payable on her death. Throughout her life, correspondence shows a continuing solicitude — letters sending him money, letters requesting the influential Bonrepaus to further her son's naval career, etc. Valliquierville, who must have been more than a little bit in love with Ninon, showed in tangible form his interest in her boy. In 1656, after Ninon had broken with Villarceaux and was perhaps short of money, Valliquierville transferred the income on a debt from the boy's father to the boy himself. The notarial contract had a characteristic provision. If Louis-François predeceased his mother, one-half the income of 240 livres ($480 to $1200) was to go to Valliquierville's heirs, the other half to "the said demoiselle Anne de Lanclos provided she not be a nun, or a novice . . ." Valliquierville had perhaps noticed the austere streak in Ninon and feared that like so many other ladies who in their old age had qualms of conscience about the gay days of their youth, Ninon might take the veil. If so, his money was not going to the Church. He need not have feared — Ninon never regretted the variety of her love life. She used to say that whereas some people in their old age regret what they did in their youth, she wanted to live her life so that in her old age she would not have reason to regret what she had missed.

As for Villarceaux, he was enraptured by the birth of his natural son. Its advent seems to have heightened his passion for Ninon. Years later he legitimized Louis-François, following the example of his king and master Louis XIV, who legitimized the children of his maîtresses en titre, his acknowledged mistresses, not of course those of the wenches. Why Villarceaux waited some forty years to legitimize Louis-François is unclear. Ninon, according to Tallemant, had two children by Villarceaux. The other child must have died young, however, as nothing is known of it.

In 1654, the faithful Valliquierville was probably away on family business in Normandy where his ancestral manor was; in any event he could not receive Ninon and Villarceaux a third * summer. Fortunately, Madame de Villarceaux and her children were not at the family château, so Villarceaux seized with alacrity the opportunity to take Ninon to his own seat of which he was justifiably proud. Today, owned and sometimes occupied by the family of the marquis de Villefranche, it is an estate of some 1900 wooded acres and was probably at least that big in Villarceaux's time. Situated between the Seine and its tributary, the Epte, it is a region of murmuring rivulets, canals, and ponds. Everywhere is the sound of living water — rushing and gurgling. Villarceaux lived in a large fifteenth-century castle dominated by two towers at each end. One was called the Tower of the Condemned, where the feudal lord used to shut up his prisoners. Angry waters still swirl beneath its foundations with an ominous roar. This scared Ninon, and she preferred to live in the turreted tower at the other end, the image of which is mirrored in a small lake. The tower is still called Ninon's Tower. Here Villarceaux had been accustomed to paint, and here the lovers made their nest.

At the top of the staircase is a landing, paneled in gray wood, in which hangs a famous picture of a naked woman emerging from her bath. The plate below the picture reads: FRANÇOISE

---

* Ninon seems to have spent the first two summers (of her three-year liaison with Villarceaux) at Valliquierville's château, the third summer at the château of Villarceaux.

D'AUBIGNE, MARQUISE DE MAINTENON 1635–1719 [at the time of the painting she was Madame Scarron]. PORTRAIT EXECUTED BY THE EFFORTS OF LOUIS DE MORNAY, MARQUIS DE VILLARCEAUX. Whether Villarceaux painted Scarron's wife from first-hand knowledge or imagination provoked much controversy.

Today there is a second castle on the estate. It was built about 100 years after Ninon was there, around 1755; it is there that the revealing portrait of the dashing, handsome Villarceaux hangs. The later château was built on an eminence; the old château, of which only parts remain, hugged the shores of the lake into which little streams emptied, filling the quiet nights with their silver tinkling. To Ninon, her erotic sensitivities aroused, it sounded like the male water of heaven, according to the novelists.

The park is enclosed by a grilled fence surmounted by spikes. The grounds with their old trees, multicolored flowers, manicured lawns, carved stone urns, stone benches, statuary, birds of brilliant plumage make Villarceaux one of the show places of France. Particularly famous are the very high, carefully tailored hedges considered to be the finest in the Ile-de-France. When Villarceaux was chasing the stag, Ninon occupied herself with reading, walking, picking the purple, pink, and yellow dahlias, the giant orange marigolds, or merely watching the red and yellow ducks in the pond. Villarceaux, knowing that Ninon did not have Valliquierville to talk to, did not hunt every day but would take her for hikes — in the forest or circling the lake. Still to be seen are the Fountain of Youth and the Pool of Ninon. In the former she would wash her face, whence arose the legendary reason for Ninon's famed complexion, fine beyond the usual span. In the seclusion of the glade where the Pool of Ninon is situated, tradition has it that Ninon would strip off her clothes and splash around nude like some forest nymph.

Sometimes they would go visiting nearby estates, whose squires were under Villarceaux's dominion. Villarceaux loved to show off his Ninon to their envious eyes. They would not have dared to make advances to her. He was their lord, and here he felt secure. But Ninon, without Valliquierville to occupy her active mind, was growing restive. Magnificent lover though Villarceaux was, Ninon needed more than just physical satisfaction. Villarceaux sensed this and resented it. The Fronde had been over since 1653, and Paris was recovering its old gaiety. By the early summer of 1655, Ninon's love was waning fast. Villarceaux fought its decline with petulance, which of course only cooled Ninon the more. Boredom was setting in. Then came a missive from Paris — a poem from Saint-Evremond, who addresses Phyllis — the usual generic name in pastoral poetry to denote a sweetheart or a rustic maiden. Ninon in the countryside qualified as either.

To Mademoiselle de Lanclos
Elegy.

Dear Phyllis, what has become of you?
This enchanter who has kept you
For three years, does he retain you
By a new spell in some old castle?
If so, I seek adventure
As the Knight of the Sorrowful Countenance . . .

The Knight of the Sorrowful Countenance, as Saint-Evremond often signed himself, goes on to say, however, that Ninon is quite capable of delivering herself from the enchanter's (Villarceaux's) magic. He recalls that she has given evidence before of her ability to extricate herself from even greater charmers such as Coligny and Enghien. (Saint-Evremond is being particularly gallant when he includes the anything but enslaved Coligny in the list of those abandoned by Ninon.) Variety, says he, is the spice of love. Saint-Evremond was talking to the right person — he knew his pupil. Then, in what is perhaps a reference to the saying about town that Ninon was getting old (as she had been faithful for three whole years), Saint-Evremond continues:

> You will regain your pristine looks
> In living as you used to:
> And the return to your frivolities
> Will bring out your beauty.
> You must burn with an active flame,*
> Lively, brilliant and always fleeting,
> Be inconstant as long as one can,
> For a time comes when one wants to be and cannot.

In 1655, Ninon might not have seen or heard from Saint-Evremond for five years or more. Astutely he had backed the victorious royal party in the Fronde, had been made a brigadier general, and been awarded a pension of 3000 livres ($6000 to $15,000). His star was clearly in the ascendant. He was highly respected as a soldier, writer,† and wit; he was the classic hon-

---

* One of the master stylists of the English language, the nineteenth-century Walter Pater, advised his reader "to burn with a hard gem-like flame." Is he echoing Saint-Evremond's lines?

> Il faut briller d'une flamme légère,
> Vive, brilliant, et toujours passagère.

† In 1654 Saint-Evremond had produced one of his better known pieces — *The Conversation of the maréchal Mocquincourt with Father Canaye*. The Sorbonne professor and literary historian, Antoine Adam, notes that "it heralds 100 years in advance, the Voltaire of *Candide*. It would not be unworthy of him."

nête homme. His poetic plea to Ninon to stop this nonsense of fidelity to one man and of isolating herself from the hub that was Paris, reflects the charm and self-assurance of a man who was successful and esteemed. Ninon did not need much persuading. Much to Villarceaux's vexation, she curtailed the usual summer-long stay in the country and returned to the rue de Richelieu in Paris. It is not hard to imagine the welcome she got from her old friends — Saint-Evremond, the vigorous Miossens, the witty d'Elbène, the entertaining abbé Boisrobert, the ever-admiring Scarron, trying to repair his position at Court which had been prejudiced by his thunderous Mazarinades* during the Fronde. Incredibly the cripple had taken a wife in 1652 — a beautiful, penniless, chaste ex-Huguenot, called Françoise d'Aubigné, who, poles apart from Ninon, was to illustrate that opposites sometimes do attract. There was, of course, much teasing to the effect that Ninon had not been true to her Epicureanism in her seemingly complete surrender to the pleasures of the flesh. Balance, moderation, the golden mean, they pontifically reminded her. Ninon took it all in good part. Besides, they could hardly know to what an extent Valliquierville in the first two summers had filled the intellectual void.

Her friends may have made their little jokes to Ninon's face, but when she was not there to defend herself, they were loyal. At the time of Ninon's return to Paris, the current mistress of one of her former lovers, the chevalier de Méré, was Madame de La Bazinière. But when she began to make malicious remarks about Ninon, Méré, like the honnête homme he was, put on his clothes and repaired to the rue de Richelieu, at considerable personal sacrifice, for there is no evidence to suggest

* Anti-Mazarin poems.

that Ninon welcomed him again to her bed, though she did welcome him as an old friend.

Miossens, fiery as ever, was a frequent and hopeful caller. His visits sharpened Villarceaux's jealousy acutely. But Ninon refused to make any exception to her rule that former lovers are never returned to grace. Similarly, Villarceaux clamored for reinstatement but in vain. Villarceaux took it hard. After all, he was considered a catch and his pride was hurt. He did not act like a good sport. He went around saying he had left Ninon, which bothered the self-confident Ninon not in the slightest. Villarceaux can hardly be considered an honnête homme — he consistently acted like a cad so far as his ex-mistresses were concerned. He was not only the kiss-and-tell type, he was malicious — showing all over town letters to him from his former mistresses. Later he added venality to ungallantry. He offered to sell his young niece to Louis XIV, who had cast an appreciative look in her direction. "Villarceaux," said the king, then thirty-three, "we are too old, you and I, to attack young ladies of fifteen."

But such was Ninon's magical skill, that even the vindictive Villarceaux forgave her and became her friend. She was going to need all her friends, for with more and more of the Court flocking to her house on the rue de Richelieu, Ninon was imperiling her position. These courtiers were mainly wealthy libertins, men of power, and, whereas the Society of the Holy Sacrament knew it was hopeless to take aim at them, its members revived their hopes that they might yet bring down the much more vulnerable woman who attracted them. They redoubled their spying and prying, they whispered to the bigots and harpies at Court that the time to strike again was at hand.

# ᨑᨑ Chapter 8 ᨑᨑ

## A Princess Came Riding

THE INDEFATIGABLE Society of the Holy Sacrament had never given up hope of ensnaring Ninon who to them was a dangerous — but better still — a vulnerable symbol of impiety and intolerable freethinking. Lacking the protection of a powerful father or husband, Ninon was highly vulnerable. As professor René Pintard says, "Freethinking was a luxury for gentlemen." He quotes the wry maxim that "before attacking God, it is prudent to be assured of protectors against men." Of course Ninon never attacked God, though she made no attempt to hide the fact that she had no use for organized religion. Opposition to religion was dangerous because it was against the established order. It was all right for the Great Condé to utter blasphemy and indulge in sacrilege like trying to burn a piece of the True Cross. The Society of the Holy Sacrament would not have risked attacking the mighty for a major crime like blasphemy or sacrilege. But because a defenseless woman ate meat during Lent and resolutely insisted on the right to believe or not to believe and conduct her private life as she saw fit, the society determined to run her into the ground. Its zeal might win it favor with the Establishment. This was a time when denouncers of offenses against religion received one-third of the fines.

Besides, it was no longer chic to be libertine. The Erudite Libertins of the 1630s, like Gassendi, had had their day. The elegant Libertins of the 1640s, the time of the relaxed Good Regency, had run for cover. The triumph of the royal party in the Fronde had ushered in the period of absolutism. It was expedient to conform religiously, no matter what one thought in the recesses of the mind. The hour of libertinism had passed, and with the 1650s the Age of Hypocrisy, the Age of Tartuffe,* as Professor Pintard puts it, supervened. It was a favorable climate for the self-righteous Society of the Holy Sacrament, which had constituted itself the guardian of public morality and religious observance. In 1656, the very year of its renewed attack on Ninon, the society won the infamy of history by instigating the "solution" of the beggar problem by coming up with the idea of the workhouse. Saint Vincent de Paul, when sounded as to whether he would assume the direction of the rat-infested workhouses euphemistically called "general hospitals," brusquely declined, not subscribing to the principle of coercion. By 1660, the society had become such a menace that it was officially banned, though *sub rosa* it carried on its dreaded persecutions for years. Such were the bloodhounds on the track of the hapless Ninon.

This time they did not waste effort on making complaints to officials like the bailiff of Saint-Germain-des-Prés, whom Ninon's highly placed friends had easily bought off with a purse of gold back in 1651. They renewed their campaign to inflame the queen mother, Anne, who was beyond bribery. Always extremely religious, Anne — in her middle fifties now — was thinking more and more of her salvation, and in her rather limited way she wondered how better she could serve her own

---

* Tartuffe is the archetype of the hypocrite in Molière's play of the same name.

interests vis-à-vis the Lord than to suppress religious nonconformity.

The Society of the Holy Sacrament found a ready ally in the
maréchal de Grammont's wife, who was close to the queen.
Tallemant described Madame de Grammont as a "malicious
prude." Her husband used to say that she could spot the devil
thirty points and still beat him. With the duchesse de Vendôme
and the marquise de Senecé, she formed a cabal at Court, constantly needling the queen to put Ninon away. They were
bigots, all three, who could not abide that Ninon was living
with impunity like an honnête homme, gathering her rosebuds
wherever she pleased, just as did the gentlemen of the Court.
They affected profound devoutness, certain that this would appeal to Anne. "A sanctimonious person," said that trenchant
observer of character La Bruyère (another of Ninon's devotees), "is one who under an atheist king would be an atheist."
Knowing that it might be hard to pinion Ninon on the charge
of sexual license, since many of the Court ladies would then
have had to be shut up in convents too, they concentrated on
Ninon's impiety, picturing her as a perverter of the religious
conscience of youth. They knew very well that the youths did
not need Ninon to lead them religiously astray, but since the
youths were mostly members of great families, it was useless to
attack them. But the fair Ninon was fair game.

And so it was that one fell morning Madame de Vendôme
and Madame de Senecé set out, armed with the much feared
lettre de cachet from Queen Anne, to call upon Ninon. The
queen could have merely sent an officer, but these ladies did not
want to forgo the pleasure of personally arresting Ninon. Long
had they labored to destroy independence of thought and unconventional living. As part of the entourage forever prodding

Anne to acts of reactionary repression, they had proposed stiffening the laws against blasphemy by sending offenders to do perpetual service in the galleys and even went so far as to suggest the whipping of officers not zealous enough in the tracking down of nonconformists. Even for those days it was too much, and the religious party never had the courage to publish these exercises in unbridled persecution. But getting Ninon confined in the Convent of the Madelonnettes, an institution for the correction of wayward women, would be a triumph that would compensate mightily for previous disappointments. They knew the humiliation that Ninon would suffer in being punished like a common prostitute, in being flogged, a discipline not unknown at the Madelonnettes.

The ladies' coach stopped at Ninon's door. Dressed in somber, dark clothes, and doubtless with exquisite refinement, they handed Ninon the fateful lettre de cachet. Ninon made no remonstrance, knowing it would be futile. The duchesse de Vendôme and the marquise de Senecé then begged Ninon to accompany them. On the way over to the convent, which was not far, Madame de Senecé and the duchesse de Vendôme who, according to Tallemant was a "thorough idiot," made conversation. Ninon said not a word during the drive, struggling to keep a stiff upper lip. It was their hour of triumph; she would not contest it. According to the tradition, she held her head high.

A ditty of the day went:

> To the Madelonnettes!
> No meat, no wine, no beds;
> Only blows on your posterior
> By the gracious mother superior.

The mother superior had heard of Ninon — not just as the toast of Paris but as a person of wit and integrity. She was not accustomed to having a lady of quality under her roof, for the Madelonnettes catered to a low-class clientele of women of the streets. Before long she found herself utterly taken by Ninon's grace and dignity. Instead of corporal punishment she accorded her specially good treatment, as did the rest of the nuns, who received her as a great lady. So kind were they that Ninon, not losing her habit of playful raillery even in confinement, wrote her homosexual friend, the abbé Boisrobert, "I think, following your lead, I shall commence to love my [own] sex."

Ninon's friends were outraged that the religious party had prevailed with the queen mother, that their "adorable" Ninon had fallen into the clutches of the Society of the Holy Sacrament and the prudish bigots, that without formal charge she had been summarily deprived of her liberty and thrown into a prison for vulgar wenches and prostitutes. Liberty, ever precarious, was a fragile thing in seventeenth-century France. No trial — a weak queen easily persuaded, and Ninon found herself a prisoner. Not long after in England, the right of habeas corpus, which had existed for hundreds of years, though perhaps more honored in the breach than otherwise, was given teeth in the Habeas Corpus Act of 1679. The cream of France's aristocracy decided to introduce a Gallic kind of *ad hoc* habeas corpus in Ninon's case. "Thou shalt have the body" suddenly became like an Eleventh Commandment to Ninon's supporters — particularly when the body in question was surpassingly fair, not meant, parbleu, to be roughened by coarse convent clothes, to be disfigured by lashes, or to wither in a sunless cell.

Rumors flew, according to Tallemant, that "all the gallants of the Court wanted to lay siege to the House of the Madelonnettes; the Watch was sent to patrol around it all night." Richly dressed cavaliers were to be seen surveying the convent, taking the height of its walls, preparatory to attacking. The mother superior, scared out of her wits, sent word to Cardinal Mazarin that she could not guarantee the impregnability of the Madelonnettes. The astute cardinal, never popular, had not forgotten the Fronde when he had had to flee France. At that very moment he had his hands full fighting France's perennial enemy, the Spaniards. To add to his worries, the Great Condé —in exile—was plotting his downfall. Now he was confronted with a loss of face because Queen Anne had let herself be misled. Mazarin knew how popular Ninon was. He could not have relished the prospect of new blasts, new slashing Mazarinades from an anonymous author with a style suspiciously like that of Ninon's great and loyal friend, Scarron. It was common knowledge that the Great Condé had shown his support of Ninon in an earlier attempt to bring her down, by conspicuously going over to her sedan chair in the Cours-la-Reine and, hat in hand, had opened the door and helped her out as all Paris watched. Everyone, of course, knew where the sympathies of the fiery Miossens, now a marshal, lay. As for Saint-Evremond, it was a forgone conclusion that he would employ his rapierlike wit to hold up to ridicule the petticoat influence on the government of the greatest power in the world. Mazarin could not release Ninon after such a short confinement — the queen might be affronted and the government look weak. So he ordered Ninon transferred, under heavy escort, to another but very different convent — of the Benedictine order on the outskirts of Paris, at Lagny. It was a pleasant place, in the midst of a great garden; it was not a prison. There she was allowed to receive visitors and live with a minimum of restraint until the furor would have abated. Thus did Mazarin, like the good politician that he was, play for time.

Ninon's friends came to Lagny in droves. The proprietor of the local inn, the Epée-Royale, could not bless Ninon enough, so rich did he become from the influx of her admirers. He had an indiscreet chambermaid, however. One of the first to come to cheer up Ninon was the abbé Boisrobert, followed by the inevitable little lackey. After the abbé had done all he could to console and encourage his "goddess," he returned to Paris. When the chambermaid took the next guest of the inn to the room Boisrobert had been occupying, she asked, "Monsieur, shall we make up but one bed for you and your lackey as for Monsieur the abbé Boisrobert?" The innkeeper was delighted to repeat the story to Ninon to make her laugh. When Boisrobert came back, Ninon could not refrain from twitting him. "At least I would draw the line at lackeys," she gibed.

"You don't understand," explained Boisrobert. "It is the livery I go for."

The months passed slowly, despite the constant stream of company. Even Villarceaux came, he who had taken the breakup of their affair in such ungentlemanly fashion. But he was Ninon's staunch friend now. Whenever he was not hunting with Louis XIV, now eighteen, he would look for game in the vicinity of Lagny, and drop in on his once great love. Doubtless he promised he would try to enlist the king's sympathy on Ninon's behalf. Villarceaux also brought the earnest regards of the ailing, impecunious Scarron and those of the handsome Madame Scarron, to whom he was now laying siege. The days dragged on. Ninon caught up on some of her back reading. Herself the victim of intolerance, she reread the tolerant Montaigne — perhaps as an antidote. Valliquierville had interested her in Stoicism, and she sent for a copy of Seneca. Perhaps she felt she could learn acceptance and resignation from the old Roman. This was the summer of her discontent.

> When, in disgrace with Fortune and men's eyes,
> I all alone beweep my outcast state,
> And trouble deaf heaven with my bootless cries,
> And look upon myself, and curse my fate,
> Wishing me like to one more rich in hope . . .

At the end of September 1656, relief came in the person of Queen Christina of Sweden who some three weeks earlier had made a triumphant, historic entry into Paris and had been staying with the French Court. Indignant at not finding Ninon at large, she determined to visit her, escorted by Ninon's sometime lover, the rampaging Miossens, now the maréchal d'Albret. Christina's riding to Ninon's rescue after Ninon's nine months' confinement in the convents was, though perhaps unexpected, not unlikely in the light of circumstances.

Christina knew a good deal about Ninon. They were kindred spirits. Like Ninon, from an early age Christina had been skeptical about organized religion. Different advisers interpreted right and wrong according as it served their interests, invoking the Deity to their purpose. She concluded that they did not serve God but used him to manipulate her. She was highly educated, speaking fluently Swedish, French, German, Italian, Spanish, Latin, Greek, and one of the Slavic tongues.

She had read deeply in philosophy and in several literatures. She was independent to the core in her thinking. Of all the erudite freethinkers of the century, she was probably the most spectacular. Succeeding her warrior father, the formidable Gustavus Adolphus, in 1644 when she was only eighteen, she surrounded herself with intellectual libertins. She wanted to make Stockholm the Athens of the north. To attract scholars she accumulated an extensive library from all over Europe. Her greatest coup was to get Descartes to come to live in Stockholm. When he died there, she tried unsuccessfully to induce the head of the rival school of philosophy, Gassendi, Ninon's spiritual godfather, to replace him.

Most of the Parisian visitors to her court knew Ninon well or friends of hers well. Christina heard about Ninon's courage in daring to live like an honnête homme. Christina too had rebelled, bridling at Lutheran austerity and intolerance. In certain ways she went much further than Ninon in invading the world of men and adopting their prerogatives. She was an avid horsewoman, thinking nothing of spending ten hours in the saddle. She swore like one of her own troopers. She loved to tell risqué stories and to watch the court ladies blush. Unlike Ninon, her manners were not those of a perfect lady, but masculine, rough, and more suited to barracks than drawing rooms. Another striking difference was her indifference, by and large, to men, although she may have had an affair later with Cardinal Azzolino in Rome. Her unfortunate physique may have partly accounted for the paucity of amours in her life. She was short, somewhat humpbacked, with traces of smallpox in her face. She was anything but chic, dressing grotesquely in semi-masculine fashion. But her eyes sparkled with intelligence, and an engaging sweetness hid beneath the assumed gruffness.

In 1654 Christina startled the chancelleries of Europe by laying down the crown. The main reason was her refusal to accept a politically desirable marriage to her cousin, Charles Gustavus, whom she did not love. But like Ninon, she was opposed to marriage in principle. In one of her *Secret Letters* she wrote, "I have an antipathy so great for marriage that if the King of the Universe wanted to lay at my feet his scepter and crown, no matter how gallant he was, nor how good-looking besides, I would refuse to marry him . . . Liberty and philosophy are two belles that I caress in turn, and which charm me. Other things titillate me more keenly than the pale pleasures of marriage." But though both Ninon and Christina would have none of marriage, their position was not identical. Ninon's aversion was essentially a moral one. Why promise fidelity and then break a vow? Christina's was, it would seem, physical. But where they joined forces was in their passionate adherence to liberty which the tyranny of seventeenth-century marriages would shackle.

The world was stunned by the abdication, but few denied Christina's courage and many applauded her sovereign contempt for things sovereign. The abbé Le Camus, almoner to Louis XIV, was moved to write a sonnet:

> . . . If Gustavus brought princes under his laws,
> Christina made kings of her own subjects;
> If he conquered states, his daughter gave them back . . .

No sooner had Europe begun to recover from the shock of the abdication than Christina delivered another. Between the

hands of the pope she converted to Catholicism. The Catholic
world rang with acclaim. Christina was a prize catch. But
probably never was there a less fervent, more detached convert.
It was not that she loved Catholocism more, but Lutheranism
less. At church during the sermon, Christina would read Virgil
or Petronius,* or play with two spaniels. She denied the existence of heaven and hell and did not believe in the Incarnation,
the resurrection of the dead, or the immortality of the soul. She
held that one must love God, but not fear him, that "what is
called religion today is nothing but the pure illusion of men,
who love to deceive themselves," that it is absurd to impose on
reason beliefs which paralyze it. It will be noticed that her beliefs almost coincided with Ninon's.

Her conversion did not change her one whit. At Dijon she
asked the scholar Monsot his religion. "The Catholic religion,"
he replied, adding gallantly that if he had been born in another
religion he would have changed it to follow the example of
such a glorious princess. "Do you know what cult I practice?"
she asked. "Everybody knows your majesty has preferred the
Catholic religion to the superstition of her country." "You are
mistaken: my religion is the religion of the philosophers, which
I prefer to all others . . ."

Christina had written Mazarin asking him to forgo a ceremonious welcome upon entering Paris. He called out the mili-
tia 15,000 strong. Two hundred thousand citizens went outside
the city gates to greet her. Anne of Austria and her son, Louis
XIV, received Christina in great style. The Court ladies, not

---

* Petronius was also a great favorite of Saint-Evremond's, who considered him the
ideal honnête homme — pleasure-loving but refined, elegant and witty, emancipated.

noted for their chastity, found Christina immodest. They were shocked by her short skirts and her habit of lounging with her feet lifted higher than her head and "of having herself served by men at the most intimate moments." Reports Lomenie de Brienne:

> To play the bonne vivante, she said one time to our good queen [Anne of Austria] that she would have married if she had found pleasure in that; she let loose the coarse word: "To f . . . Madame." The queen mother blushed to her eyelids, and Créquy . . . said to her quickly: "Your Majesty has then tried it?" "That," said she, "is another thing; all I can say is that if I had a craving for it, I would give myself to it with a full heart" . . .

Madame de Motteville, however, says in her *Memoirs:*

> I found she had beautiful, lively eyes, that she had sweetness in her face . . . mixed with pride. At last I perceived with astonishment that she pleased me . . . Everybody admired the vivacity of her mind . . . she taught Frenchmen things they didn't know about their own country.

After having spent about ten days attending fêtes at the French Court, Christina resolved that before setting out for Italy she must call on the fabulous Ninon of whom she had heard so much from the French libertins at her court in Stockholm, and whose name she heard mentioned again and again in France. Miossens volunteered to take the queen to Ninon. During the ride he impressed Christina not with his high praise for Ninon — she had heard all that before — but with his passionate self-involvement in her plight, for Miossens, like many another former lover, had been eased out of her boudoir and into her drawing room.

And so the confrontation took place. Enter Christina like a bombshell, bursting in, with hearty gusto and animal energy, upon the stunned Ninon. The queen wore the red jacket of a man and the dun-colored skirt of a woman. A black, plumed woman's hat sat upon a masculine wig. She had on men's boots. The tradition is that Ninon was the picture of regal dignity as, with exquisite grace, born of much practice in dancing, she executed a low reverence before the queen. There exists but a meager record of what followed. They evidently got along extremely well. One of Ninon's recorded witticisms was hatched at this meeting. Christina asked Ninon her opinion of the précieuses, those aristocratic, affected ladies who made a fetish of platonic love and did violence to the noble tongue of Montaigne, Malherbe, and Corneille with their elaborate verbal circumlocutions. The queen's ebullience and warmth seem to have ignited the spark in Ninon again, all but quenched by her confinement. "The précieuses," she quipped, "are the Jansenists of love." The Jansenists were the great doctrinal opponents of the Jesuits, believing in predestination and divine grace, in contradistinction to the Jesuits' belief in free will. In love the Jansenists were fiercely austere — French Puritans. It is the Jansenist position on love, not theology, to which Ninon of course alludes. The queen, who could not abide the strait-laced précieuses, was so taken with the bon mot that she spread it to polite society across half of Europe.

The meeting is said to have gone on for hours. With their community of friends and philosophy, they did not lack for conversation. Tallemant relates that a couple of years before, Ninon had met a great big hulk of a man, Des Mousseaux, at the theater. Next morning Des Mousseaux, while Ninon was still in bed, brushed aside her servants and entered her bedroom. "Who are you," Ninon asked, "who has the effrontery to come to see me without someone to introduce you?" "I have no name," he replied saucily. "And where do you come from?" Ninon asked. "Picardy." Ninon disliked Picardians. "And where were you brought up?" "In Candia."* That was worse. "Jesus! what a man! But aren't you perhaps a swindler?" "Pierrot," Ninon said to her valet de chambre, "watch out that he doesn't steal from me." Then turning to Des Mousseaux Ninon said, "I don't know you; I must have a surety." Des Mousseaux started naming people Ninon knew, beginning with her loyal friend, Boisrobert. Playing difficult, Ninon said he wouldn't do. Then Des Mousseaux offered Coligny's friend, the playboy Roquelaure, a perennial hell-raiser. Feigning horror, Ninon rejected him out of hand. Finally he advanced Rambouillet, the great balladeer, Ninon's lover of five years previous. It appeared that Des Mousseaux wanted to enter her service. He had formerly been captain of Christina's guards. Whether that clinched the job or not is not told. Perhaps Christina asked her.

Report had it that Christina would jump out of bed at 2:00 A.M. in Stockholm, don a short, black velour skirt, stick a hat on her head, and rush off to direct fire-fighting. If Ninon twitted her about it, Christina, who knew French society as well as her own, could easily have come back with the story of how Ninon had dressed herself up like a cavalier during the Fronde and run after that handsome young officer Villars, all the long way to Lyons.

Whatever they talked about, it is recorded that Christina,

* Crete.

who was on her way to Italy, suggested she had sufficient influence with Mazarin to secure Ninon's release if it was understood she would accompany Christina to Italy. She painted an enticing picture of Italy. Christina's strong affection for the comtesse de Sparre was common gossip, and Ninon may have been uncertain whether Christina's invitation was a Lesbian advance, or just an offer of a joint adventure in comradeship or both. She replied that she could not express how honored she was at the invitation, that she feared Christina would tire of her after a space, that much as she would love to see Italy, she could never accept exile from her beloved Paris as a condition of her release. Christina evidently understood, for they parted on the best of terms. Indeed Madame de Motteville comments, perhaps a little jealously, "It was to her [Ninon] alone, of all the ladies she [Christina] saw in France, to whom she gave certain marks of esteem."

When Christina regained the courtyard of the convent, she called for pen and paper and wrote a short note to Cardinal Mazarin stating "nothing was lacking to the king but the conversation of this girl [Ninon] to render him perfect. She has in truth much wit, and all those who pride themselves on their wit repair to her to exercise theirs, as under an avowed mistress of high gallantry." Christina then departed for Italy, accompanied, says Madame de Motteville archly, by but a paltry number of attendants (actually five).

The cardinal, probably looking for an excuse to terminate Ninon's unpopular confinement, immediately sent orders for her release, much to the chagrin of the Court prudes and the Society of the Holy Sacrament.

At long last the spiritual ancestor of George Sand, the crusad-

ing Pankhursts, and latter-day feminists had won her protracted struggle to be treated with the respect accorded a grande
dame but on her own terms — the right to live like an honnête
homme.

## Chapter 9

### Schoolmistress of Gallantry

A GREAT BALL was in progress. Genuinely glad to have one of its chief ornaments restored, Parisian society was dancing attendance upon the sweetheart of the Marais. Cavalier after cavalier invited Mademoiselle de Lanclos to join him in the ceremonious and graceful dances of the day. They bowed before her as before a queen — at last come into her own. Vindicated, it is said she had never looked so radiant. Finally, after having tired herself dancing sarabands and courantes, she sat down next to her friend Henriette de Coligny, sister of her first love, Gaspard. A cool drink, the exhausting excitement, the soft lulling music — she dozed. Henriette, a beauty herself, placed Ninon's head on her (Henriette's) naked shoulder. They constituted, tradition says, a striking tableau — a sleeping beauty and a protecting beauty, both in full bloom. Henriette, or Madame de La Suze, as she is known in history, was a respected poet, specializing in love songs and erotic verse. While Ninon slept, she composed:

> Enjoy, enjoy this peace profound
> Which a happy slumber provides,
> And let it close the most beautiful eyes in the world,
> Since tomorrow upon their awakening
> The sun's rays will pale before them.

Henriette was another victim of a marriage forced upon her by parents. A Protestant, she was in love with a Catholic. Her parents married her, against her will, to the Protestant comte de La Suze, an odious drunkard deep in debt. Eventually Henriette became desperate, and, striking at the foundations of her marriage, she converted to Catholicism, giving rise to Queen Christina of Sweden's remark that "the countess changed her religion so as not to see her husband either in this world or the next." Christina, no doubt with tongue in cheek, was, of course, echoing the prevailing Church position that in the afterworld, Catholics and Protestants would go to separate (but unequal) places. Evidently problems of segregation are neither peculiar to the twentieth century nor to the planet Earth.

Eventually Henriette got an annulment on the grounds of her husband's alleged impotence, notwithstanding the fact that he inconveniently fathered several children in a subsequent marriage. Like Ninon, she flitted from lover to lover. Unlike Ninon, Henriette declined early and sadly. She became fat and a bit unhinged. As did most seventeenth-century ladies who had strayed from virtue, in her advancing years she practiced a contrition which she evidently believed would help in her salvation. But it took a curious twist. She fell passionately in love with Christ, the man. She imagined him, says Tallemant, "as a tall youth, dark and very handsome." She of course discussed the matter with Ninon who playfully hazarded the thought that Christ was fair. "Not at all, my dear," she said earnestly. "You are wrong. I know for a fact that he was dark." She died at fifty-five before being locked up.

*

In 1657 Ninon rented a house at 36 rue des Tournelles, in the Marais. She loved the house and was to live in it the rest of her life — forty-eight years. It still exists, sadly déclassée in a shabby district of down-at-the-heel little tradespeople. Even in Ninon's time the house was never magnificent, for Ninon was not wealthy, but it nonetheless merited the description of "hôtel" or "mansion." Five stories high, with handsome wrought-iron grillwork on the lower part of the windows, it had its own porte-cochère. It was solidly respectable, in an excellent neighborhood, a few minutes' stroll via the rue du Pas de la Mule to the fashionable Place Royale, then Paris's most beautiful square.

The late 1650s were one of the happier times in Ninon's life. A little recognition is good for the soul, and Ninon basked in the afterglow of her victory over the bigots who had not succeeded, despite the confinement at the Madelonnettes and Lagny, in humiliating her. Her unconditional release gave her the public respect for which she had been fighting. This was probably the period when she became friendly with Molière, who admired her taste and courage. These were the years when she derived great satisfaction out of helping and advising Françoise Scarron and comforting and stimulating Françoise's invalid husband. Joyfully she resumed her love life, all the sweeter because of her enforced abstinence in the convents. Suitors besieged her just as much as ever, strenuously strove to impose on her a constancy which was just not part of her makeup. The incident of La Châtre occurred about this time, giving birth to one of her sayings quoted to this day, although many are unaware of its origin.

The marquis de La Châtre had won Ninon's favor but alas,

right in his hour of ecstasy and before his time was up, the
trumpet blew and off to the wars he had to go. La Châtre must
have been attractive physically, for he certainly was not too
bright. Aware of Ninon's reputation for inconstancy, which
had already assumed legendary proportions, he assailed her ears
with demands not only that she be faithful but also that she put
it in writing. To humor her importunate lover, Ninon, mis-
chievously, wrote a little note promising fidelity which the vain
fellow quickly showed to anyone he could buttonhole in the
officers' mess. Not long after, Ninon was again in the arms of a
new lover. Suddenly, reminding herself of the writing that La
Châtre had wrung from her, she exclaimed merrily, "Ah, the
fine little promissory note I gave La Châtre!" The count (he
remains anonymous), who was making love to her, wanted to
know what she meant. Ninon explained — much to the
count's amusement. But he was no more discreet than La
Châtre, telling the bon mot all over town. This annoyed
Ninon. She had not thought it necessary to tell the count to
hold his tongue and reproached him sternly. The count went
down on his knees to her, more charming and tender, we are
told, than ever, and soon they were in bed again. When the
count was about to leave, Ninon gaily bethought herself of the
proprieties and feigned renewed anger at the count's indiscreet-
ness in blabbing. Running after him to the head of the stairs,
she called down, "At least, count — remember — we haven't
made up."

There is nothing peculiarly Ninonesque in taking lightly
vows of undying love. What is peculiarly Ninonesque is the
lighthearted, unhypocritical "Ah, the fine little promissory note
I gave La Châtre!" It has become a proverb — applied to some-

thing on which it is unwise to count. Voltaire and Le Sage quote it later in their plays.

In 1658, Saint-Evremond spent some time in the Bastille for fighting a duel. He could not have been confined very long in the king's "château," for Saint-Evremond was present with Mazarin at the signing of the Treaty of the Pyrenees the following year. But whether his incarceration was just for a few months or over a year, Ninon doubtless missed him keenly, as he had probably been the most active of those who had welcomed her back when she had returned from her confinement. Another of her dear friends, the delicate Charleval, was absent too — looking after his estate in Normandy. Perhaps because of these lacks, and also her increasing prestige in the community, she opened a School of Gallantry for young aristocrats. Chavagnac records, "When a courtier had a son to be polished, he sent him to her school. The education she gave was so excellent that one marked the difference in the young men she had trained. She taught them to make love prettily, with delicacy of speech; provided her pupil was of a docile nature, in no time she made of him an honnête homme."

To begin with, Ninon enunciated her basic Epicureanism: "All good sense should lead in the direction of happiness . . ." We should not make a business of pursuing happiness, however; we should let it come unforced but be ready to seize it when it comes. "We must store up victuals, but not pleasures. One must take them day by day." Then she plays a variation on the theme — "The more things change, the more they are the same." "There is nothing," she used to say, "so varied in nature as the pleasures of love, even though they be always the same." Variety, she never tired of saying, is the spice of love. "I have always sworn to my lovers to love them eternally, but for me eternity is a quarter of an hour." "The woman who has loved but one man will never know love." A surfeit of love is fatal. "Love with passion, but only for a few minutes." Don't pine over a lost love — march on. "Nothing is so ridiculous as a woman who bemoans a lost lover." There is a correlation between intelligence and susceptibility to love, for smart people know a good thing when they see it. "I have observed that men of intelligence show less resistance in the alcove than imbeciles."

Lust may be for the stupid but not love, which requires finesse and is the finest of all the arts. "It takes [as has already been quoted] one hundred times more intelligence to make love well than to command armies." Like everything else, expertise in lovemaking requires painstaking (or rather pleasure-giving) effort. "The bed is a battlefield where the victories are won only at great cost."

Ninon wishes for her pupils that they fall into the category of those who find that love nourishes itself. "There are those privileged souls who are capable of finding in love the very reasons for loving still more." She cautioned her charges against falling for looks alone, although she herself had not always been proof against the temptation of pure, unalloyed physical appeal — as in the case of Miossens, whose technique was that of a line-crashing football player. But for the most part she had subscribed to her dictum that "Beauty without grace is a hook without bait."

It is important, said Ninon, to understand what a woman wants in a husband and in a lover. (In her time it was taken for granted they did not coexist.) "A sensible woman must never take a husband without the consent of her reason nor lovers without the advice of her heart."

Ninon taught her pupils to be gentle and patient the first night. Women are sentimental, even shy. "Women ordinarily show all their modesty on the wedding night, just as men show all their love."

Again and again through the course Ninon gave vent to one of her major complaints against current conventions. "It is laughable that they have made a law of modesty for the very women who esteem nothing in men as much as boldness."

Cultivate savoir-faire, advised Ninon, never be coarse, practice delicacy, but don't be overnice in believing protestations about a fate worse than death. "Leave to the Céladons* the sublime passages, the beautiful sentiments; let them be all hearts and flowers. I tell you as a woman, there are times when women prefer being treated a little roughly rather than with too much respect: men lose more hearts by awkwardness than virtue preserves."

Sometimes her advice has an uncharacteristic, Victorian ring: "Only by showing respect, by taking great pains, by infinite obligingness and by eternal homage can you hope to share the extreme love that your mistress has for her own beauty. Speak unceasingly of her and rarely of yourself. And rest assured — she is a hundred times more enchanted by the charms of her face than by the display of your thoughts. However, if someday she yields to your urgings, remember, in receiving her heart, that she puts in your hands her life's happiness, that she makes you the supreme arbiter of her destiny."

Saint-Pavin, one of the four innocuous poets whom Ninon

---

* Céladon was the shepherd separated from his shepherdess, mooning inconsolably, in the best-selling *L'Astrée* by Honore *d'Urfé*.

cultivated when the snarling Society of the Holy Sacrament was sniffing at her heels some eight years before, was not going to let Ninon get away with this high-flown excursion into unwonted sentimentality. To a popular air he wrote lyrics which he put into the mouth of Ninon:

> All the young bloods come to my school
> To be saved,
> I want to save Duras, Dangeau, Briole*
> And that is my sole aim.
> Evil be to him that evil thinks,
> I am repentant
> Honestly I am.

Ninon's lessons in gallantry were not all theory. There is reason to believe she went in for some lab work in her famous chambre jaune. This of course aroused the jealousy of other society ladies, who protested against Ninon's virtual monopoly of the capital's youth — to no avail. There is no record of how Ninon marked her students' efforts, but whole generations of French collegians, cramming Caesar and Horace for their baccalaureate, have lulled themselves to sleep with thoughts of being examined in Advanced Gallantry by a youthful thirty-five-year old enchanting schoolmistress (maîtresse) called Mademoiselle de Lanclos.

Ninon has not left much in the way of writing. There is little doubt that in a highly epistolary age† the extremely literate Ninon wrote many letters which have been lost. There are obvious gaps in her correspondence with Saint-Evremond as

---

* Three of Ninon's aristocratic pupils.
† Absence of the telephone was not the only reason — not every epoch produced letter writers like Madame de Sévigné, or, later, Lord Chesterfield.

shown by a number of references to letters which no longer exist. This was a pity which the eighteenth century was quick to recognize, and some enterprising writers even went so far as to try to remedy the loss by manufacturing a great many letters which they attributed to Ninon and sold for gain. There are many more spurious letters than authentic ones. Of her poetry and other writing, too, there probably remains but a fraction. Her poetess friend, Henriette de Coligny, comtesse de La Suze, influenced her not only to write verse but to adopt a personal emblem, which was the style then. Thus, in addition to the armorial bearings of her father's family, she assumed her own device — a crown traversed by a flower, bearing the motto — JUSQUES AU BOUT, which sums up rather well her concept of loyalty, whether it be to a principle or a friend. She incorporated the design into her seal, which she affixed in red wax to appropriate papers such as her will but not, alas, to all her poetry. A chronicler claims that Donneau de Visé published some of her poetry anonymously in the well-known *Mercure galant*. The little of Ninon's poetry which remains shows wit, grace, and an ability to score quickly.

The courtier Saint-Aignan was in the habit of rhapsodizing extravagantly in verse about the splendor of the formal gardens of Versailles. Just as years earlier, when a young girl, Ninon had pricked the cloud of overblown, heart-rending oratory which the histrionic Eastertide preacher was exhaling on the Lenten congregation, so in her maturity she deflated Saint-Aignan who, perhaps because he had been recently made a duke by the king, was laying on the praise of the royal gardens rather thick. Addressing Saint-Aignan as Damon (following the convention to call the man Damon, the woman Phyllis), Ninon wrote:

*Damon, laisse juger nos yeux*
*De ces jardins délicieux*
*Où l'art surpasse la nature.*
*Le froid qui règne dans tes vers*
*Fait plus de tort à la verdure*
*Que le plus affreux des hivers.*

(Damon, leave it to our eyes to judge of
Those delightful gardens
Where art surpasses nature.
The cold which reigns in your verses
Does more harm to the greenery
Than the most terrible of winters.)

Her old implacable enemy, the religious party, had never re-lented in its persecution of her. Knowing it was useless to pro-ceed against her crudely as before, her pursuers adopted indi-rect and sly means. They contrived to insinuate into Ninon's midst one of the henchmen of the Society of the Holy Sacra-ment. His name was Louis Lesclache, a scholar who had gained prominence as a popularizer of philosophy to ladies. Lesclache had reduced Aristotle's philosophy to synoptic tables. These tables were a kind of do-it-yourself course of instruction with information made readily available under a variety of headings, the whole expensively bound in fine morocco. Les-clache made a small fortune out of them. He was the rage in many ladies' drawing rooms, particularly those of the religious party. He did not look like a fanatic. Ninon, in her principal literary effort, *La Coquette vangée* (The Coquette Avenged), tells us he was not a doctor of the Sorbonne (notorious for its bigotry), that he dressed simply and neatly — his silk stockings were never wrinkled — that he wore good gloves, was not affected. "A droop of the eyelids, a smile or some other slight gesture" attracted women, including Ninon — at first.

He soon aroused her suspicions, however, by intolerantly blasting practically everything modern. One of the great persisting arguments of the century aligned the Ancients versus the Moderns. Ninon had great respect for Greek and Roman culture but was taken aback by the vehemence with which he attacked the contemporary stage — a sure giveaway — for the Church thundered against the stage, denying actors and actresses last rites and Christian burial. Ninon, say the chroniclers, felt a cold shiver go through her, for Lesclache had fooled her into allowing him to attend her salon and had noted well the independent, often irreverent, opinions of her coterie. She inquired more deeply into his background, found that on the Mardi Gras he had gone around sermonizing about the Beatitudes and the Lord's Prayer. Ninon was frightened. Under his exterior of seeming normalcy she perceived the wild ferocity of the religious persecutor. She must get rid of this spy before he got rid of her — if it was not too late. Her staunch champion, Christina of Sweden, was now far away. Her loyal friend, the Great Condé, was still in exile, for the time was early in the year 1659, and he was not pardoned till later in the year. Saint-Evremond was in the Bastille. It is perhaps hard to imagine Ninon's fear, but though Christina had secured her release from Lagny in 1656, evidently Ninon did not know in 1659 how decisive her victory over the reactionaries had been. The long years of persecution had left her permanently wary.

Retaining her sang-froid, Ninon decided to handle the situation with kid gloves. Knowing that Lesclache was going to

visit her, she arranged that she and her friends would be dis-
cussing whether love is a passion or a virtue when he arrived.
They asked his opinion. Lesclache referred to his tables.
"Love," he read, "is a very lively inclination of desire."

Ninon kept quiet but her friends pounced. "Is that all one
can say of the passions, of all the impetuous forces which agi-
tate our lives? We certainly have here a great sea confined in a
little space. Only one line for love! How you cramp the goddess!"

Lesclache, mightily discomfited, argued still. The debate
grew more heated. Ninon grabbed her lute and played a
sprightly courante, to which her company danced. When they
had finished, someone asked Lesclache if his tables included a
definition of dancing. He shook his head whereupon Ninon
pleaded, "Monsieur — you must make one for love of me."

Lesclache, unaware of the irony, answered, "When my tables
are finished, whoever reads them will be a good dancer." The
room exploded in derisive laughter. Getting the point at last,
Lesclache took his departure angrily, despite Ninon's excuses.
"I see clearly," said he, "that I cannot instruct you from now
on." But he promised to send a pupil — Félix de Juvenel. Like
his master, he specialized in criticizing others' behavior and in
exuding omniscience.

Ninon's friends were ready for him. Unknown to her, they
laid a trap. Showering him with compliments, they begged
him to favor them with a little talk. Juvenel turned to one of
his master's favorite topics — the eight Beatitudes. Enthusiastic
applause. Emboldened by his seeming success, the pious Juvenel drew one of the ladies into an alcove and planted a not so
pious kiss on her lips. The lady requited his passion with a

resounding smack of her fan and fled for security into the midst of the room. This was the signal for a general onslaught by the ladies on the sanctimonious Juvenel. One guest, turned Amazon, clipped him on the nose. "Take that, you amorous philosopher!" Another made his ears smart by hitting him with a piece of whalebone, adding, "And that, you amorous poet." A third stuck pins in him. Ninon did her best to rescue the embattled Juvenel from her friends enraged by his presumptuousness and hypocrisy, but Juvenel vowed vengeance.

His reply was to write *Le Portrait de la coquette*. Taking the form of a letter from an uncle to his nephew, it attacked Ninon's great cause, the feminist movement, excoriated free-thinking and free-loving ladies, their resistance to the tyranny of seventeenth-century marriage, their demands to be treated with respect, dignity, and equality. Ninon girded herself to reply. She must unmask this forerunner of Molière's *Tartuffe,* this self-righteous Bible-spouting philosopher, who under the cloak of piety and pedagogy maneuvered ladies into a corner and then tried to seduce them. Several years later Molière has the self-righteous Tartuffe, who has been stealing glances at the décolletage of his friend's wife say, "Cover this breast which I must not look at." A few minutes later he is doing his best to look at more than just the pectoral region.

Ninon's answer to *Le Portrait de la coquette* was *La Coquette vangée*. Paralleling Juvenel's satirical form, but much shorter, Ninon has an aunt give advice to her niece from the country who is going to Paris. She warns her to beware of wolves in philosophers' clothing. Her portraits of Lesclache and Juvenel, stripping them of their false religious zeal, were easily identifiable and seemingly devastating, for both Lesclache and Juvenel were soon personae non gratae in the salons of Paris. Ridicule, Ninon's only weapon, had effectively silenced them.

There is some doubt as to when Ninon and Molière became friendly. Some have it that Ninon's dipsomaniacal and unsuccessful wooer, Chapelle, had introduced them in the early 1650s. Certainly their friendship did not start later than 1659, the year when Ninon published *La Coquette vangée* and Molière his *Les Précieuses ridicules,* one of the earliest comedies of manners and perhaps the best. Ninon and Molière were fighting the same fight, and sooner or later their common cause would have brought them together. Their subject in 1659 was not the same — Ninon actually got the jump on Molière by about five years in attacking the false devouts, but their approach to life in general was the same and their enemy was the same — falseness, whether in language, modesty, or religion. Though Molière's target in *Les Précieuses ridicules* was less charged with explosives than Ninon's, the play nonetheless stirred up a tempest among influential ladies, nettled by the sting of Molière's barbs. They did not appreciate his attack on their prudery, actual or false. "How," asks one of the ladies in *Les Précieuses ridicules,* "can one tolerate the thought of sleeping with a naked man?" They winced at his satire of their affected speech. The religious party, which was always seeing a libertin ambush behind every bush, was already suspicious of the intrepid Molière and put him on its list. Thus the initial bond between Ninon and Molière may well have been that they had the same dislikes and a common foe. Later they undoubtedly met on more solid ground, respecting each other's literary taste, passion for naturalness and simplicity, fundamental decency.

Sainte-Beuve comments: "He [Molière] is of the continuing posterity of Rabelais, of Montaigne . . . Molière is naturally of the world of Ninon, of Madame de La Sablière before her conversion . . . The pupil of Gassendi [Molière], the friend of Bernier, of Chapelle, is tied fairly directly to the philosophy and literature of the sixteenth century."

Thus Ninon and Molière had a common past, as well as a common present. Both were spiritual heirs of the free air of the Renaissance. Both revered the liberal Montaigne. All the people Sainte-Beuve mentions as being close to Molière were also close to Ninon. Chapelle worshiped at her shrine until she had to expel him for drunkenness. Gassendi was her master through Saint-Evremond, who studied with him and relayed the world. The world traveler Bernier was one of Ninon's great boosters. Madame de La Sablière was a mutual friend of Ninon's and Molière's, collaborating later with Ninon in helping Molière write one of the funnier scenes of Le Malade imaginaire.

Molière no doubt was also drawn to Ninon because, like him, she lived dangerously. Not that they were political revolutionaries; far from it; but unlike the average Epicurean skeptic, who just wanted to be left alone to think his own thoughts and live his own innocuous life, and in whose vocabulary the word indolence crops up perhaps a little too often, Ninon and Molière were prepared to preach what they practiced. Both were persecuted: Ninon for following the code of the honnête homme and for demanding feminine equality, Molière for his war on sham in any guise. Spearheading the secular arm of oppression against Molière was, not unexpectedly, Ninon's old enemy, the Society of the Holy Sacrament, who howled for his blood, literally speaking. It would be reassuring to think that the official banning of the society in 1660 was at least in part due to its distempered baying at Molière and Ninon. It may have been. Public opinion was turning increasingly in favor of Ninon. Her reputation for integrity and dependability was growing apace as the Gourville incident two years later underlines. Molière had a powerful, though not at this time all-powerful, ally in the young king who had not yet assumed the reins of government while Mazarin lived. Ninon's joy in the suppression of the society was second only to that when she was released with honor from Lagny. It was public recognition of the validity of her stand against persecution by inquisitors, lay or clerical. But the society merely went underground, and for years continued indirectly its relentless pursuit of nonconformists.

The apparent defeat of the society may have encouraged Molière to continue Ninon's struggle for feminine emancipation. Ninon was elated though anxious as she watched him dangerously do battle against the accepted male attitude of the day — the inalienable right of the husband not just to dominate, but tyrannize. Molière would discuss his ideas for plays with Ninon, read them to her scene by scene. In her salon he found a microcosm of French aristocracy, a rich source of characters which he mined thoroughly. It will be remembered that Molière was not of noble birth, but the son of an upholsterer. Thus Ninon not only gave Molière stimulation and the benefit of her critical taste, but also an invaluable observation post on high society.

*

Some minor historians, with a weakness for exaggerating the influence of women, see the reign of Louis XIV as nothing much more than a terrain for the duel between Ninon, leading the forces of progress, liberalism, and light, and Madame de Maintenon, representing the forces of reaction, bigotry, and shadow. Out of focus as this view is, it may afford, after a substantial discount has been taken, some indication of the important if not primary role that Ninon played. Madame de Maintenon's second husband was Louis XIV, but her first had been Scarron, Ninon's brilliant, brave, tortured friend. "I preferred a cripple to a convent," Madame de Maintenon later explained.

The woman who was to preside over the opulence of Versailles was born in jail where her Huguenot father, Constant d'Aubigné, baron de Surimeau, had been put for counterfeiting. When a young girl of about thirteen, Françoise d'Aubigné had been converted to Catholicism under duress — not before first resisting courageously. It was no doubt around this time that the iron entered into her soul.

At the time of her marriage, Françoise was seventeen, Scarron forty-two. This was the year when Ninon met Villarceaux and began her three-year affair with him. Ninon and Villarceaux would spend the six warm months of the year in the countryside; they would come back to Paris when the leaves fell. It was probably in the dying months of 1652 that Ninon met Françoise, lately become Madame Scarron. Françoise had a mountain of adjustments to make. Even if Scarron had not been an impotent invalid, the disparity in their ages, backgrounds, and religious convictions would have presented towering difficulties. Scarron was the leader of a merry cosmopolitan set, a respected writer, an active protagonist on the losing side

of the Fronde; Françoise was a sober, unfledged, country demoiselle, déclassée. Scarron was religiously unobservant and
irreverent; Françoise was extremely observant and very pious.
When to all this is added an unconsummated sex life, or rather
the complete absence of it, Françoise had a sea of problems. It
is a tribute to Françoise's courage, her exceptional poise, that
she did not break under the strain. Her husband, well aware of
the situation, looked to Ninon for help.

Ninon was twelve years older than Françoise. They were the
antithesis of each other but had mutual respect. Françoise, who
definitely had a streak of prudery in her, might have been expected to disapprove acutely and even violently of Ninon's libertinism. As a very devout Catholic who during Lent ate her
herring alone while Scarron and his friends feasted on meat,
who was, even when young, just this side of bigotry, Françoise
might easily have been shocked by Ninon's outspoken criticism
of clerical hypocrisy and pretentions to omniscience. Ninon, on
the other hand, might easily have smelled a future president of
the seventeenth-century counterpart of a women's auxiliary to
the reactionary Society of the Holy Sacrament. After a short
period of reciprocal scrutiny and wariness, with Françoise displaying the more reserve of the two, they took to each other
thoroughly. Françoise, who had learned to calculate before she
could compute, undoubtedly realized that she could learn a
great deal from the accomplished Ninon about the grand
monde, that probably nobody would be more proficient in rub-
bing off her rustic traces in a pleasant fashion and in transmit-
ting to her the polished urbanity without which she could not
make her way up the ladder of high society. But that was not
all. They found a common denominator in intelligence and
intellect. Françoise was an uncommonly shrewd young

woman, and though perhaps not quite as well educated as Ninon, due to her (Françoise's) nomadic childhood, was far from unlettered. Ninon came to be fascinated by Françoise's bottomless self-discipline and aloofness, characteristics that more often than not incite dislike or fear, but which she succeeded in wearing as an adornment. "Other women," said Scarron, "make a show of their intellect; this one loves to hide it." Françoise thoroughly understood the proposition of not putting all one's wares in the shop window. She was far too cute for that. She always held something back. All this Ninon found intriguing.

There was perhaps one other point of attraction between them — physical. Françoise was very handsome. "They were the best of friends," writes the marquis de La Fare, a contemporary memorist, "even to the point that they had only one bed during three entire months." This suggests, but not necessarily denotes, Lesbianism. Voltaire seems to whitewash the relationship: "When Mademoiselle d'Aubigné, who then had no fortune, believed she could make a good thing out of marrying Scarron, Ninon became her best friend. They slept together for several months straight: it was then the style in friendship. What was less in style was that they had the same lover and didn't quarrel." Voltaire is referring to Villarceaux.

An alleged letter of Madame Scarron to Ninon in 1653, while Ninon was staying with Villarceaux in the country, gives the flavor of their relationship even if the letter is spurious.

MADEMOISELLE:

Here are verses that Monsieur Scarron has done for you, after having vainly tried to turn them against you . . . All your friends sigh for your return . . . The marquis wears an air quite as bored as that during the first few days of your departure . . . his is a heroic constancy. Come back, my amiable one, all Paris begs you. Saint-Evremond wants to send Châtillon,* Miossens, and du Raincy, in the capacity of knights errant, to abduct you from your old château. Come back, beautiful Ninon, and bring back grace and pleasure . . .

Since 1652, Villarceaux had been one of the guests at the Scarrons'. In describing Ninon's Tower in the château of Villarceaux, mention was made of a portrait done by Villarceaux of a naked young woman just emerged from her bath. It is rather amateurish and probably does not do the subject justice.

How comes it that the prim Françoise was painted nude? It ill accords with her maxim: "Nothing is cleverer than irreproachable conduct." It ill accords with her campaign at Versailles to raise necklines, or with the image we have of her court days, both from brush and pen portraits, when what the French would call her "ferocious reserve" impelled her to dress in somber-colored, high-necked dresses surmounted by a nunlike hood. Françoise was a Puritan — with one or two possible and even probable falls from grace.

Actually there is no incongruity at all between the picture's nudity and Françoise's modesty. When Ninon broke with Villarceaux around 1655, Villarceaux turned his attentions to Madame Scarron, among others. But the others soon faded as the all-conquering Villarceaux found Madame Scarron's resistance highly challenging. Some say that Ninon put in a good word for Villarceaux to Françoise, vaunting Villarceaux's exceptional vigor as a lover. This may well be; it would have been in keeping with Ninon's character. She gladly recommended ex-lovers

* Gaspard de Coligny, Ninon's first love, became duc de Châtillon on his father's death. He had been dead several years at the time of the alleged letter which was forged at a later date, when counterfeiting letters of Ninon and selling them had become profitable.

to her friend Madame de La Suze, so why not to Françoise? By 1657 or so, Françoise had shed some of her retiring manner and was mingling freely in Paris society, exciting attention wherever she went. Suitors redoubled their efforts to seduce her. Financiers vainly tried to buy her.

Françoise, however, *was* wavering under the attack of Villarceaux's charm. A healthy young female of twenty-two or twenty-three, whose marriage to Scarron had, as he put it, been one long Lent, she might well have been expected to surrender earlier. But her fierce virtue sustained her for at least a little while longer. Villarceaux was taking his reverses hard; he was not used to being put off. It will be recalled what a poor sport he proved to be when Ninon brought an end to their romance. Villarceaux was consistent in his vindictiveness. It was a trait which doubtless shortened his period of intimacy with Ninon, who was not one to put up indefinitely with petulance and unbridled jealousy. In characteristic pique, he decided to get even with Madame Scarron, and around 1657 painted her from imagination in a manner that left nothing to the imagination.

He evidently kept the embarrassing portrait not in his country château but in his town house which he shared with the abbé Boisrobert. The abbé proudly showed off the painting. Christiaan Huygens — he who wrote the verses in praise of Ninon's anatomy — has this entry in his Journal on February 17, 1661: "Was to see the abbé de Boisrobert, [who] showed me the portrait of Ninon naked in his room at Villarceaux's with that of Madame Scarron." It appears that Villarceaux let the abbé keep the two nudes in his [Boisrobert's] room rather than either keep them both all for himself, or Solomon-like allow each to have one. This seems the most generous thing that Villarceaux ever did in his life, but we do not have to go overboard in our admiration, for there is good reason to believe that by 1661, some four years after he painted the damning picture, Villarceaux knew far more about Madame Scarron's anatomy than he did in 1657 and perhaps considered that since he had been on very friendly terms with the living, pulsating subjects of both pictures, the least he could do was to let his friend have the likenesses. Incidentally, in fairness to Villarceaux's skill as an artist, the fact that he was not working from the model when painting Madame Scarron may account in part for the picture's weaknesses.

According to Françoise's first biographer, she denied bitterly that she had ever posed as alleged; weeping tears of anger and anguish, she had sent Villarceaux packing. Emile Magne says this is not true and that "their relations were never interrupted at all." If they were, they were soon resumed. The fact that Villarceaux contrived to reinstate himself in the outraged Madame Scarron's good graces speaks volumes for his irresistibility and explains more clearly than anything else the puzzle as to why Ninon favored him above all other lovers.

The question as to whether Madame Scarron and Villarceaux were lovers or not has exercised the French for centuries. The pro–Madame de Maintenon faction has had a difficult time maintaining that she lived chastely until at the age of forty-eight she married the Sun King in 1683. They could make a better case that she may not have cuckolded Scarron but only had sexual relations after his death in 1660, though even that is not easy. It appears, according to Tallemant, that society must have been making bets on whether she had yet capitulated to Villarceaux. Sometime between 1657 and 1659, Tallemant wrote, "Up to now, they think she [Madame Scarron] hasn't taken the leap." But the learned Emile Magne believes Scarron himself gives the answer: "Scarron seems at first to have been quite easy in his mind about the matter, and even to have treated the whole affair as a joke, but suddenly his attitude changed. In a pathetic poem and in a letter to Ninon he complained of the betrayal of a woman, and wrote in a mood of desperation even to the point of longing for death."

Magne assumes the "cruel one" in the poem is Madame Scarron. But the accompanying letter to Ninon contradicts this. "There they are, my dear Ninon," wrote Scarron, "these unhappy stanzas, enclosed herewith, which I recited to you yesterday. There is no one in the world but you who can boast of having as much power over me. They [the stanzas] would never have seen the light of day were it not for your orders. But really, should I tell you? Although I love you dearly, I doubt that I'll die of it. If you had less understanding, I'd be afraid you'd take this admission in bad part. I'm going to drink your health with my friends . . . and if I can get my poor bones carried as far as your place for dinner, they will have the honor of warming themselves at your hearth. Adieu — the most amiable in the world for — Scarron."

It seems clear from this letter that the "cruel one" is Ninon. How else can one explain "Although I love you dearly, I doubt that I'll die of it," etc.? Monsieur Jean Goudal has a plausible hypothesis as to what probably happened: "One night, smitten by the beauty and wit of Ninon, Scarron felt himself excited by an entirely new feeling for her. He disclosed this to Ninon, who laughed it off. Next day, he told her he had composed some verses about his torment. Flattered, she insisted on receiving the rhymed homage: it would always be an interesting document for her autograph album. Besides, he himself had no illusions as to the ultimate character of his passion . . . It was doubtless one of these loves of the head, semi-sensual, to which he had been prone, the cripple, all his life . . ."

But there are a good number of other signs pointing to the likelihood that Madame Scarron weakened. Both Saint-Simon and Primi Visconti state that Françoise capitulated to Villarceaux. Probably the final coup to the legend of her continence was given by Ninon. Decades later, perhaps in 1692, Saint-Evremond wrote her from London, asking what she knew about the great Madame de Maintenon's alleged affair with Villarceaux. The latter had died in 1691, and perhaps his death had stimulated tongues to wag again, or maybe they had never stopped. Ninon, who was then sixty-eight, seemed annoyed by the question. "Why do you persist in forgetting that I must read these love stories with spectacles? You would be wise if you contented yourself with your England and a little with the friendship which you owe me and which I deserve on account of the affection I bear you. Scarron was my friend; his wife gave me a thousand pleasures by her conversation, though I considered her too gauche for lovemaking. As to the details, I know nothing, I saw nothing, but I often lent her my yellow room, to her and to Villarceaux."

Of all the many poems which friends and suitors had written for Ninon, perhaps the most valued was the one Scarron had sent her as an étrenne, a New Year's gift, back in 1643. In it he had expressed concern that the ripe, unprotected young woman of twenty might be spoiled or led astray by the blandishments of the dandies. He therefore hoped that she would get, if not a husband worthy of her, one who was handsome and kind, and that the world would learn to see through her veneer of insouciance and appreciate her depth and character as he did.

She had not married as Scarron had hoped. She had concentrated on living honorably like her male counterpart, fearlessly doing what her mind and body told her was right. She had been achieving recognition. Scarron was not the backslapping type — he was far too subtle for that, even if he had been physically able. He had never left Ninon in any doubt as to his approval of her struggle, had organized support in her defense, had sent her encouragement during her enforced stay in the convents. When she had been released with honor from Lagny, his glee had been great. Ninon was a constant visitor to Scarron — reading to him when he was too tired or dispirited to entertain her. Her earthy femaleness filled the grateful Scarron with a warm glow almost to the last. Ninon would often relieve Françoise, giving her a chance to get out.

When in 1660 Scarron's end approached, Françoise importuned her husband to take the sacraments, but his and Ninon's friends, d'Elbène and Miossens, shamed him out of it. But later when he was too ill to resist, Françoise had last rites administered. Before he died he brightened and said to a bystander, Legras, "The only regret that I have in dying is not to leave some wealth to my wife, who has infinite merit, and whom I have every imaginable reason to praise."

Six years later the widow Scarron may have written the following letter to Ninon. Some deny its authenticity, not, notably, the knowledgeable Sainte-Beuve, who accepts it.

Your approbation consoles me for the cruelty of my friends; in the state I am, I can't repeat to myself too often that you approve my courage . . . What do you think of the comparison they dare to make between this man and Monsieur Scarron? O God! What a difference! Without fortune, comforts, the former attracted good company; the latter, on the other hand, would have hated and alienated it. Monsieur Scarron had that gaiety that everyone knows, and that goodness of spirit that practically nobody knew; my suitor is in no way brilliant, funny or sound; if he speaks, he is ridiculous. My husband had excellent depth; I had cured him of his license; he . . . had probity which was generally recognized and unparalleled disinterestedness. C—— . . . is known only for having wasted his youth . . . Assure those who attribute my refusal to an engagement that my heart is perfectly free . . . and will be so always . . . Give, I pray you, my compliments to Monsieur de La Rochefoucauld and tell him that the Book of Job and the book of his *Maxims* are my only reading. I will not thank you, since you don't want to be; but my gratitude is not diminished because of the silence you impose. How I am in your debt, my very kind friend!

This letter may contain the last kind words Madame Scarron spoke of her late husband. Soon she was to place her sure foot on the threshold of greatness. Not only did she not look back, but when she had become the awesome Madame de Maintenon, she forbade the mention of Scarron's name at Court.

With a precise sense of history, Madame de Maintenon once said that she wanted "to be an enigma for posterity." She succeeded.

# ᘒ Chapter 10 ᘒ

## A Friend in Need

THE CLOSING YEARS of the 1650s had been good ones for Ninon
— what with the honor paid her by Queen Christina of Sweden, her triumphal return to an adoring Marais after her enforced confinement, the opening of her School for Gallantry,
her friendship with Molière, and the effectiveness of her *La Coquette vangée*. The opening years of the 1660s were sad ones.
Scarron's death in October 1660 was a great grief to her. Then
a year later came the exile of Saint-Evremond, and shortly after
that, the exile of her current lover, Gourville.

Mazarin died in 1661 when Louis XIV was twenty-three.
Taking the reins of government in his own firm hands, the
young king decided to bring down the mighty superintendent
of finance, Fouquet, who had made the double error not only
of stealing from the royal treasury a little too much, but also of
poaching on the king's amorous territory by trying to buy the
royal mistress, Louise de La Vallière. In Fouquet's fall, a dam-
aging letter from Saint-Evremond to the maréchal de Créquy
came to light. In it Saint-Evremond, who had accompanied
Mazarin to the signing of the history-making Treaty of the
Pyrenees in 1659, criticizes the cardinal for the soft peace he
made with Spain when France's military advantage would
have permitted a tough peace. The letter itself is not nearly so

anti-Mazarin as Colbert and Le Tellier, both political heirs of the cardinal, made it out to be to Louis who ungratefully ordered Saint-Evremond to the Bastille notwithstanding Saint-Evremond's loyalty to the crown in the Fronde.

Saint-Evremond was returning to Paris from a visit to the country when Ninon's friend Gourville intercepted him in the forest and told him that an order for his arrest had been issued. Saint-Evremond had known Gourville for years — in the Fronde when he had won Mazarin's admiration for shrewd diplomacy, and as one of Ninon's caprices. He knew that Gourville had had some business relations with Fouquet and that Gourville was probably risking his own safety in coming to warn him, when he should himself be spurring for the frontier. Saint-Evremond reversed his direction — to seek refuge in Normandy while he tried to get together a few belongings and a little money. Then he made for Holland — the Frenchman's traditional seventeenth-century asylum.

In a trice Saint-Evremond's world had collapsed. Aged only forty-five, still in his prime, a respectful military commander, an acknowledged master of wit whose company was widely sought out at Court and in the salons, the classic honnête homme was fleeing his beloved France with not much more than the clothes on his back. He was never to return. Ninon was heartbroken. The man she respected most in all the world, he who brought out the best in her, her conscience, her instructor, her delight, her fellow honnête homme, was wrenched out of her life without even a leave-taking. It was 1632 all over again, when her adored father had been forced to run.

\*

With Gourville it was different. He came to say good-bye — in the dead of night some months after Saint-Evremond had gone. Under his cloak he had a casket — a right romantic casket, filled with shining gold crowns, to the value of 20,000 écus ($120,000 to $300,000). Gourville explained that earlier he had left a similar amount with the Grand Penitentiary of Notre Dame, a holy man, begging him to keep it for him during his absence which Gourville's sanguine nature led him to believe would not be too lengthy. As a person of presumed equal trustworthiness, he besought Ninon to keep the second casket. Ninon said she would. Worried, she urged Gourville not to take any unnecessary chances, since he had a reputation for daring.

A man of great native ability, a supreme opportunist who nonetheless, according to Madame de Sévigné, "was adorable from the point of view of the heart," Gourville contrived in exile to convince the princes of Brunswick and Hanover that friendly relations with France would be to their advantage. Louis XIV was well pleased and gave him the title of plenipotentiary just at the time that the court of justice, which was trying him for having accepted suspect gains from Fouquet, condemned him to death in absentia and burned him in effigy. The playful Gourville did not like this treatment and made a secret trip to Paris where he sent a lackey to take down a portrait of him pasted on the scaffold. In his *Memoirs* Gourville remarks that the portrait did not do him justice.

With both Saint-Evremond and Gourville in exile, Ninon probably saw more of Molière. Tallemant says that Molière owed his inspiration for *Tartuffe,* still the most frequently

played French classic, to Ninon. "An abbé of Pons, a big hypocrite . . . attended upon Ninon quite sedulously . . . he is the
original Tartuffe, for one day he declared his passion to her; he
had become enamored of her. In discussing the matter, he told
her that she should not be surprised, that the greatest saints had
been susceptible to passion: that Saint Paul was given to tenderness and that the blessed François de Sales had not been proof
against it."

But the abbé de Châteauneuf, who knew Ninon well — it
was he who brought the eleven-year old Voltaire to see her the
year of her death — has this to say of the *Tartuffe* affair:*
"You remind me . . ." said Callimaque (one of the two
speakers in Châteauneuf's *Dialogue*), "of an incident involving
Molière himself, who recounted it a few days before he presented his *Tartuffe* . . . We were speaking of the power of im-
itation. We asked him why the same ludicrous situation, which
often escapes us in the original, often strikes us unerringly in
the copy. He replied that it is because we see it then with the
eyes of the imitator which are better than our own; for, added
he, the talent of perceiving it by oneself is not given to everyone.
Whereupon he cited Leontium† [Ninon] to us as the person
upon whom, so far as he knew, the ridiculous made the most
acute impression; and he apprised us that having been the night
before to read *Tartuffe* to her, in accordance with his custom to
consult her on all he did, she had repaid him in like currency
by the recital of an adventure which had happened to her with

---

* In his *Dialogue sur la musique des Anciens,* 1725.
† Leontium was Saint-Evremond's (and others') nickname for Ninon. The original
Leontium was the pupil and mistress of Epicurus. John Hayward says of their relationship: "It is reasonable to assume that like Abelard and Héloise, they enjoyed
the pleasures of the flesh and spirit."

a scoundrel of nearly the same type; of whom she painted the portrait in such vivid and natural colors that if his play had not been finished, he told us, he would never have undertaken it, so incapable did he feel himself of putting in the theater anything as perfect as the Tartuffe of Leontium."

Officially suppressed or not, the Society of the Holy Sacrament felt that with his attack on hypocritical piety in *Tartuffe,* Molière was clearly the anti-Christ incarnate, and deemed it safe to reemerge from the shadows to destroy him. Not acting as a body, but working individually to pull strings, they succeeded in raising such a hue and cry that Louis had to forbid the public performance of *Tartuffe.* For almost five years Molière fought, at all times seconded by Ninon, to have the archbishop of Paris rescind his threat to excommunicate anyone caught reading it. In 1669, *Tartuffe* was finally readmitted to the boards and enjoyed a long run.

Indeed, these must have been rather bleak times for Ninon. To make things worse, the debt-ridden d'Elbène was now more a care than a comfort, and her friendship with the widow Scarron was no longer close. It was good that Ninon was occupied in helping Molière in the battle of *Tartuffe,* for as the French say, she had heard the forties tolling, and notwithstanding her vaunted retention of youth, there was probably not the same queue lining up to woo her. This was the transitional period in Ninon's life, the time of her graduation from the Ninon stage, when the emphasis had been on the physical, to the Mademoiselle de Lanclos stage, when the emphasis was on dignity, respect, and the philosophical. Her forties may not have been, from all the contemporary testimony about Ninon's youthfulness, the time of her physical menopause, but they were the time of her mental menopause. She was fighting a rearguard action against the advance of time, had not yet reconciled herself, as she did in the next decade, to its unremitting progression.

Attacked as he was on all sides, Molière sometimes doubted his own position and found the encouragement that comes from a woman who believed in him vital to his carrying on. Molière's association with Ninon illustrates rather well the peculiarly tonic effect of an interested woman on the creative power of an artist. Like Molière, she was not an atheist but a rebel against institutionalized religion; she prayed to God all her life. She held to her independence of thought and nonconformism, even in the face of approaching death with its threat, according to the Church, of hellfire.

Molière valued this courage. Besides being a witty conversationalist, Ninon was also a stimulating listener. Perhaps that is what Creuzé de Lesser had in mind when in his play *Ninon de Lanclos ou l'epicuréisme,* written at the end of the eighteenth century, he gives Molière the lines: "And what man would have this grace, this piquancy which characterizes women and Ninon more than any other?"

Unlike Saint-Evremond, who did not have Gourville's interest in, or flair for, business, Gourville seems to have recouped his fortunes in exile, for he was able to return to France in 1668 allegedly upon payment of 600,000 francs ($1,200,000 to $3,000,-000). This ransom probably took all he had and he hastened to the Grand Penitentiary to get back his 20,000 crowns which he had left with him. The priest at first had difficulty recalling him, but eventually Gourville succeeded in identifying himself.

Gourville then asked for his deposit. The Grand Penitentiary asked what deposit. Since Gourville had not wanted to insult the reverend gentleman by asking for a receipt at the time of leaving the money, he had no written proof. Sweat and strain as Gourville did, the holy man's position was unshakable — he had never got the money in the first place, but if Gourville was certain he had, then he had used it to give alms or to order masses for Gourville's soul. He wished Gourville well and good day. Gourville made his exit declaring that he had now lost all faith in mankind. If this is what a holy person does, what could he expect from the notoriously unreligious Ninon? He was afraid to find out and kept away from her.

Meanwhile Ninon heard that Gourville was back. She was put out that he had not called and sent for him. Gourville came diffidently, afraid his fears would be confirmed. Ninon must have divined his thoughts for she seems to have played a little joke on him. "Ah," she cried as soon as she saw him, "something terrible has happened in your absence . . . I am sorry if you are still in love with me," Ninon went on, affecting great earnestness. "The misfortune is irreparable; I have lost the desire I once had for you but not my memory. Here are the 20,000 crowns. Take them with you, but do not ask anything more than the sincerest friendship." Gourville wept tears of gratitude. He then proceeded to recount to Ninon why he had not come sooner, fearing that if a devout man had acted as a cheat, what could he expect of lesser mortals. Gourville continued to sing praises to her probity. Ninon stopped him.

On pain of displeasing Ninon, Gourville said no more of the matter to her, but as soon as he left he spread the news far and wide. She became a legend for integrity in her own lifetime.

The story crossed the Channel. Eighteen years later, far away in London, lonesome Saint-Evremond hailed her "as the beautiful keeper of the casket" and, after vaunting her integrity, finds he can no longer do justice to her in confining prose.

> In your loves they found you fickle
> In friendship always constant and sincere;
> For your lovers, the love of Venus
> For your friends, the solid virtues.
> In a convent, as a Sister Trustee
> You could have handled any transaction,
> And on the outside, to keep deposits
> They would justly have preferred you to the bigots.

Even the sharp-tongued duc de Saint-Simon softened markedly when he wrote of Ninon being "virtuous and full of prob.. ity . . . she kept faithfully deposits of money."

Voltaire does not seem to have been able to get the incident out of his head. First he tells the story in a letter written forty-six years after Ninon's death. The passage of time may perhaps have permitted the addition of some embroidery. After observing that Gourville died "one of the most well thought of men in France," he tells us that upon Gourville's return from exile, "he found the casket at Ninon's in exceedingly good condition; there was even more money than he had left, because gold coins had gone up in value in the interim. He maintained that at least the excess belonged as of right to the trustee; her reply was to threaten to have the casket thrown out the window." But his zeal to make the incident known widely was not satisfied by mere letter writing and conversation. Voltaire wrote a five-act play on the theme entitled *Le Dépositaire*. In the preface, Voltaire remarks:

Everybody knows that Gourville entrusted a part of his wealth to this so gallant and philosophical a girl . . .

We do not present this play as a theatrical work; we rather feel it is not meant to be acted. We give it solely as a very unique monument in which one can find again, word for word, what Ninon thought about probity and love.

Ninon may not have been an observant Catholic but she *was* a firm believer in the New Testament maxim that "it is more blessed to give than to receive." She always kept in reserve one year's income with which to help needy friends. Among those who joined the swelling chorus of people praising Ninon's conduct about this time — 1670 — was the son of the Great Condé, known as "Monsieur le duc." Condé still loved to attend Ninon's salon, had passed on his regard for Ninon to his son who wrote Gourville: "I am very glad to be able to tell you that according to what I have heard, Ninon has behaved very well in several matters which concerned me. If you write to her, tell her, as if it came from yourself, that . . . I am very much pleased with her." Gourville replied, "I have written to tell you how pleased I was to learn that Your Highness was so well pleased with her behavior and with what she said on those particular occasions. I should not be a friend of hers if I did not endorse Your Highness's feelings on the subject."

It would be intriguing to know details of the circumstances in which Ninon had so pleased the duke, but the record is silent.

Saint-Simon and Voltaire also record an incident in which Ninon, the soul of integrity, says that she hates virtue. The boring comte de Choiseul, afterward a marshal, was lagging

badly in his campaign to conquer Ninon. What made his chagrin all the more unbearable was that an upstart dancer,
Pécourt, was succeeding where he failed. Pécourt seems to
have had more than just a good physique. One day Choiseul
saw Pécourt in Ninon's anteroom preening himself in a uniform which, with all its braid, looked military. Knowing
Pécourt was no soldier, Choiseul cuttingly asked him in what
"corps" he served. "Monseigneur," said Pécourt, looking in the
direction of Ninon's boudoir, "je *commande* un corps où vous
*servez* depuis longtemps" (My Lord, I *rule* a body which you
have been *serving* for quite some time).*

Choiseul was trying too hard to impress Ninon. He had
finally won the coveted "Order," and "could be seen," says
Saint-Simon, "gazing at himself in the mirror, decked out in
his blue ribbon." Ninon found him doing so on more than one
occasion and finally lost patience. "Watch out, monsieur le
comte," she said, wagging a pretty finger while the others
waited mouths agape, "if I catch you at it again, I'll give you a
list of who else are members." The proud duc de Saint-Simon,
who was always complaining about parvenus, adds, "And indeed some members of the order were enough to make one
weep . . . This marshal [Choiseul]," continues Saint-Simon,
"was the very pattern of virtue, but he was dull company and
not overintelligent. After one very long visitation, l'Enclos
yawned, looked at him and then exclaimed: 'Oh God! how you
do make me hate virtue!' which is a line of some play or other,

---

* According to Emile Magne, this incident is apocryphal. Magne says that the
usual date given is 1665, though he does not give his authority for said date. Magne
points out that in 1665 Pécourt was only twelve — a little young even for Ninon.
However, if it was in 1673, Ninon would have been fifty and Pécourt twenty — well
within Ninon's range, her early biographers contend.

I forget the name.* You may imagine the laughter and the tittle-tattle. None the less, even this sally did not provoke a quarrel between them."

Ninon, who hated unctuousness, would not have been found dead with the label of virtue on her. It would have smacked too much of Tartuffe, of the hypocrites and the prudes who reeked of it. "However," Voltaire states, "she herself was the very personification of virtue, to use that word in its true sense; and this virtue won her the name of *the beautiful keeper of the casket.*"

Ninon's old friend d'Elbène was in financial trouble. She had a special fondness for this intellectually gifted, charming, irresponsible rake who had run through a large fortune and was now reduced to borrowing. He had always been generous, entertaining lavishly, putting his carriage at the disposal of all the little minxes of the Marais with whom he had passed a joyous hour, week, or month. Ninon remembered with gratitude the loyal friendship he had shown the undaunted, crippled Scarron, visiting him day after day, ceaselessly trying to cheer him up. When Scarron was *in extremis,* it was d'Elbène who had held him like a mother. Ninon did not forget that after Scarron's death, the usually indolent d'Elbène had toiled selflessly in sifting through the musty mass of Scarron's papers, and had brought out *The Last Works of Monsieur Scarron* — without even mention of his own name as compiler and editor. Ninon was not rich, but when d'Elbène needed a loan, she did not fail him.

D'Elbène had pledged as security for the loan certain reve-

* From Corneille's *La Mort de Pompée.*

nues which, probably inadvertently and certainly not mischie-
vously, he had also pledged to one Dromont. In 1667 we find
Ninon in court — as plaintiff. Dromont had taken over the
property which was Ninon's security for her loan, and Ninon
was contesting the seizure. She lost. It appears that Ninon had
what might be equivalent today to a second mortgage, but evidently Dromont had a first mortgage. He jumped first and was
declared owner to Ninon's exclusion. Learning no lesson from
the Dromont affair, or more accurately, not wanting to learn
any lesson of self-interest where friendship was concerned, she
involved herself in another matter of d'Elbène's, an involvement which not only again cost her money but also a painful, if
temporary, estrangement from Saint-Evremond.

After leaving Gourville in the forest where the latter had
warned him that the king's officers were looking for him, Saint-
Evremond had made his way to Holland, thence to England in
1662, and then because the English climate seemed to be affecting his health, had gone back to Holland in 1665. Sometime
before Saint-Evremond had been forced to flee, d'Elbène had
borrowed 200 pistoles ($4600 to $11,500) from him. In exile
Saint-Evremond was now in more straitened circumstances than
d'Elbène. Repeatedly he asked d'Elbène to pay him back.
Being a nag must have been extremely distasteful to a man of
Saint-Evremond's dignity and gentlemanliness. Ninon, feeling
keenly for both her friends, unwisely decided to intervene. She
proposed a compromise whereby in return for her assuming
one-half of d'Elbène's debt to Saint-Evremond (100 pistoles),
the latter would forgive the other half. Ninon did not offer to
pay the one-half immediately. She was expecting to recover
some other moneys she had lent d'Elbène and meant to pay
Saint-Evremond out of that recovery.

## From Saint-Evremond to Ninon

1669 or 1670

With no offense to that old dreamer who never found a happy person this side of death,* I consider you, fully alive as you are, the happiest person that ever was.

You have been loved by the most honorable men in the world and been in love long enough to leave none of its pleasures untasted, and yet with judgment enough to avoid the vexation of a languishing flame. Never has the happiness of your sex been carried so far. There are but few princesses in the world who would not feel their life hard compared to yours, not a saint in her convent who would not gladly exchange her tranquillity of mind for the agreeable tumult of your soul. Of all the torments, you have felt only those of love, and you know better than anybody that compared to love, the other pleasures aren't worth the trouble.

Today, now that the flower of your wonderful youth is passed (the word is harsh, but you have written it to me so often† that I'm only repeating), your face retains so much charm and your mind so much grace that, were it not for your fastidiousness, there would be as big a throng of . . . persons at your house as there are in courts where fortunes are to be gained . . . Your word is the most reliable possible covenant; and when you have given a man hope of receiving 100 pistoles . . . he can count on them as if already received . . .

Let us go, my dear, let us go to the Indies and follow the cult of that people of whom I've told you: there they live for centuries, and never a moment passes without a taste of pleasure. I must admit you have made a marvelous gain in our own country to find yourself three years younger than you thought. Alas! you

---

* Solon, according to Saint-Evremond's master, Montaigne, said that "men, however much Fortune has favored them, cannot call themselves happy till they have been seen to pass over the last day of their life."
† Not one of these letters survives.

must pity us other mortals who add days unto days and rush precipitously toward our end.

. . . My days march on; but, notwithstanding some diminution of my first vigor, I'd console myself for that which I have lost, if I could stay in the same state for that which remains.

Would to God we were united by marriage . . . doubtless we would occupy ourselves much with delicacy of the mind, but the body would not fail to furnish some of the pleasure out of jealousy of leaving all the credit to its companion.

. . . Adieu, I'd like to know if all is still well with your lute.

This letter, the earliest extant from Saint-Evremond to Ninon, is interesting on a number of points. It assumes that distant pastures are greener, that Ninon was blissfully happy when in fact she had her share of every mortal's problems: her fading youthfulness; her worry over Molière's security and health; her concern for the welfare and education of her natural son who was being brought up, as was the custom then, by his father, Villarceaux. The letter also reflects the century's preoccupation with the passage of time. Lastly, it sheds important light on Ninon's birth date, long in dispute. Until the middle of the nineteenth century, the year of Ninon's birth was thought to have been 1616. Then Jal found her baptismal certificate showing 1620. A legal document of October 7, 1670, however, refers to an "extract" from her baptismal certificate of January 9, 1623. Historians have wondered which is right — 1620 or 1623 — but they seem to have ignored the seemingly decisive passage in Saint-Evremond's letter indicating that Ninon had apparently found evidence she was born three years later than she had thought.

Ninon did not send the 100 pistoles to Saint-Evremond right

away — waiting first to collect something herself. Poor Saint-Evremond must have felt demeaned writing to his friend, d'Hervart:

> If you see Mademoiselle de Lanclos, I pray you assure her that nobody can be more her servant than I, although I no longer hear tell of the 100 pistoles as if 100 pistoles did not exist in the whole world. Her good faith is great, but my absence is long . . . there is nothing so easy as to forget people when remembering them costs 100 pistoles. Perhaps I am wrong in suspecting her of human weakness . . .

Only urgent want could have engendered this bitterness in Saint-Evremond, but he still had the magnanimity to write d'Hervart not to try to collect for him from the down-at-the-heel d'Elbène.

D'Hervart told Ninon about Saint-Evremond's dissatisfaction in not having received anything from her yet. She decided to send him immediately one-half of her commitment, i.e., 50 pistoles, even though she had not collected anything herself. Saint-Evremond, hard pressed, wrote her stingingly in 1670:

> . . . If I only get the 50 pistoles of which Monsieur d'Hervart speaks, don't reproach yourself with not keeping your word: it is the influence of my star, and not lack of good faith on your part; some of the most upright gentlemen . . . have treated me in the same manner. I bear them no ill will; this blasted star [of mine] has forced them to . . . act contrary to their nature.

Then his charm returns to draw the sting:

> I shall have another consolation which will deflect my thinking from this mournful influence toward something pleasant: if I draw the whole amount, your correctness and wonted honor

would exclude me entirely from the role of a lover [who is] subject to the laws of your infidelity. If I were to draw nothing, the
part of friend would find itself too concerned, and the sense of
security that has always prevailed in your dealings would be lost.

The middle course you have adopted is in keeping with the delicacy of your mind and does justice to the role I have always played
as regards you, neither that of a mere friend, nor that of a veritable lover. Perhaps you will be so hard-hearted as to deny the
least suggestion of passion. I am accustomed to such hardships,
and if you send the other 50 pistoles, as a sign that the love I
have is doomed, I will accept the sentence in submission to your
wishes and receive them as a mere friend who deserves no better.
A friend I shall always be as long as I live, and were there more
truth in our imaginings, I should consider myself to be something
more than that at the moment of writing.*

Ninon was deeply hurt and said so to d'Hervart who relayed
the information to Saint-Evremond. Concerned, Saint-Evremond quickly wrote d'Hervart he was surprised that Ninon
had taken offense, for none was intended. ". . . As to my feelings toward her, they will never change, and nothing will prevent me from being her eternal friend, whether she wants it or
not."

Ninon was not entirely appeased. She sent the whole 100 pistoles, not just the fifty, and then, still piqued, wrote Saint-
Evremond a rather stiff letter in 1671 (the first — which remains — from her pen):

> An over-scrupulous man is always inclined to be a little cruel,
> for it is no easy thing for virtue to subsist with an even temper.
> I had written you a very nice letter in which I pointed out to

* Joint translation of John Hayward in his *Letters of Saint-Evremond* and of
Edgar H. Cohen.

you the merit of my paying in advance. Although I had given my pledge, I doubt that [even] Marcus Aurelius, philosopher and emperor that he was, paid his creditors in advance.

And yet that is what I have done for you and poor d'Elbène. By rights I should have put myself in your position, and before keeping my word, should have waited until I had settled my own affairs, from which I have not yet got a sou; but I have considered you two more to be pitied than myself, and have dispatched 100 pistoles . . . which, as I have said, were not due until my business had been concluded.

That is some consolation, and if you think of it, you will realize that a banker, free from reproach, must not be made fun of.

The cold, a bad pen and a man from d'Hervart whom I am keeping waiting, prevent me from saying more; but love me enough to bear with my severity.

I have told you that my charms have changed into solid and serious qualities, and you know that it is forbidden to jest with a personage.

The cloud on their relationship is said not to have lasted long, although there is a long lapse in the correspondence of which there is a record. But as most of the correspondence has been lost, the absence of letters between them for ten years or more does not necessarily prove a protracted period of coolness.

Ninon and her contemporaries were still gay at the beginning of the 1670s — making full use of Paris's greater amenities which included the recent installation of 6000 lanterns. Around this time Madame de Sévigné, who had irrepressible joie de vivre, wrote, "We found it pleasant to go and pick up Madame Scarron at midnight at the end of the faubourg Saint-Germain . . . We came back gaily — thanks to the lanterns and security from thieves." Madame de Sévigné had even forgiven Ninon for having seduced her husband some two decades before, had greeted her at musicales, and was all ready to become friendly, but then Ninon got into her bad books again, this time because of her liaison with Madame de Sévigné's son Charles.

The episode with young Sévigné is both puzzling and disturbing. It does not show Ninon at her best. Charles, who was twenty-three in 1671 when Ninon was at least 48, was not her type, either physically or mentally. Emile Magne describes him as having a "girlish countenance and languishing eyes . . . his figure supple and willowy." Though he was to prove himself brave in battle, he was vacillating and irresolute in love about which he had a virulent guilt complex deriving from a deep-seated streak of piety inherited from a maternal great-grandmother, who was made a saint. Some have speculated that Ninon saw in him a reminder of his dashing, irresponsible father, the marquis de Sévigné, of whom she retained a lively recollection as an accomplished lover. But the son was a pale copy, ineffectual and effete — or at least he seemed that way to Ninon. He must have had some attractiveness though, for he had taken the reigning actress of the day, Mademoiselle de Champmeslé, aged twenty-nine, away from the leading playwright, Racine.

The thought of measuring her powers against an actress almost twenty years her junior may have presented a challenge to Ninon whose self-confidence in her magnetism for men may well have needed bolstering now that she heard the fifties tolling. She was up against formidable competition. After la Champmeslé's triumph in Racine's *Andromaque,* La Fontaine had written Racine; "All the world belongs to the king and to

Mademoiselle de Champmeslé." Like Ninon, she was not a great beauty, but her voice was evidently pure music.

When Madame de Sévigné saw her son switch from la Champmeslé to Ninon, she was even more worried.

*To Madame de Grignan (her daughter)*

March 13, 1671

Your brother wears the chains of Ninon; I doubt they will prove good for him. To some minds they are mischievous. This same Ninon corrupted the morals of his father. Let us commend the boy to God . . .

*To Madame de Grignan*

Paris, Friday, April 1, 1671

. . . But that Ninon is a scornful creature; if you only knew how she argues about religion, it would make you shudder . . . She says your brother has all the artlessness of the dove, that he is just like his mother, but that Madame de Grignan has all the fire in the family, and has more sense than to be so docile. Somebody wanted to take your part, and change her opinion of you; but she bid him hold his tongue and told him that she knew more of the matter than he did. What a falling away from taste! Because she finds you beautiful and witty, she needs must give you another attribute* without which, according to her rule, there is no being perfect. I am greatly concerned about the harm she does my son in this respect; but do not take any notice of him. Madame de La Fayette and I are using all our endeavors to disengage him from so dangerous an attachment. Besides her, he has on his hands a little actress,† and people like Despréaux‡ and Racine, to whom he gives suppers; in short, he is perfectly infatuated.

---

* Fire or passion.
† la Champmeslé.
‡ Nicolas Boileau-Despréaux, generally known as Boileau, one of the most famous critics and satirists of his time.

Madame de Sévigné was herself so infatuated with her attractive daughter (who, being far away, could not talk back to her) that she used up all her affection on her and seems downright unsympathetic to her wishy-washy son, torn morbidly by what to him were two irreconcilable forces — desire and religious fervor. Had Saint-Evremond been in Paris to guide him, he would have explained (as he had to Ninon) that the two pulls were but different manifestations of passion, that the two are not mutually exclusive, that they often coexist healthily in one person, and that where they do not coexist, one often succeeds the other — as in the case of the woman whose sensual youth changes in later life to intense devoutness. Madame de Sévigné was chaste but not puritanical and seems to illustrate well the maxim of "a healthy mind in a healthy body." But Charles had the conscience of a Puritan, without his mother's self-discipline. He was sick of soul, poor Charles, having inherited his mother's religiosity without her strength and his father's weakness without his insouciance.

"He is," lamented his mother, "in fashionable circles up to his ears; no sacrament at Easter, no plenary indulgence, gulping sin like water." And again: "My son is not mad in the head, but in the heart. His opinions are wholly true, are wholly false, are too cold, are too burning, are too knavish, are too sincere. In a word, his heart is all folly." Today's psychiatrists would have a field day with Charles, though his mother probably knew then, without benefit of analysis, that her husband's death when her son was only three largely accounted for Charles's disorientation. The memory of Charles's not too worthy father was probably not treated with excessive respect in the Sévigné household. Thus, Charles could not help but equate sex with sin.

Once Ninon had won him away from la Champmeslé, or more accurately was sharing him with her — Ninon getting the lioness's share — she quickly lost both her patience with his vacillating nature and her taste for him. But she did not dismiss him immediately. She seems to have had a score to settle with Mademoiselle de Champmeslé. What the cause was we do not know, but we have here the only known example of vindictiveness on Ninon's part. She demanded that Charles surrender to her the actress's letters to him. He did. Ninon, according to Madame de Sévigné, had the intention of forwarding them to one of Mademoiselle de Champmeslé's lovers, the comte de Clermont-Tonnerre, "in order," relates Madame de Sévigné "to make him give her [la Champmeslé] a few little whacks with his belt." Like the mama's boy that he was, Charles told Madame de Sévigné all about it.

"I told him," wrote Madame de Sévigné to her daughter, "that it was an infamy to cut the throat of this little creature [la Champmeslé] as a reward for having loved him; that she hadn't done likewise with his letters, as someone wanted to make him believe in order to stir him up . . . that it was base treachery and unworthy of a man of quality, and that even in improper things, there is a certain propriety to maintain. He saw my point, he ran to Ninon, and half by ingenuity, half by force, he got back the letters from this poor wretch. I had them burned."

Madame de Sévigné was evidently furious that Ninon was playing with her son as one does with a toy or a fly. "Poor wretch" was the ultimate in scorn. Ninon may have played the arch seducer in this incident, but in downgrading her to a "poor wretch," Madame de Sévigné was hitting below the belt. But Ninon had a fairly tart tongue too when she wanted. She was probably angry with herself that she had stooped to malice vis-à-vis la Champmeslé, and that she had ever allowed herself to get mixed up with such a weak-kneed individual as the young marquis de Sévigné, whom she probably despised as much for giving her her rival's letters as she was annoyed by his forcibly taking them back. She gave Charles his marching orders, commenting, according to Madame de Sévigné, that Charles "had a soul like pap, a body resembling wet paper, with the heart of a pumpkin fricasseed in snow."

Charles went into a decline, characterized by erotic hallucinations. He had been trying to serve two mistresses, and it had been too much for him. With touching simplicity he confided the details to his mother who immediately unburdened herself to her daughter.

April 17, 1671

My son is still not cured of the sickness which causes his precious mistresses to question his passion.* He told me last night that during Holy Week, he had gone in for such excess that he had taken a distaste for all that formerly used to make his heart leap up; he was afraid to even think about it . . . he was always seeming to see about him basketsful of breasts, and what not! Breasts, thighs, basketsful of all manner of things, in such abundance that his fancy was seized with it all and still is. He could not look at a woman; he was like horses sickened by [too much] oats.

The mother brought him around, however, no doubt substituting good wholesome advice, interspersed with Father Bourdaloue's views on chastity, for tranquilizers and the psychiatrist's couch. At first it was hard. "Ninon has dismissed him.

---

* One biographer, reaching far, interprets this to mean temporary impotence.

He was unhappy when she loved him; he is in despair that he is no longer loved, also that she does not speak of him with much esteem." But Ninon tried to help. She took him back, not as a lover but as a friend, though in this case not for long.

*Madame de Sévigné to Madame de Grignan*

April 27, 1671

I trust that the chapter on your brother has diverted you; he is presently more or less at peace; he sees Ninon every day — but as a friend. He went the other day with her to a place where there were five or six men. They made a face which convinced her that they thought Charles was her lover. She divined their thoughts, and said, "Gentlemen, you deceive yourselves if you think there's anything improper between us; I assure you we are like brother and sister." It's true he is fricasseed . . .

Like the males in the Sévigné clan, Madame de Sévigné also felt the attraction of Ninon's personality. Now that Ninon and Charles were no longer lovers, her anger against Ninon was soon spent, and, evidently fascinated by Ninon's description of her son, she finds herself lining up with Ninon's estimate of him — "a pumpkin fricasseed in snow." Madame de Sévigné quotes the phrase three times — in her letters of April 8, April 27, and May 1, 1671.

But Ninon, try as she did to make a man of Charles, simply could not stand him. "Ninon says your brother beggars discription," wrote Madame de Sévigné in her last letter on the affair. It was finished, and so was the chapter, by and large, of Ninon's love life. When Ninon found herself straining to compete with an actress young enough to be her daughter, when she began despising herself for trying to attract a feckless boy young enough to be her son, she decided to act her age even if she did not look it. Perhaps the crowning indignity to the usually proud Ninon was an incident in that fashionable crossroads of aristocratic Paris, the Cours-la-Reine, where twenty years before she had effortlessly caused the handsome comte de Navailles to spring to her side at the merest drop of a billet doux. While promenading perhaps a little too ostentatiously with her young gallant, Charles, Ninon noticed his eyes straying in the direction of other women — no doubt her junior. "You certainly know how to ogle," she said, and struck him with her fan. She hated herself for doing this, and it was not long after that she sent Charles away. She for whom all Paris had sighed was not going to make herself ridiculous. She was a "personage" now, as we have seen her style herself to Saint-Evremond in a letter written the very same year. She had a reputation to live up to as a woman of taste, elegance, dignity, and good sense.

It was time to withdraw from the lists. To everything there is a season. Ninon, who knew her Bible, was well aware of seemliness. There was a time to love and a time to hate; a time to embrace and a time to refrain from embracing. The farewell to arms was harder for Ninon than for most people because for her sex had been almost a way of life, a raison d'être, chief nourisher in life's feast. She played it up, not down. She engaged in it openly, proud to acknowledge her joyous acceptance of nature's sweet gift. Unlike Charles de Sévigné, Ninon saw nothing evil or sinful in desire, but a healthy, positive, constructive force which legitimately quickened the blood, brightened the eye, colored the cheek, sharpened the wit, motivated gallantry, gave to life its flavor. And yet there is no indication that, upon her withdrawal from what was to her life's gamiest game, she suffered a serious menopausal depression as might have been expected. The reason is that Ninon had been preparing, probably subconsciously, for this moment all her life. The resources of her body — vitality, passion, fire — her sophisticated erotic technique — these she had given to her lovers. But the resources of her spirit — integrity, reliability, steadfastness — she had reserved for her friends. She had a host of them, and they respected and adored her. It was upon them that she was now able to fall back, as the Age of Ninon, which had been waning for over a decade, drew to a close, and the Age of Mademoiselle de Lanclos, which had been waxing steadily, ensued.

Ninon evidently acted in good time — before she had drained the last drop and got down to the dregs. A year later Madame de Sévigné, who seems to have wanted to make up with Ninon, wrote her daughter that Monsieur de Longueville besought Ninon: "Mademoiselle, save me from that fat marquise de Castelnau" who, according to Marcil Gobineau,* had stripped off the breeches of the young Longueville and violated him. Monsieur de Longueville was the natural son of Ninon's friend La Rochefoucauld. Devotees of Ninon like to point out that Longueville was half Ninon's age and that she was still, at age forty-nine, able to attract young men. Some chroniclers say Ninon and Longueville became lovers. If so, she only came out of retirement temporarily — probably more out of the goodness of her heart than the urgings of her body which, however, were not yet stilled, she records elsewhere.

Charles de Sévigné, it may be noted, proved to himself and

* In his novel, *Ninon de Lanclos*.

the world that he was a man after all, fighting like a lion at the battle of Senef and the siege of Aire. Then he took up Latin intensively, grew more and more devout, engaged in an inky theological duel with a certain Dacier over a passage in one of St. Paul's Epistles, and ended up a monk in a cell of the seminary of Saint-Magloire. It is not recorded whether Ninon ever said she saw it coming.

# ⌘ Chapter 11 ⌘

## "What Does Ninon Say?"

SOME TWO DECADES before the Charles de Sévigné liaison, one of
Ninon's passing fancies had been Antoine Rambouillet, sieur
de La Sablière, who had succeeded Charles's father in her boudoir. A few years later Rambouillet married one of the more
engaging ladies of the century, but for reasons inexplicable to
us, he treated her badly, stripping her of much of her fortune
and depriving her of her children — in addition to the standard
philandering. Madame de La Sablière had an arresting oval
face, radiating sweetness and light; her hair was fair and her
eyes a blue deepened by melancholy. As sensitive as she was
winsome, singularly chaste, she was possessed of an amazing
erudition in mathematics, science, philosophy, and the classics.
Ninon, seventeen years her senior, felt deeply for her in her
marital plight and became her loyal friend for many years.

Married at fourteen, Madame de La Sablière endured for
fourteen years the cruelty of Rambouillet de La Sablière, then
finally effected a separation in 1668. Still only twenty-eight, she
tried to make a new life for herself, holding open house for a
select intelligentsia. Molière and the court painter Mignard
often dropped in. La Fontaine, who was poor, lived in her
house for almost twenty years though not with her. She was
his fairy goddess, feeding and sheltering him and encouraging

him to write the fables which still delight us. The satirist Boileau was a constant caller, as was our chronicler Tallemant,
her brother-in-law. Bernier, the disciple of Gassendi, gave the
circle its philosophical character — anti-Cartesian and libertin.
All these people were good friends of Ninon who was a frequent visitor.

The atmosphere at Madame de La Sablière's was both edify-
ing and gay. The Sorbonne professor Antoine Adam, in his
*Histoire de la littérature française,* credits Ninon with exerting
a strong influence on the thinking of the group: "Bernier and
Ninon were of one mind in teaching that gentle pleasure is the
supreme factor of life in reducing morality to a smiling wisdom. Reason must not, they thought, stifle passion; its role is to
give order to passion, to use it to achieve the greatest and most
enduring happiness." Many years after the heyday of Madame
de La Sablière's salon, Saint-Evremond in a letter to Ninon
from London, recalls what Bernier, "the prettiest philosopher
I've ever seen," had said about asceticism: "I am going," he
quotes Bernier as saying, "to divulge a confidence that I
wouldn't divulge to Madame de La Sablière, not even to
Ninon, whom I consider to be of a superior order. I tell you in
confidence that *abstinence from pleasure seems to me a great
sin.*"

Madame de La Sablière used to dread the time when her
guests would take their leave in the late afternoon. One day, to
induce some of them to stay on, she invited Ninon, Molière,
Bernier, and Boileau to remain for dinner. Molière began ex-
plaining the difficulties he was having with the writing of one
of his funniest plays, *Le Malade imaginaire,* an attack on medical mountebanks. He feared that the locale — a sickroom —
would militate against the success of the play as a comedy.

They prevailed upon him to read them what he had written. His audience immediately knew that he had a masterpiece in his manuscript, though perhaps in need of a little doctoring. Bernier, himself a physician, proposed an interlude satirizing the ridiculous examination ritual to which aspiring doctors had to submit. All of the five present collaborated to write the dialogue in mumbo-jumbo dog Latin. Bernier distributed the parts: Boileau was to be the candidate, Bernier the presiding officer, Molière the board of medical examiners, while the ladies were to be the chorus. Instead of the usual eulogy of the faculty, Bernier launched into a mock panegyric of the medical profession, itself a hotbed of dangerous charlatans. Then, in sepulchral tones he sternly interrogated the student, Boileau, on various phases of medicine. In response to a question on treatment, Boileau gave the stock answer:

> *Clysterium donare*
> *Postea seignare*
> *Ensuitta purgare.*

> (To give an enema
> Afterwards bleed
> Then purge.)

Each time the aspiring bachelor would give a "correct" answer, Ninon and Madame de La Sablière would chorus:

> *Bene, bene, bene respondere.*
> *Dignus, dignus est intrare,*
> *In nostro docto corpore.*

> (Well, thrice well said.
> He is worthy to enter
> Into our learned society.)

In French and in dog Latin the satire continued, with everyone contributing a quip here, a thrust there. Finally, when Boileau, as the student, took the oath (*Juro*), the ladies recited:

> *Vivat, vivat, vivat, cent fois vivat!*
> *Novus doctor, qui tam bene parlat!*
> *Mille, mille annis, et manget et bibat,*
> *Et seignat et tuat.*

(May he live, live, live, a hundred times live!
New doctor, who speaks so well!
A thousand years may he eat and drink,
And bleed and kill.)

The play was received hilariously by the public and of course infuriated the faculties of medicine. But Molière was not to enjoy his success for long. Seized on the stage by a coughing fit during the fourth performance, he died shortly after. The Church refused him Christian burial, on the grounds that he had been an actor who had never recanted his profession nor received the last sacrament. His wife Armande appealed to his patron, the king, and Molière was finally allowed to be buried in holy ground at night, though no hearse, bells, or prayers were permitted. Ninon's grief was doubly bitter — she had not only lost her rare friend but the Church had renewed its persecution of him right to the edge of the grave. Years later her spiritual heir, Voltaire, raged against Rousseau for seeming to approve the Church's attitude in this matter.

That same year, 1673, Ninon lost another of her friends, Madame de La Suze. They had had many good times together in the vigorous days of their youth, discussing till the small

hours their amours, composing poetry together, speculating on
the mystery of life. The shadows were beginning to lengthen.
Ninon was fifty.

Some three years after Molière's death, Madame de La
Sablière fell deeply in love with the marquis de La Fare. Four
years younger than Madame de La Sablière, he charmed her
with his easy grace, elegant manners, stimulating mind. He
believed in the essential goodness of passion and evidently convinced the virtuous Madame de La Sablière to throw restraint
to the winds for she gave herself utterly to him. She loved him
with a tender, sensitive, romantic love.

Ninon was apprehensive. She did not mind Madame de La
Sablière's giving La Fare her body — far from it. She liked the
Saint-Evremond in him, she found him most attractive, but
she feared that La Fare would not match the unalloyed, single-
minded love that Madame de La Sablière was perilously giving
him. Madame de La Sablière gloried unashamedly and openly
in the fullness of her passion. There were always killjoys.

"What!" said a magistrate who was a relative of hers.
"What, madame! Nothing but love and more love! Even the
animals [les bêtes] have but one season." Like a true daughter
of her century, Madame de La Sablière replied, "C'est que ce
sont des bêtes," which of course means "That's because they are
animals," but underlying it is the probable pun on *bêtes* meaning "stupid" as well as "animals." "That's because they are stupid." Ninon chuckled when she heard the bon mot but wished
that the easily hurt Madame de La Sablière would remember
the teachings of Epicurus, the master of Madame de La
Sablière's master, Gassendi, and accordingly moderate her passion with reason. However, Ninon soon saw it was useless to

try to stem the flood, and stepped aside, keeping her fingers crossed.

Her son by Villarceaux, Louis-François de Mornay, known as the chevalier de La Boissière, was growing up. On December 28, 1671, he is listed as a naval ensign at Toulon. Madame de La Sablière introduced Ninon to François d'Usson de Bonrepaus, who occupied a high post in the ministry of marine. La Boissière went in for some lively pranks which resulted in his being broken from his rank of ensign to a lower grade. Disturbed, Ninon appealed successfully to Bonrepaus who saw to it that La Boissière was reinstated within nineteen days of his demotion. Thus began a long correspondence showing Ninon as an anxious mother — sending her son money, bringing him home to nurse when he was wounded, urging him to write thank-you notes. Careful not to use "the style of a suppliant," she asked Bonrepaus to transfer La Boissière from Toulon to Brest where her old admirer, the maréchal d'Estrée, was in command. Bonrepaus not only complied, but La Boissière received a promotion to a lieutenancy as well. Ninon does not want to appear too obvious in thanking Bonrepaus for the influence he had exercised; so she tells him, in her usual succinct style, that she is grateful for the privilege of being a friend and not just for favors.

> I had always hoped, monsieur, to tell you in person that my gratitude is in no way conditional upon events, that I shall never forget your goodness, that I beg you to consider and believe that in me you have a friend as devoted as she is useless to you.

Bonrepaus became a very important man in the kingdom — rich, respected, honored by Louis XIV. Like most people,

Ninon liked people who liked her. She admits to Bonrepaus that she has been very fond of him since Madame de La Sablière told her of Bonrepaus's tenderness for her. Later we see Ninon in the role of protective mother, making excuses for her son:

> A poor boy, ill since a month, monsieur, and who had come to Paris to pay you his respects, prays me to reassure you concerning his apparent negligence. He has excused himself for not having had the honor of writing you on the grounds of violent pains which an old wound in his foot is inducing in his knee. Accept at the same time my assurance of my very humble service and of the genuine concern I have for anything pertaining to you. I often give proof of this to myself. Would to God I could similarly prove my concern to you — usefully, if you will allow me the term.

There is not much known about La Boissière. We do know he rose to be captain of a frigate and that he inherited his mother's passion for music. According to Bret, "All the musicians who, during his [La Boissière's] sojourn at Toulon, were going to and fro between Italy and France, never failed to descend on him; they were always perfectly received . . ."

While Ninon was standing on the sidelines anxiously watching the affair between Madame de La Sablière and the marquis de La Fare move toward its dénouement, material matters claimed some of her attention. She evidently believed in annuities, for beginning in 1669 she started buying them — enough to give her an income of 7000 livres ($14,000 to $35,000). Whether we take the lower or upper figure, Ninon thus guaranteed herself a comfortable living, though nothing permitting magnificence, for which she had no hankering anyway. Fortunately for her, the currency remained stable. If anything, there was deflation, due to scarcity of gold coins.

Besides putting her finances in order, Ninon finally took sole title in 1678, after a complicated legal proceeding, to the house on the rue des Tournelles,* which she had rented all the way back in 1657 and which four years later she bought in partnership with one Gérard du Bourg. The understanding with du Bourg was that Ninon would occupy the house — presumably paying du Bourg compensation — and that upon the death of one, the survivor would own the house outright. Du Bourg died first but his heirs contested Ninon's right to sole ownership. Ninon had to fight shrewdly to defend her position successfully. Ninon was an intellectual but like Voltaire, who would drop his writing to travel halfway across France to make a good deal, she was proficient in business. Several times in her lifetime we see her in legal wrangles, as we do others in her circle. The French upper class seems to have spent a good deal of the Splendid Century in enervating litigation.

The rue des Tournelles is just west of the present boulevard Beaumarchais. By our standards it is a relatively short street, about one-third of a mile long. The famous Porte Saint-Antoine, through which Queen Christina had made her entry into Paris, was hard by. So was the Château of the Bastille, guarding the Porte Saint-Antoine; Ninon could easily see its turrets from her house. The rue des Tournelles is said to have been one of the most "frequented and brilliant" streets in Paris. Nonetheless, the street may not have been well paved, if at all, for Ninon writes to Bonrepaus: "A coach on the rue des Tour-

---

* Today designated by 36 rue des Tournelles. Buildings did not have civic numbers then.

nelles is troublesome. I always take my little conveyance [sedan chair]." Perhaps she was cautioning him against coming in his grand coach for fear the muddy ruts would injure it. Even today one can still see evidence of solidity, dignity, and elegance in the houses which are of stone construction, five or six stories high, their portes-cochères giving on an interior court. The windows are fine, with Renaissance pediments. Over the windows and doorways there is stone carving, often delicate.

Ninon loved her house — her abode for the last forty-eight years of her life. The Inventory of Possessions shows she had a well-stocked cellar (not wine) containing, at the time of her death, eight loads of wood, 300 faggots, and five loads of coal. The kitchen, opening on the courtyard, boasted all the necessaries for Marguerite, the cook, and Catherine, the housemaid, to prepare the delicious meals which Ninon was known for: a commodious fireplace with spit, complete with pot hanging by a chain; a great oaken buffet on which shone a copper basin and which had shelves bearing chafing dishes, a fish kettle, frying pan, coffeepot, salt box, white marble mortar and pestle. On the wall was an imposing array of pots and pans, skewers, a gridiron, a dripping pan, chestnut roasters, sweetmeat tins, and a hook from which to hang meat.

Ninon's apartments, which were on the second story, consisted of an antechamber, a study, a small room or den facing the courtyard, and her bedroom overlooking the street. Guests first entered the study, its walls hung with Flemish tapestries. On the marble mantelpiece stood one of Ninon's prized possessions — a stately clock in an ebony case embellished with gilded copper. The decoration and fabrics imparted an air of gaiety and good taste, which carried throughout this floor. The den was a particularly charming room, the focal point of which was a fireplace flanked by a thermometer and barometer, with a fire screen of Chinese satin. Here Ninon kept most of her books — sixty volumes handsomely bound in leather. There was more than a touch of luxury in this retreat with its little bed covered in rich Indian silk, two small tables of rare woods inlaid with mother-of-pearl, armchairs cool and elegant in magnificent silks.

It was in the bedroom, however, hung with taffetas in a striped and checked design, that Ninon spent most of her time. Following the practice of the day, it was here that she entertained her guests, not just lovers. In winter she probably received in bed — the warmest place; in summer on a couch. The room must have been tremendous to accommodate all the furniture: Ninon's large bed, standing on oaken bases with carved pillars surmounted by a duchesse canopy; a silk-covered couch and a small bed with taffeta bolster and spread; six gilt chairs covered in red, a huge easy chair, three average-sized armchairs — two covered in red plush, one in tapestry — two little armchairs with black wood frames upholstered in green brocaded satin; two small oaken footstools covered in satin; seven graceful tables of assorted sizes and wood; an eighteen-drawer cedar bureau; a six-drawer secretary of inlaid wood ornamented in gold; a walnut desk; two little Chinese lacquered boxes. The floor was partially covered with Turkish rugs. Incidental pieces such as fine china, slender, gleaming candlesticks, and silver inkstands supplied harmonious accents.

The great bed sounds inviting, even without Ninon. Instead of our modern box spring, it had a box filled with horsehair; on top was a fustian-covered mattress filled with the finest of wool.

A soft bolster sat upon a quilted, lace bedspread. Ninon's comfortable and highly livable bedchamber had two foci — the imposing bed with its soft, taffeta curtains, and the fireplace with its andirons ornamented with four copper apples, its shovel, and tongs of polished iron. Over the fireplace was a gilt-framed mirror; on the walls were landscape paintings and portraits of friends, and a tableau of the Virgin, the infant Jesus, and Saint John. The clerk who made the inventory evidently did not think much of the religious painting, giving it a value of twenty sols — under $5.00. Since it probably had no artistic value, Emile Magne speculates that it was acquired late in life to act as a sacred counterpoise in a room which had long served as a temple of love. This is curious, for Magne himself claims that "she experienced no pangs of remorse and never felt called upon to expel from her surroundings pieces of furniture and other objects which were the silent witnesses of her former licentiousness." If Ninon did attempt to redress the balance in this manner, the effort was certainly half-hearted, if the official's estimate of the picture's worth is at all accurate. The presence of the third-rate picture with its sacred theme is a bit of a puzzle. Possibly one of the many priests trying to reform her gave it to her, and she did not want to hurt his feelings by putting it in the attic.

Where Ninon ate is unclear. The inventory lists sumptuous* table silver but does not indicate where it was used. Nor does it mention her famous "yellow room" which she had lent to Madame Scarron and Villarceaux some forty-five years before her death. Presumably she had redecorated in the meantime. This modest mansion had a good-sized garden at the rear. Her

* Valued at 1392 livres ($2784 to $6960).

staff was small — by contemporary standards. Unless she omitted a servant or two from her will, she had four domestics: a valet, his sister who was chambermaid, a cook, and a maid of all work. Earlier she probably had two menservants, as her sedan chair* required one bearer fore and one aft. Perhaps when the vinaigrette — a chair with wheels requiring only one man — came on the market, Ninon bought one or, alternatively, maybe she had given up using her chair in her very old age. The servants lived on the floor above Ninon; the fourth and fifth floors seem to have been used mainly for storage.

There is no record of the conversations at Ninon's table. From what contemporaries said, for brilliance and charm they have seldom been equaled. But they were not all pyrotechnical displays. That would have been somewhat of a strain on the participants, and if there was one indispensable characteristic of the well-bred Frenchman, it was his relaxed, aisé manner. Tallemant does record a short scene but it shows Ninon not in one of her scintillating moments but in a situation where her good heart has made her concerned. The year is 1672, and it was just after the young Monsieur de Longueville, natural son of the duc de La Rochefoucauld, had begged Ninon to save him from the clutches of the "fat marquise de Castelnau" who lusted after him. On this particular evening he had come to sup at Ninon's with his father, the duke, with Boileau, and the comte de Dangeau, a graduate of Ninon's School for Gallantry. La Rochefoucauld brought his son to Ninon's in the hope that he would acquire the social graces in her company. The conversation was on the subject of France's gilded youth and how it would per-

---

* She had the right, according to d'Hozier, to have a carriage with her coat of arms but evidently did not own one — perhaps because it was too expensive.

form in the coming military campaign — who would distinguish himself with feats of valor, and so on. Dangeau, who had no use for heroics, was very frank: "As for me, I intend to do my duty and nothing more." To which Mademoiselle de Lanclos replied; "I have no doubt that you will conduct yourself very prudently, but it is this young lord here [motioning toward Monsieur de Longueville] who I fear will do something rash." Ninon's premonition was right. Longueville was killed in that very campaign at the Crossing of the Rhine, so often celebrated in painting and words by Louis XIV's sycophants.

Ninon's forebodings about Madame de La Sablière were also all too accurate. The latter's love affair with La Fare started out at a dizzy height from which there was but one way to go. Both had artistic temperaments; they understood and adored each other. Sophisticated Parisian society, not used to such purity of passion, marveled and watched uneasily. Madame de La Sablière, who had become free on the death of her estranged husband, expected marriage. But she was a romantic in a classical age — an Epicurean manquée. On the other hand La Fare was a confirmed Epicurean bachelor capable, however, of occasional, unsustained involvement of the heart. La Fare's cronies jeered at his unwonted constancy. He took to gambling and occasional side affairs with other women; eventually Mademoiselle de Champmeslé, Ninon's former rival for the affections of young Charles de Sésigné, administered the coup de grâce.

The poor "turtledove," as Madame de Sévigné used to call Madame de La Sablière, having flown in the clouds for about three years, fell to earth with a thud, the song gone from her

throat forever. Ninon, the confidante of both lovers, strove in
vain to reconcile them. Patiently she listened to both sides.
Deeply worried, she unburdens herself to her good friend Bonrepaus:

> I have received a letter from Madame de La Sablière. This un-
> fortunate woman evokes a great pity in me. I see Monsieur de
> La Fare every day and I am like the judges of Parlement who
> never cease hearing the pros and the cons . . . I am sorry for
> them both. Truly heaven's gift is cruel when an excess of sensi-
> tivity and tenderness causes much more suffering than joy. As for
> me, I need nothing but consolation. I am entirely at the disposal
> of her who has earned my esteem and friendship. To me she
> seems alone too much.

Try as she did, Ninon could not comfort the brokenhearted
Madame de La Sablière, who decided to follow Madame de
Sévigné's advice to devote her life to good works at the Hospital for Incurables. She gave up her fine town house — scene of
many a distinguished and gay gathering — and moved to
smaller quarters, taking La Fontaine with her in her baggage.
The famous writer of fables about animals was grief-stricken
at this second sorrow which had befallen his princess with the
ashen hair. But when Madame de La Sablière started spending
more and more time at the hospital, and less and less at home,
the good man lost his equilibrium. Ninon would go to visit
him, find him wandering around the house, dazed by the virtual abandonment. She did all she could to console him, to
cheer him up, but her efforts were largely futile. All through
the 1680s Ninon tirelessly labored to help Madame de La Sablière and La Fontaine, who were both sinking. Grimly Ninon

stuck to her duty. "Durability in friendship," she wrote Bonrepaus, "is not less rare than durability in love. There was a time when I cared only for the latter, now I care only for the former, and I but seek the opportunity to demonstrate it to you." Ninon was not being accurate. She had always prized durability in friendship, had never cared about durability in love — unless she was going back to her pre-Coligny times, to the days before her disillusionment. But especially the seventeenth-century French could not resist the temptation of minting an epigram.

In 1683, Saint-Evremond, hearing of La Fontaine's sorry situation, endeavored with the help of rich friends to induce him to come to London. La Fontaine did not go. Ninon refers to this in her letter to Saint-Evremond of 1687: ". . . I have known that you wanted La Fontaine in England; Paris enjoys him but little [nowadays]; his head is badly weakened. It is the destiny of poets; Tasso and Lucretius both experienced it."

Finally Madame de La Sablière moved completely to the hospital in order to be closer at all times to her charges. She had cancer now, aged but forty-six, and was living only on milk and mysticism. To Bonrepaus, ever grateful for his kindness to her son, Ninon wrote: "I have only words while you oblige with deeds; please forgive me. How I wish Madame de La Sablière would come back. Surely at this time she'd be as well off [in her own house] as at the Incurables." A year later she was dead.

Through all her travail with Madame de La Sablière, Ninon never broke with La Fare, who had loved Madame de La Sablière in his cavalier fashion — a fashion which Ninon was well equipped to understand. She had always been keenly sus-

ceptible to his relaxed, graceful manner, his elegance, his refined mind, and, importantly, his handsome face and knightly
bearing. "The days that I see Monsieur de La Fare," she writes
in an undated letter to an unknown, "are my best days. His
lofty poetry comforts me."

Ninon had probably been a little bit in love with La Fare —
twenty-one years her junior — the whole time.

\*

"From Montaigne and Charron to Saint-Evremond and
Ninon, and from Ninon to Voltaire is but a handbreadth . . .
Thus is it that in the process of time, a few minds constitute
the chain." The speaker is Sainte-Beuve. What Sainte-Beuve is
saying is that Ninon is an important link in the continuity of
free thought and liberalism from the Renaissance to the
eighteenth century. The tribute came about 150 years after
Ninon's death. She would have been well pleased but perhaps
a little surprised. She probably had no idea when she was fighting the Society of the Holy Sacrament, lending aid and comfort
to Molière in his struggle against hypocrisy, providing at the
rue des Tournelles a gracious atmosphere for independent
minds to exchange ideas, that she was entering into history.
How did she know when she took the torch from Saint-
Evremond at the time of his flight from France that she was to
hand it on to an eleven-year-old precocious child — Voltaire —
some forty-four years later? She was not even aware that she
*had* taken the torch from Saint-Evremond, who had left in a
hurry with no goodbyes, no handing on of a spiritual testament, no benediction. And what, at the age of eighty-two, did
she know of the future that lay in store for the little Voltaire,

although she did discern something remarkable about the boy, for she left him 1000 livres* ($2000 to $5000) in her will "so that he might have books." The fact that Ninon was largely unconscious of her role in history contributes to her charm — she was always simple and unaffected.

Mention has been made earlier of what seemed to be a rather remarkable coincidence — that the life of Ninon and the history of libertinism or free thought in the seventeenth century ran parallel. Upon closer inspection, however, the coincidence is less remarkable when we consider that Ninon's life, to a large degree, was the embodiment of free thought, and that therefore her life and the history of seventeenth-century libertinism can more accurately be described as being congruent rather than parallel. When libertinism enjoyed fair weather, so did Ninon, for the simple reason that she was a living, if not *the* living expression of it. Thus, in the 1630s and up to the time of Louis XIII's death in 1643, when libertinism groped stealthily behind shuttered windows, Ninon moved tentatively in life, unsure of herself. It was not just the awkwardness of adolescence and early youth. The Libertinage Erudit, the libertinism of Gassendi and his colleagues,† was a covert affair; it was contemporary with Ninon's teens. After the harsh suppression of the Libertinage Flamboyant, which hit its high point at the time of Ninon's birth, the Erudite Libertins deemed it prudent to dissemble. Most of them went through the motions of practicing Catholicism publicly while thinking their own thoughts privately. Though not a professional scholar nor a professional

---

* Voltaire says 2000 livres. He wrote so fast and so much he did not always have time to check details, and by that time he was so rich that 1000 livres difference did not loom large.
† Gabriel Naudé and La Mothe Le Vayer.

philosopher, Ninon nonetheless shared their general outlook. When the Good Regency smiled on libertinism, elegantly exemplified by Ninon and her set, Ninon's life became one gay romp. Paris was a great, golden, Elysian field for her. Then came the Fronde, its defeat, the rise of absolutism, orthodoxy, the renewed suppression of the independent thinkers. Ninon's fortunes hit their nadir — she was imprisoned. But Ninon never gave up. Other libertins, less courageous, more discreet, struck the flag and either changed coats to be in style with the prevailing season or went underground. Ninon persisted. Aid arrived unexpectedly in the shape of the misshapen Christina of Sweden. The Society of the Holy Sacrament had to retreat when Ninon was released from Lagny with honor but retreated only to lick its wounds. Molière burst upon the scene, and the society attacked him tooth and claw. With characteristic consistency Ninon rallied to his defense. In 1660, Ninon and Molière won an engagement when the extremist Society of the Holy Sacrament was officially banned. But Ninon and Molière could not rest on their oars. They fought a brilliant holding action, while exiled Saint-Evremond applauded from England. Gassendi was gone but his disciples were carrying on with a vigor which would have frightened him. Gassendi opened the door to the light of Reason but feared to cross the threshold. Like a good, tolerant Catholic, he preferred to inhale the fresh air from the window, praising God that He had let him see the light. It was as if the glory outside was too strong, and he modestly (and prudently) preferred to contemplate it from within. But his disciples — Molière, Chapelle, Bernier, Madame de La Sablière, La Fontaine, Saint-Evremond, Ninon — rushed through the door at which old Gassendi had stood, and gloried joyfully, if hazardously, in the sunshine of untrammeled thought.

The bigots attacked again around 1672, aiming to blacklist the philosophy of Gassendi's old opponent, Descartes. In a significant joining of skills the Cartesian Boileau collaborated with the Gassendist Molière to pulverize the stifling department of theology at the Sorbonne with lethal ridicule. Ninon had seconded Molière and Boileau in this sortie and delighted to see the forces of reason (for both Descartes and Gassendi held reason dear) unite in the battle against obscurantism. Molière died soon after, but the tide was turning. Libertinism was fearlessly, proudly emerging in strength from its hushed gatherings of inquiring minds. It was no longer on the defensive, unsure of its destiny, or racked by pessimistic fears that the odds against it were too heavy. By 1680, a new spirit of optimism infused the old bones of Gassendism; it was confident it held the key to the future — Reason. With Reason man would hack away encrusting superstition and oppressive dogmatism. Reason would unlock man's energies, and nature, whose harmonies the rationalists adored, would gladly yield up her enormous bounty. New standard-bearers arose — Fontenelle, who as a young man paid tribute to Ninon, and Bayle — doughty libertins both. Fontenelle and Bayle helped the tired Ninon hold aloft the banner of free thought until Voltaire was old enough to accept it. The tide of libertinism was running strongly now in 1680. Its many adherents could feel that the world was at last at the bright dawn, rejoiced that the voice of the uncowed thinker was heard in the land — loud and clear. It is this voice which Paul Hazard calls in a memorable phrase, the "Libertinage Triomphant." Ninon was its high priestess, its link with its distant past, its guardian angel through weather fair and foul, its ornament, its pride. She had made port at last. It was her hour of triumph.

There was no blare of trumpets, no parades, none of the trappings of military victory that the word *triumph* evokes. It can be summed up in two words: respectability and recognition. But it should be remembered that Ninon was far less conscious than historians are of the drama in which she was playing a significant part. She never took the field, as did some of the ladies in the Fronde. Ninon's terrain was the salon. It was there that quietly but resolutely, in an atmosphere not of war but of peace, of exquisite refinement, she provided a milieu in which free thought was kept alive. There was nothing of the cloak and dagger or cabal about Ninon's salon. Outwardly it resembled social gatherings such as occurred in many other drawing rooms. It had no agenda, program, or stated objectives. But, says Sainte-Beuve, "it corrected the tone of the hôtel de Rambouillet." It was far less formal and, according to Voltaire, "more natural and philosophical." Its main distinction was the lack of any restraint on subject matter other than that dictated by good taste, its encouragement of tolerance, its insistence on conversational expertise, its charm. Without the latter characteristic — charm — it would not have existed, for people came to Ninon's primarily to enjoy themselves. That edification went along with enjoyment is merely an indication of the caliber and interests of the guests.

The company would arrive around five o'clock. It was very diverse: philosophers like Bernier and (later) Fontenelle; generals like Miossens and the Great Condé; literary men — Boileau, Racine, La Fontaine; the master of maxims, La Rochefoucauld; the musician, Lulli; the painter, Mignard; the scientist, Huygens; ambassadors, courtiers and abbés — many abbés. Crusty Saint-Simon records what for him was a paean:

Ninon had famous friends of all kinds, and so much intelligence that she kept them all, and maintained harmony between them, or at the very least there was not a speck of quarreling. All went off in her house with a respect and apparent propriety which the loftiest princesses with their foibles seldom commanded. She numbered among her friends the most hand-picked and eminent persons at Court, so much so that it became à la mode to be received at her house, and this made sense owing to the contacts one made there. Never any gambling or boisterous guffaws, or disputes . . . much wit, highly polished, news old and current and always without opening the door to backbiting; everything there was delicate, light, moderate, and nourished the conversation which she knew how to sustain by her wit and her command of information about every age.

The respect, strange as it may seem, that she had acquired, the number and distinction of her friends and acquaintances operated, when her physical charms ebbed, to attract society to her, when seemliness . . . deterred her from mixing any longer the body and the mind . . . Her conversation was charming, impartial, dependable, discreet in the highest degree . . . one could say she was virtuous and full of probity . . .

There are several other passages in contemporary memoirs, all similar. "Her mind," reports Angélique Petit, "is lively and penetrating and always attunes itself to the people whom she is with." Saint-Simon's reference to the absence of gambling is illuminating, for gambling was viciously prevalent. At Ninon's, people found there was thrill enough just in her company. The princesse Palatine, whose son Philippe, duc d'Orléans, became regent upon the death of Louis XIV, has this to say of the decorum at Ninon's: "My son is one of her friends. She likes him very much. I wish he would go there more often and keep company with her rather than with his bosom friends. She would inspire the loftiest and noblest sentiments in him — something they don't." The Palatine's party-loving son may not have spent as much time with the aging Ninon as his mother would have liked, but some of Ninon's teaching — or rather attitude, for she did no formal proselytizing — must have sunk in, because the regent was well known later for his emancipated ideas.

Women, too, flocked to the rue des Tournelles. Madame de Sévigné concedes this: " . . . thus she [Ninon] gathers everybody to her in her old age — both men and women; but were she now to have only women, it would not bother her, having had enough men in the days of her youth." Madame de Sévigné need not have concerned herself, for the men continued visiting. Eventually even she, who had lost both a husband and son to Ninon, thawed before the soft, late afternoon warmth of her former rival. She was delighted to see her grandson, the marquis de Grignan, received by Ninon.

Despite the occasional infirmity, Ninon's autumnal days were on the whole mellow ones, now that the time of hot passion and strident struggle was behind. Her old friend Charleval, who had vainly hoped for years to become her lover, still visited. His desire long cooled, he was more content in her company now, wanting nothing but her priceless friendship, which she gladly accorded him. They would now theorize about love, giving Ninon the opportunity to reiterate her unchanged view that desire was a delicious but a sometime thing, mysterious in its coming and mysterious in its going, whereas affection could be soundly and reasonably based, and therefore lasting. Charleval's poetic talent had not deserted him:

> No longer am I a bird of the fields,
> I have joined those warblers of the Tournelles
> Who sing of love year in, year out,
> Who pity the turtledoves
> That love only in springtime.

The guests would urge Ninon to play the lute for them, and occasionally she did. Saint-Evremond too had musicales frequently in London, composing, playing and directing quartets. By letter he inquires about Ninon's lute, and it is unlikely that Ninon ever abandoned one of her principal passions, even if the season for madrigals was past. The guests loved to discuss music with her, drawing her out on opera and matters of technique and taste. Ninon sometimes would arrange little concerts. At one of these a German, Pantaléon Hebenstreit, gave a performance on a new instrument, the dulcimer. The abbé de Châteauneuf tells about it:

> One could see on the face of Leontium [Ninon] the different emotions and passions which the musician was trying to express, for she wore an expression always in harmony, and one would have said that each sound was for her a sentiment. The lively impression that he made on the soul of Mademoiselle Lenclos passed into his own and seemed, in reentering him, to redouble the tenderness of his playing . . . never had he felt so powerfully inspired.

Another evening the discussion was on opera of which Ninon was not overfond, feeling that the singing of words in dramatic form should be confined to prologues, invocations, and choruses; she approved Molière's use of it in interludes, but she did not want to sit through a whole evening of it. Opera had only been introduced in France around the mid-century and was primitive, although some of Ninon's comments have a modern ring: "They have presumed to put into song an entire tragedy from one end to the other, right down to the dialogues of a prince and his confidant and the orders he gives, even to the most indifferent recitations. How is it possible for such a profusion of harmony not to weary attention? This ends up by making the spectator of a divertissement, where art and magnificence have not been spared for the pleasure of the eyes and ears, wish it were finished."

The eminent composer Lulli is said to have felt that Ninon's opinion could make or break a new work. He particularly loved to get Ninon to talk on expression in music. "Sensitivity," she explained, "is the soul of song and no matter how little taste the listener has, he will always prefer it to the most expert technique, for the latter caresses the ear only, whereas the former goes straight to the heart. A fine talent, a beautiful voice, and an excellent touch are appealing and admired, but a musician is moving only if he himself is moved and feels himself what he is trying to communicate."

One of the guests was retelling the story of the Spartan, Timothy, who had made the mistake of adding a string to the lyre. He was thus accused of following the penchant of Sparta's enemies, the Athenians, who let themselves be softened by music's charms. Timothy was consequently punished.

"In that case," said Ninon, "there wouldn't be enough punishments for our musician [the German, Hebenstreit] who has added more than a hundred strings to the dulcimer."

The guest replied, "He could traverse the world [today] as much as he pleased — he would not find any Spartan in his path." The hour was getting late and Ninon, no longer robust, could not stand late hours.

"What time did the Spartans used to go to bed?" inquired Ninon softly. Châteauneuf adds that Ninon had a knack for bringing conversations, which were lasting too long, to an end without hurting anyone's feelings or giving the impression of boredom. But boorish showoffs she made short shrift of. A certain Rémond, variously nicknamed Rémond the Greek (because of his erudition in Greek), and Rémond the Devil (for his amorous exploits), was getting on her nerves. Saint-Simon tells us, ". . . He manifested . . . much effrontery, a high opinon of himself and contempt for others . . ." To make matters worse, Rémond was not very prepossessing, having a big nose, protruding eyes, and a raspy voice.

What triggered Ninon's anger was his advertising that "she had formed him" at her school. This was too much. Ninon dismissed him, asserting, "I've been the dupe of his Greek erudition and I've banished him from my school, because he has an awkwardness both in philosophy and society: he did not fit into company as intelligent as mine. When God had made man, he rued what he had done; I feel the same about Rémond." However, in a letter written in her eighties, Ninon mentions familiarly a Monsieur Raimond who may be Rémond the Greek, restored to grace. If so, Ninon, like God, repented of her anger.

Ninon never seems to have lost her art of elegant ridicule which so delighted her friends. Time and translation have in varying degrees dulled the point of her sallies, but some still retain considerable flavor. Of the skirt-chasing abbé Testu, Ninon gaily circulated the rumor that he was slated to be given

a bishopric of women only. The abbé wanted to "convert" *
Ninon. "He believes," said she, "that that will bring him
honor, and that the king will give him an abbey; but if he is
relying on my soul to make his fortune, he runs the risk of
dying without a benefice."

The court portrait painter, Mignard, was complaining to
Ninon that his daughter had no memory. "You may think
yourself lucky," Ninon assured him, "because [at least] she will
never be able to quote." Seventeenth-century society was particularly impatient with showoffs.

Ninon did not think too highly of a certain Madame du Fresnoy. The minister of war, Louvois, had persuaded the king to
make her a lady of the Queen's Bedchamber. "The king,"
wrote Madame de La Roche, "has created, in the house of the
queen, the post of Lady of the Bedchamber for Madame du
Fresnoy . . . Ninon has made a joke about it . . . she says
that Monsieur de Louvois has done in this case what Caligula†
did when he made his horse Consul."

Louis XIV himself is said to have feared Ninon's gibes. "At
each change in his seraglio," states Arsène Houssaye, "he
would constantly inquire, 'What does Ninon say?' What singular times! Ninon was the conscience of the king and of public opinion."

Louis had a good memory. One day a courtier related a discussion which had taken place between Ninon and the abbé de
Dangeau on the immortality of the soul. Citing as her authority a Carthusian monk, Dom Pelot, Ninon had denied survival

* The French used *convert* also to mean bringing a nonobservant Catholic back
to the fold, not just to get a person to change his religion.
† The Roman emperor.

of the soul after death. Three years later Father Ananat proposed Pelot for a bishopric. "How now, Father," said Louis coldly — "you propose to me a man who does not believe in the immortality of the soul?"

When Ninon's quondam lover, the chevalier de Méré, an old friend of Pascal, was in his early seventies, he dropped in at the mansion of the duchesse de La Feuillade, just a stone's throw from the rue des Tournelles. The duchess was a religious mystic of the Jansenist stripe, having been personally indoctrinated by Pascal, one of the adornments of Jansenism in its prime. She was a good woman, and Ninon, her inquiring mind still searching, loved to explore matters of the spirit with her. Neither made the slightest attempt to convert the other. Ninon happened to be with the duchess when Méré called. Méré, the supreme arbiter of the credentials of the honnête homme, had been tutor decades before to the young Françoise d'Aubigné, later Madame Scarron. A thorough man, he had essayed to instruct her both mentally and physically, achieving, to his disappointment, more success in the former endeavor than the latter. He had found Ninon just the reverse. Though once again he would have liked to have been the complete tutor and have possessed Ninon body and soul, he had gained more success with her body than her mind. This seems at first blush a bit strange, for Ninon, as a would-be honnête homme, might have been expected to have yielded totally to the doyen of honnêtes hommes, but the chevalier tended to be somewhat conceited,* a characteristic for which Ninon had a low tolerance. Nonetheless she is said to have had a child by Méré, so it is not astonish-

---

* Méré thought nothing of presuming to give lessons in mathematics to Pascal — something like carrying coals to Newcastle.

ing that he exhibited considerable emotion on seeing her again after a long absence. He was passing through Paris and had thought to talk about their mutual friend Pascal with the duchesse de La Feuillade. The three wallowed for hours in the past. On returning home, the chevalier, ever gallant, wrote Ninon:

I swear to you, mademoiselle, that I have never in all my life felt a purer joy than when I met you at Madame la duchesse de Le Feuillade's. It was one afternoon, you will recall, when you two were alone together, that I intruded upon you. You were perhaps even a little put out to be interrupted in such an agreeable conversation. I did not attempt to conceal my gratitude for the pleasure I had in seeing and speaking to you again, and I believe it would show a lack of appreciation, or at least civility, were I not to tell you I felt a little hurt by your attitude. In truth, mademoiselle, to get to the point and not engage in too great subtlety, it is not for yourself alone that you are endowed with such rare qualities and such a lovable nature; they are also for the pleasure and happiness of deserving mankind. Decorum and decency are much in your debt, and I make bold to assure you that nobody in this world knows better than I how wonderful you are. If only I had the wit to publish abroad your excellence as I know it, I could perhaps add something very exquisite and fragrant to your reputation. When I saw you again the other day I fell anew under your spell and especially appreciated that after such a long absence you seemed as sweet to me as if I had never lost sight of you and also that you did me the honor of permitting me to visit you as if I had never ceased to do so. I humbly tender you a thousand thanks, mademoiselle, and I beg you will remember, and not be annoyed at, my gratitude.

Ninon treasured the letter, happy to see that the chevalier's right hand had not lost its grace, sad when he returned to

Poitou. There he died in 1685, the fateful year of the Revocation* of the Edict of Nantes, which some historians (probably unjustly) lay at the door of Ninon's former friend, Françoise d'Aubigné Scarron, now become the mighty Madame de Maintenon, wife of Louis XIV.

* Depriving Protestants of civil and religious liberty, the Revocation was a brutal attempt to force them to convert to Catholicism. It led to many atrocities and the flight of thousands of Protestants, whose loss contributed significantly to France's decline.

## ~~ Chapter 12 ~~

### Grace in One Autumnal Face

NINON's and Madame Scarron's paths had diverged radically since the days when they had shared one bed for three months. When Madame de Montespan needed someone to put in charge of her natural children by Louis XIV, she shortsightedly secured the position for the widow Scarron, thereby bringing about her own undoing. In 1674, Louis gave Madame Scarron a Christmas present — 240,000 livres ($480,000 to $1,200,000) to buy the estate of Maintenon. When Françoise Scarron returned to Paris from her new marquisate, Louis addressed her before all the court as Madame de Maintenon. "It is true," she wrote, "that the king called me Madame de Maintenon and that I had the imbecility to blush. The friends of my husband are wrong to accuse me of having connived with the king for this change." It is impossible to know whether Madame de Maintenon was including Ninon among these particular friends of Scarron, but for a long time now Madame de Maintenon had deemed it politic to divert attention from her former role as wife of the libertin Scarron, and as intimate of their irreverent friends like Ninon.

Moral reformation was in the air at Court, for Louis's conscience was bothering him more and more. Sensing this, Françoise played up her piety, combining religion and charm — a powerful cocktail at this juncture in Louis's life. The king, powerless to give up his mistresses, much though his mother and the Church had urged him to do, gradually came to the conclusion that if sin he must, he should sin with the minimum of impiety. He began to associate the ravishing scarlet Madame de Montespan with temptation and the devil, whereas he linked the somberly dressed, fanatically devout Madame de Maintenon with piety and God. Whether Françoise became his mistress at this time is uncertain. The wags undoubtedly thought so and dubbed her "Madame de Maintenant" — Madame of the Moment.

Though unquestionably Françoise's star was rapidly rising, she did not have plain sailing all the time. Her brother Charles, for one, was a constant worry. A wastrel and ne'er-do-well like his father, he was forever embarrassing his decorous sister with reminders of her past, was continually asking for a handout. A letter to Ninon from Françoise, probably spurious, nonetheless reflects their relationship at the time.

> Versailles, November 12, 1679
>
> Continue, mademoiselle, to give good advice to Monsieur d'Aubigné [Françoise's brother]. He has need of lessons from Leontium [Ninon]. The counsel of a charming friend persuades more than that of a severe sister.
>
> Madame de Coulanges has given me assurances of your friendship which have flattered me. What you have heard in my favor is nothing but empty noise; I am a stranger in this atmosphere . . . without friends other than self-centered people whom the slightest change in fortune will turn against me, without relatives other than people who ask favors unceasingly and are always without merit. You enjoy complete liberty; I live in perpetual

slavery. Believe me, my beautiful mademoiselle (for you will never cease to be), the intrigues of the Court are much less agreeable than the commerce of the mind . . . Continue, I pray you, your kindness to Monsieur d'Aubigné.

In 1683, the ignored queen, Maria Theresa, obligingly died. Louis did not wait long to marry Madame de Maintenon — secretly. Françoise was disappointed that she was not made queen, but then she did understand that her blood was not royal. Françoise was an understanding person.

It is a rather remarkable coincidence that the careers of both Ninon and Françoise should have reached their apex around the same time. The Libertinage Triomphant, which Ninon could rightfully wear as a garland around her temples, dates from around 1680. Françoise, too, at last achieved her dream of honor and power. Her fairy-tale progress from the jail at Niort to the steps of the throne at Versailles was to bring her greater power — much greater — than had she been queen. But happiness and peace eluded her. "She could," says Le Roux de Lincy, "have acquired great glory if she had wanted to bring to the throne the shudderings, the cries of despair of the Protestants who had been her brothers." Then, evidently of the school which believes that Madame de Maintenon was involved in the nefarious Revocation of the Edict of Nantes, he adds, "She could have been an angel for France, she was its flail." Ninon's admirer, the princesse Palatine, sister-in-law of Louis, was briefer, calling Madame de Maintenon "the old whore." When she felt more kindly disposed, she termed her "the old mess."

Françoise did not rise when the king entered the room in private, though she had the good sense to appear meek and unassuming in public. In her *Memoirs* Madame de Caylus writes,

"This . . . dame was so feared at Court that one would have offended God sooner than her. One word from her sufficed to bring banishment or favor, and never was an idol more the object of so much homage . . ."

But Louis was both inconsiderate and difficult. Françoise was forty-eight in 1683 and had probably never been passionate. That was probably what Ninon meant when she called her "gauche" in her famous letter answering Saint-Evremond's query as to whether Françoise and Villarceaux had been lovers. But Louis was three years younger and had always been passionate. Saint-Simon records that "no matter how bad she might be feeling, the king went to her at his ordinary time and did whatever he had planned." Furthermore, the strain of always appearing agreeable to Louis, of forcing a smile first thing in the morning whether she had spent a bad night or not, was all but unbearable. With remarkable self-knowledge Françoise wrote:

> I am perhaps now punished with an excess of favor, as if God had said to me in anger: "You want glory and praise. Good! You shall have them until you are cloyed and they will be your torment in this life."

And again:

> I can't possibly make you see the boredom which devours the great! . . . Don't you see I am dying of sadness in the midst of riches difficult to imagine and to which I don't succumb only by the grace of God? . . . I have attained to favor, and I protest to you that all the stages leave a frightening void, a disquietude, a lassitude, an envy to know something else, because in all that there is no satisfaction.

254 Mademoiselle Libertine

Some historians (and moralists) love to contrast the years of Françoise after she married Louis with those of Ninon's early old age. On the one hand they show Ninon happy with her friends in the unpretentious rue des Tournelles, and on the other hand Françoise tormented in sumptuous Versailles. This is not entirely true. Ninon had enjoyed so intensely the thrill of living life fully and adventurously that she could not but be painfully vulnerable to the grayness of advancing age. She must have communicated this to Saint-Evremond in a letter (now lost), for Saint-Evremond refers to the subject in his answer.*

"Your life, my dearest, has been too illustrious for it not to continue so right to the end. Don't let Monsieur de La Rochefoucauld's inferno terrify you: it was a studied inferno from which he wanted to mint a maxim." La Rochefoucauld had earlier said to Ninon: "Old age is the inferno of women," and evidently Ninon, in her sixties at the time of writing Saint-Evremond, thought she detected evidence of what La Rochefoucauld had said long ago and had, as usual, unburdened herself to Saint-Evremond who, as usual, gallantly reassured her.

Ninon had come to understand all too well Saint-Evremond's teachings of decades earlier, when he had exhorted her to terminate her three-year liaison with Villarceaux and to come back from the countryside to her host of admirers in Paris. His haunting lines were returning to mock her.

> One must burn with an active flame,
> Lively, brilliant and always fleeting;
> Be inconstant as long as one can,
> For a time comes . . .

* Of uncertain date — probably between 1681 and 1686.

That time had come. To begin with, Ninon was finding her early old age, with its relative inactivity, the harder to bear because of the sharp contrast with her unusually extended activities, now ended, in the piquant playgrounds of love; additionally, she was experiencing a letdown from the exciting if perilous days of her struggle with the bigots. But perhaps more importantly, she was likely paying the price for practicing what she preached. As probably the century's leading feminist, Ninon, in her disapproval of seventeenth-century marriage, in her determination to live like a bachelor honnête homme, had denied herself the comfort of a family in her later years. True she had a son, but he did not live in Paris and she saw him seldom; she had no other relatives who meant anything to her. She had outlived a number of close friends who had substituted heretofore for kin. Saint-Evremond was far away. The new, young friends could not fill the void.

Ninon, like Madame de Maintenon, was learning that one never wins but one loses. In partially winning her battle for women's rights and dignity, she had had to forgo family. In winning her way to power, Françoise had had to prejudice her femininity, her joie de vivre, her ease of conscience. The historians and moralists are of course right in holding that Ninon was far better off than Françoise, but the main difference lay in the fact that Ninon had come to terms with herself and that Françoise had not, rather than in the contrast of an idyllic golden age on the modest rue des Tournelles and a pathetic, tortured middle and old age at golden Versailles. Françoise, like the troubled sea in Isaiah, could find no rest.

*

Ninon seems to have met the advancing years with both spirit and intelligence. Always a reader, she had more time now in her late sixties to give to books, particularly philosophy. Her salon gave her great satisfaction, growing more renowned and prized year by year. It also gave her life structure. The guests came in the afternoon, seemingly almost every day, and left just before darkness, for they wanted to get home before the footpads prowled. Thus, the long winter nights, necessitating an early termination to social gatherings, were hard on Ninon, whose guests were not all mighty aristocrats with armed escorts, but included many intellectuals, some of whom may or may not have had the price to pay public torchbearers to light them home. The torchbearers bore notched, burning candles and charged by the notch, with extra for lighting the customer inside the building to an upstairs apartment.

Ninon cultivated her friendships. Dipping her quill in the silver inkstand on the writing desk with the gold and marquetry in the corner of her vast bedroom, she penned short notes frequently. To an unidentified person she writes, probably not untypically:

> My first action, this morning, has been to go and look for that book for you in the attic. It is a good way to begin the day. I mightn't have done it for anyone else but it seems that we didn't get along any too well yesterday. I have been reproaching myself on that account. I don't like friendships which start with a rush and end equally fast.

One day Marie Poron, the upstairs chambermaid, lay before Ninon a letter in a hand familiar to her from the days of long ago. It was an invitation to Versailles from Madame de Maintenon. At an appointed time a carriage would pick her up and convey her to the palace. Puzzled, Ninon bid Marie Poron tell the royal messenger she would accept. She and the aloof Madame de Maintenon had had very little contact in the last two decades. Saint-Simon tells about it:

> She [Ninon] had been the intimate friend of Madame de Maintenon all the time the latter lived in Paris. Madame de Maintenon did not like Ninon to be spoken of in her presence, but she dared not disavow her. She wrote to her with friendliness from time to time until her death. L'Enclos . . . was not so reserved with her intimate friends, and when she interested herself strongly on someone's behalf, or for some cause, which she only did sparingly, she used to write to Madame de Maintenon who obliged her efficiently and promptly; but, since her [Maintenon's] accession to greatness, they did not see each other more than two or three times, and then very secretly.

A few days after Ninon had accepted Françoise's invitation, a comfortable carriage, but not bearing the royal coat of arms so as to preserve secrecy, called early one morning at the rue des Tournelles for the sixteen-mile drive to Versailles. The exact date of the visit is unknown — probably around 1690. It was a time when gaiety had departed from Versailles. The princesse Palatine held that the Jesuit, Père Lachaise, and Madame de Maintenon had convinced Louis that only by the Revocation of the Edict of Nantes and by strict piety could he wipe out the stain of his sins with his former mistresses. The princess may have been unfair to Madame de Maintenon so far as her part in the Revocation was concerned, but the king's morganatic wife had certainly got rid of the mistresses. Louis, gloomy and irritable, was still waging his interminable wars, but no longer

successfully. His treatment of the French Protestants had alienated his Protestant allies abroad. Ninon, of course, knew about
the outcries of the peasantry, ragged and starving from the ex-
pense of the wars. Along with Saint-Evremond she deplored
the heartless persecution of the Protestants which led many
thousands of France's best citizens to flee, thereby accelerating,
if not initiating, France's long decline. Things had been much
worse since Louis had been induced to give up the official mistresses. Doubtless, the jokers were saying things would have
been better if Louis had stayed in bed.

Like many another, Ninon had heard all sorts of rumors
about her once close friend — good and bad. Françoise's enemies claimed that she had tipped off her troublesome brother
Charles to buy up cheaply the property of Huguenots forced to
flee France in the wake of the Revocation of the Edict of
Nantes. On the other hand, it was common knowledge that the
widow Scarron had shown singular devotion to Louis's children
by Madame de Montespan long before Louis had evidenced any
amorous interest in her. Furthermore, she had been kind to the
late neglected queen, unlike the hardhearted Madame de
Montespan. Reports had it that in appearance Françoise,
though twelve, perhaps fifteen years younger than Ninon, was
a far cry from the days when Ninon's circle had dubbed her
"the beautiful Indian." * This was a condition with which
Ninon undoubtedly felt great sympathy. Lately she had com-
mented, "How better it would be if age etched its lines on the
heel instead of the forehead."

The carriage entered the grounds of Versailles by a postern
which, instead of taking them down the middle of the vast

* Françoise had spent part of her childhood in Martinique.

Courtyard of the Ministers, brought them to an unfrequented side door of the palace. Thence she was conducted down seemingly endless halls and drafty passageways. Gold, ormolu, parquetry, marble, mirrors, tapestries, busts, chandeliers — splendor — overpowering splendor everywhere. It was a long way from Scarron's unmentionable Hôtel de l'Impécuniosité.

Françoise received Ninon seated. If she did not rise for Louis, she could hardly be expected to rise for one of his subjects. She was dressed all in black, with a high-necked dress and a wimple. Whether the wimple was for warmth or severity is unclear. Her garb habitually gave the impression of mourning for a lost happiness. Her pale, drawn, strained face was still handsome in a puritanical sort of way. Instead of giving off a voluptuous scent — as did most Court ladies — Françoise seemed to exude an incenselike odor of ascetic sanctity which the lascivious, superstitious Louis, breathing deeply, believed good for his soul.

As in the case of Ninon's confrontation with Queen Christina of Sweden, little of their conversation is recorded. We do know that Madame de Maintenon discussed her difficulties in entertaining Louis, who was growing grouchier every day. When Madame de Maintenon complained to her confessor about Louis's excessive and unwelcome physical demands, the priest had counseled her to try to seem passionate and discharge her conjugal duties happily lest Louis call back his perennial weakness, the unforgettable Madame de Montespan. Stories went the rounds that to head off such a situation Madame de Maintenon would personally cull from her garden of high-born impecunious young lady students at the convent of Saint-Cyr the fairest flowers to be delivered to Louis. But Françoise had no guarantee that Louis might not transfer his present homage from her to someone many years her junior, although as absolute ruler of Saint-Cyr — Madame de Maintenon's favorite project — Françoise controlled the situation, and it was unlikely that any of her pupils would dare to supplant her. Madame de Maintenon had ordered floggings for lesser misdemeanors. But could a green convent girl compensate for the sophisticated, scintillating, highly charged Athenaïs de Montespan?

Madame de Maintenon was worried that she might break under the unrelenting pressure of her position. And, added to all that was boredom — unrelieved boredom. She missed the gay, stimulating atmosphere of Ninon's circle. She was a victim of her own doing, for it was she who had substituted rigorous propriety for lighthearted dalliance, thinking thereby to gain credit with the conscience-stricken Louis. She had been right, but in banishing gallantry, she had also banished laughter and sparkle. Louis, too, fretted over the prevailing solemnity with its constant reminder that in his fifties he should already be thinking more of his salvation than his titillation. Françoise was hoist with her own petard. "I must amuse," she cried out in anguish to Ninon, "a man who is no longer amusable." Not amusable in the climate she had created, that is.

Françoise had a proposition. She wanted Ninon to come and live at Versailles and help her to entertain Louis. But how, Ninon inquired, could she live at staid Versailles, when even their meeting had to be kept secret? Françoise was ready for the question. Efficient as ever, she had done her homework for the interview. Become devout — that was the solution. Had not Ninon's best friend, Madame de La Sablière, changed her

ways, and was doing God's work at the Hospital for Incurables? There were rumors that the libertin La Fontaine
was following his goddess, Madame de La Sablière, in the paths
of devoutness. Ninon's old friend, the naughty maréchale de
La Ferté, had converted — Why couldn't Ninon? Were she
and Saint-Evremond going to be the only ones of the old set to
hold out?

The Père d'Orléans had been striving very hard to convert
Ninon but had found her unmoved. Finally, exhausted, he had
cried, "Very well, but while you are waiting to be convinced, at
least offer up your unbelief to God." Where the witty father
had failed, Madame de Maintenon, despite her charm, was not
to succeed either. Ninon declined the proposition. Her mentor, Saint-Evremond, had written: "Devoutness is the last of
our loves and although we may think that we are aspiring only
to the bliss of the other world, we are really, without knowing
it, seeking to find a new sweet savour in this one." Ninon
agreed with Saint-Evremond. Many women, who had lived extremely gay lives, finding that men no longer wanted them,
offered to God what men now rejected. Ninon felt this was
insulting the Deity. She would continue to think as she had
always thought. Her beliefs did not exclude God. On the contrary, she prayed twice a day, but in her own way, without ad-
hering to Church dogma or ritual.

Then in a desperate and unwise move, Françoise offered a
lure — Ninon would never again have to concern herself about
financial matters. But she who had told Fontenelle, "You
know the fortune I could have made out of selling my body; I
could [now] make more out of selling my soul: the Jesuits and
Jansenists are fighting for it," was not striking the colors at this

juncture. Ninon rose to go. Françoise stayed her, protesting she was cruel. Voltaire states that Ninon made a counter offer — that Françoise should come and live with her in the rue des Tournelles, but Françoise could neither live at peace in Versailles, nor could she live without it. Once again Françoise pressed Ninon to convert and move to Versailles. Ninon replied perhaps a little stiffly, "I have need neither of fortune nor of mask," and took her leave.

It is doubtful whether they ever saw each other again.

If legend be the "poetry of history," then indeed there has been a great deal of poetry written about Ninon — most of it without rhyme or reason. The French are a gallant people and very proud of Ninon. But some are not content to let the record speak for itself. One of Ninon's extraordinary characteristics was her retention of physical attractiveness long beyond the normal span. Some of her admirers, however, dreamed up ludicrous incidents in their resolve to paint the lily. The three most persistent legends have to do with a pact she made to secure "eternal" beauty, a son who fell in love with her, and her sexual desirability when she was over eighty. So determined is the lunatic fringe of the legend-makers to prove their point of Ninon's perennial youth, that she is said to have attempted the seduction of Father Bourdaloue when she was ninety — seven years after her death.

Some of these tall tales were of course invented for material gain. But myths often illuminate or point up fact, and at least to that extent they merit examination.

Magic was invoked to account for what the French in a lovely phrase call Ninon's *verte vieillesse* ("green old age").

When eighteen, Ninon is said to have received a visit from an old but ageless man, dressed in black, named Noctambule. He had stock stage properties: white hair, wig awry, wrinkled stockings, two fingers missing, a black spot on his forehead, a limp, a cane. He was gaunt and his eyes flashed. Mysteriously he ordered Ninon to dismiss her maid so they could be alone. Frightened but transfixed by his unearthly stare, Ninon obeyed. Noctambule explained that Ninon had been marked for fame, and that he was giving her a choice of grandeur, untold riches, or eternal beauty. Ninon inquired what she had to do in return and was told she would only have to sign her name on his ancient black tablets. Choosing eternal beauty, Ninon signed. Noctambule elaborated that in the 6000 years he had traversed the world, he had previously found only four mortals worthy of his offer — Semiramis,* Helen of Troy, Cleopatra, and Diane de Poitiers. Ninon was the fifth and would be the last. She would charm both the eye and the heart all her days. She would not see him again for decades, but when she did, she would know that her end was but three days off. Exit Noctambule leaving a faint odor of sulphur, and a fainting eighteen-year old.

To demonstrate that Ninon was still irresistible at fifty-two, the story went that a son of hers who had been brought up by his father, Monsieur de Jarzay, to be unaware of his mother's identity, came to Ninon's finishing school. Mistaking tender

---

* Assyrian queen and legendary founder of Babylon, noted for her beauty, wisdom, and sexual excesses, and of whom Dante wrote:

> Abandoned so was she to wanton vice
> that, her own stigma so to wipe away,
> lust was made licit by her law's device.
> (Translation by Melville B. Anderson)

maternal glances for passionate interest, the son, called the chevalier de Villiers, fell in love with his mother. A hack called Bret, forty-six years after Ninon's death, manufactured the fiction with a heavy hand, little thinking he would inspire a faithful echo some 150 years later in the hyperthyroid, Victorian prose of Helen Kendrick Hayes. If for nothing else, we should be grateful to Bret. Writes H. K. Hayes:

> The young chevalier was just nineteen, an age when the heart responds eagerly to the golden notes of love . . . The tender looks sent the hot, young blood galloping through the chevalier's veins, rendering him half-mad with passion, until at last there came a time when he could contain himself no longer . . .
>
> Finally alarmed, Ninon endeavored to undo the evil by treating the boy with great severity . . . "Raise your eyes to that clock," she said, "foolish boy . . . Do you know that I have now lived fifty-two years in this world? Is mine an age at which to love and be loved? Control yourself, chevalier! Recognize, I beg of you, the absurdity of your desire . . ."
>
> But this grave remonstrance only served to heighten the chevalier's passion, and he threw himself at her feet in an agony of supplication. At sight of her son's misery, great tears trickled down the unhappy mother's cheek, and seeing them, the young man thought he had triumphed.
>
> "What do I see?" he murmured ecstatically; "tears of pity — of tenderness? At last, at last!"
>
> "O Heaven!" cried the distracted Ninon. ". . . I cannot listen to you . . . In pity, leave me!"
>
> "What cruel words! Can this be my tender, philosophical Ninon? Is it only for me that she wears this ridiculous mask of virtue?"
>
> "Stop, chevalier!" exclaimed Ninon. "I thought you worthy of

my friendship — but now I see that you are determined to abuse my kindness . . . Go! . . . Leave me to rue the day I ever bestowed upon you that affection you have so misinterpreted . . ."

Ninon, who had promised Monsieur de Jarzay not to reveal her identity to her son, requests permission to do so, hoping this will cool off the chevalier. Jarzay agrees, and Ninon writes the chevalier to visit her so she can tell him. The unwitting chevalier was there in a flash, galloping all the way from Paris to Picpus, where Ninon was in summer residence.

Helen Kendrick Hayes continues:

He found Ninon alone — eyes wet with recent tears . . . The young man threw himself at her feet, seized her trembling hand and covered it with kisses . . .

"Poor, unfortunate boy!" cried Ninon . . . as she allowed herself to be drawn into his arms, "alas! . . . you force me to reveal a secret which I and another had hoped . . . you need never learn."

"Ah, you are going to disappoint me again," interrupted the chevalier . . . "But think not you can thwart my desire . . . you must — you *shall* be mine!"

He was allowing himself to be completely carried away by his ardor, ready to resort to the supreme end.

"Stop!" cried Ninon in tones of the deepest horror and indignation. "Stop before you commit a crime unspeakable. Do you know who you are? . . . What I am? This woman whom you pursue . . ."

"Well?" said the chevalier, in a voice rendered almost inaudible by suppressed passion, "this woman whom I desire? . . ."

"She is your own mother! . . . O God! it is my son who lies moaning at my feet . . . who speaks to me of love . . . Oh, my son! my poor, poor boy! It was your father who, with the noblest of motives, wished you to be kept in ignorance . . . Oh, my son, my dear son! Look upon your unhappy mother; tell her you forgive her for having brought you into the world . . ."

Weeping bitterly, Ninon held close to her heart the man who, crushed by this terrible revelation, now stood pale, trembling . . . Still suffering the horrible torture of an overpowering criminal passion, he could not utter a single word, not even the sweet word "Mother," for which Ninon waited in an agony of suspense. Presently he raised his head, gave one long look into his mother's eyes, and with a half-articulate cry of despair, tore himself from her loving embrace and fled from the room. Finding himself in the garden he rushed wildly to the little wood at the farther end; then, drawing his sword, without a moment's reflection he thrust the point into his heart. The next instant the young chevalier was lying in a pool of blood . . . His last look was for her, and in his eyes still shone the love which had killed him. A moment passed and Death closed them forever.

Voltaire, never a great man for checking sources, seems to accept the fable but wastes neither words nor tears on it. In commenting on Villiers's suicide he remarks, "He was not as philosophical as his mother." Voltaire no doubt got the story either direct from its creator, Bret, or through Bret's copier, Douxmenil. No contemporary says a word of it. To add to the suspect nature of the alleged incident, all we need to do is to examine the heavy, turgid, melodramatic speech which Bret ascribes to Ninon and contrast it with her well-known crispness and simplicity. Furthermore, weeping, bosom-heaving, hand-wringing, eyes raised heavenward have never been aphrodisiacs. If Ninon had gone in for the Wagnerian histrionics attributed to her by the hungry pulp-writers of the eighteenth and nineteenth centuries, any red-blooded man would have run miles, and not upon his sword, as claimed.

The third and most widely accepted legend — that Ninon was still driving men mad in her eighties — is nearer gross hyperbole than downright fabrication. Specifically she is said to have slept with two abbés* — Châteauneuf and Gédoyn. There are many variations on the theme but they all boil down essentially to this. The young abbé, aged about thirty, finds himself uncontrollably attracted to the octogenarian Ninon, who does not gratify his desire. The abbé, feeling despised and rejected, wonders out loud why Ninon, not known for her chastity, resists his suit. Ninon encourages him, says all is not hopeless, his hour will come. The vigorous abbé bridles but is patient. Finally one night Ninon receives him in a most charming dishabille and capitulates. O joy, O rapture! Then the abbé, in the languorous aftermath, inquires why Ninon had chosen that particular night to reward him. Because, Ninon is supposed to have replied, tonight was her eightieth birthday, and she wanted to give herself a birthday present. The abbé was quite prepared to bring more presents indefinitely, and it was Ninon who, as in the long ago, terminated the affair.

It seems a shame to kill such a story but contemporary testimony plus knowledge of Ninon's sense of dignity rule her out as an octogenarian temptress. Voltaire does not seem to be able to make up his mind as to when she entertained Châteauneuf in her boudoir, saying she was sixty in one passage and seventy in two others. But he is very definite about her looks the year of her death, when she was eighty-two.† As a boy of eleven he had been presented to her. Some five decades later he painted a merciless picture. "Her face showed the most hideous marks of

* At least one of the abbés, Gédoyn, had left the Jesuits in 1694 — before his alleged affair with Ninon.
† Voltaire says she was eighty-five, but if we accept 1623 as her birth year, she died at eighty-two.

old age, her body had all the infirmities . . . She was dry like a mummy." This seems effectively to destroy the image of a Ninon still ravishing in a plunging neckline, wreaking the same old havoc. The princesse Palatine knew Ninon well through her son, afterward regent, whom she sent to Ninon's school to be edified. "Now that Mademoiselle de Lanclos is old, she leads a very respectable life; she maintains, so they say, that she would never have changed her ways if she herself had not seen the ridiculous in them."

But that she remained unusually attractive in her fifties, sixties, and seventies, there seems to be no doubt. At the time of Huygens's hymn to her charms, Ninon could not have been less than fifty-four. Huygens was a physicist as well as an astronomer. He was probably the most important contributor to the subject of the motion of bodies in the period between Galileo and Newton. Among other matters, he investigated the acceleration of a point moving in a curve. Descriptions of Ninon's figure by contemporaries, as well as the evidence of paintings in décolletage, indicate softly flowing curves which seem to have within them more than a suggestion of the rhythm of the spheres so dear to astronomer Huygens. A man of exhaustive thoroughness, Huygens was equally interested in parabolic and feminine curves. It is not difficult to visualize the good scientist's accelerating to the side of Ninon, if not at the rate of freely falling bodies, at least at the rate of a man falling freely for an evidently still lovely feminine body. The skeptical might ask that a discount be taken for Parisian gallantry from Huygens's poetic rhapsody to Ninon's sex appeal. But Huygens was Dutch, not French, and all his training conduced to exactness.

Then there is the word of the marquis de La Fare, a reliable witness. He also knew Ninon well, for she had tried to mediate between him and his ill-fated love, Madame de La Sablière. "I never saw Ninon at the height of her beauty, but at the age of fifty, and even to beyond seventy, she had lovers who loved her greatly, and the most worthy gentlemen for friends."

Poets still were moved to chant the praises of her mind and body. One such was the abbé Regnier-Desmarais, perennial secretary of the Académie française. He was ten years Ninon's junior; he called her Clusine.

> Clusine, who in every season
> Shared the love and esteem
> Of all the worthy gentlemen;
> Who, always full of good sense,
> Knew how to make good use
> Of each of life's seasons;
> Who in her enchanting conversation
> Made a happy combination
> Of charming playfulness
> With politeness and soundness . . .

What all this adds up to is that Ninon, as has already been suggested, probably terminated the active phase of her love life when she was fifty-two. She had succeeded in taking Charles de Sévigné from the much younger Mademoiselle de Champmeslé, Paris's reigning actress. Ninon decided to quit while she was ahead. Besides, her victory over la Champmeslé was somewhat Pyrrhic in that it involved some loss of self-respect. Evidently her suitors refused to accept the fact of her retirement and continued to besiege her. She may have come out of retirement occasionally where she did not have to compete with a rival and where her dignity was not imperiled. But unquestionably for the most part, Ninon rested on her laurels. She may still have excited desire, but with a possible exception here or there, she did not satisfy it. The myth probably arose partly from the unrequited love which Ninon still inspired in her sixties and possibly early seventies, and partly from her grace which seemed to grow with the years. Donne must have been thinking of someone very much like the Ninon of the 1680s when he wrote:

> Nor spring nor summer beauty hath such grace
> As I have seen in one autumnal face.

Ninon once gave the recipe: "I keep young," she said, "because I love neither gambling, nor wine, nor women."

## ∽ Chapter 13 ∽

### Trans-Channel Duet and Grand Finale

MADAME DU DEFFAND, wit extraordinary, presided over probably the most famous salon of the eighteenth century, when
elegant society flourished as perhaps never before or since. In
1774, she wrote her beloved Horace Walpole:

> I read something this morning that gave me pleasure; the title
> of the book is *Memoirs on the Life of Mademoiselle Lenclos;* the
> beginning is extremely flat, you should begin only on page 164;
> there are letters from her and from Saint-Evremond which I find
> charming and which have strongly confirmed me in the opinion
> I hold that it is extremely false to account me a wit. Oh no, I'm
> not at all! Ninon was in great measure, and Saint-Evremond
> more than I thought . . .

What Madame du Deffand found flat was Douxmenil's long
and dull foreword to the "charming" correspondence which
began on page 164. Unfortunately, most of it is lost although
several hacks like Damours and Ségur, motivated more by the
hope of gain than grief, undertook to supplement the Ninon
canon. In 1751 Voltaire wrote from Prussia, "A couple of years
ago someone printed some letters under the name of Mademoiselle de Lenclos, almost the way in this country they sell wine
from Orleans for Burgundy." Apart from the brief, strained
interchange in 1670–71 in connection with the d'Elbène debt,

the extant Ninon–Saint-Evremond correspondence covers approximately the last two decades of the lives of these fast friends, now grown old. Not all the letters are dated. They may start as early as 1680. The fact that we have none from 1671 to 1680 does not necessarily indicate a long silence — just a large lacuna.

Saint-Evremond had been warmly welcomed by the English court when he arrived in 1662 from Holland — a way-stop on his flight from France. He had known many of the English royalists when they had been in exile in France during Cromwell's regime. Charles's court attempted to be very French — in dress, manners, cuisine, gaiety, gallantry — right down to the official mistress. Charles had spent his youth at the French Court and had there vainly proposed to the beautiful Hortense Mancini, favorite niece of Mazarin. Saint-Evremond had known Hortense when she made her debut at the French Court as a girl of seventeen in 1657. All three — Charles, Hortense, and Saint-Evremond — were to meet again at the English court.

As a classic example of the honnête homme, Saint-Evremond was much in demand at Whitehall. His wit and urbanity were greatly admired. Charles II's court could use a man accomplished in the Gallic ways it wanted to mime. Though only forty-six in 1662, Saint-Evremond was like a father professor to Charles's young fun-loving entourage. As a good Epicurean, Saint-Evremond disapproved of the more riotous revels; from this and his predilection for good conversation he was affectionately dubbed "the philosopher," as earlier in his youth in France he had been nicknamed "the wit." When Saint-Evremond got the "vapors" in damp London and returned to Holland for his health, he was sorely missed. There he met practically everybody of distinction, including the prince of Orange, later William III of England, and Spinoza. In 1670 when his finances were at such a low ebb that he temporarily soured his relationship with Ninon by politely badgering her to make good on the debt of their mutual friend d'Elbène, Charles II lured him back to London with the offer of a sine-cure — keeper of the ducks in St. James Park, paying £300 per year. The position may have meant approximately $15,000 a year (in today's currency) to the strapped Saint-Evremond who was only getting 600 livres a year ($1200 to $3000) from his property abandoned in France. Saint-Evremond accepted Charles's offer. He liked the semi-French court at Whitehall and the relative freedom. Three hundred pounds a year made up for the London weather.

With an income of perhaps $16,000, he was able to live modestly, if not in the grand manner, but he yearned for his native Paris and his stimulating pupil Ninon, to whom he had been "neither a simple friend, nor a veritable lover." It is true that London was pleasant, with its skating parties in the winter and fireworks on mild summer evenings after the long twilight, with intellectual nourishment provided by men like Hobbes; but Saint-Evremond lacked the warmth of a personal, intimate relationship with an exciting woman. To him such a relationship was indispensable to his well-being. He had once articulated his concept of the ideal companion: "It is above all the idea of an accomplished person" who is not to be found in "*men* because they always lack an element of gentleness found in *women;* and I have always believed it less impossible to find in a woman the very firm and very sane reason of men, than in a man the charms and gracefulness native to women." What of course he was looking for was a female honnête homme. "This sane reason," says Sainte-Beuve, "this sensitive spirit, joined to liveliness and charm, he had found in Ninon." But she was far away.

Saint-Evremond moped. Not forced to learn English by Charles's French-speaking court, he no longer had that youthful drive and discipline necessary to master a new tongue. This of course further aggravated his sense of being on the outside looking in. He tried to busy himself with his literary endeavors. Saint-Evremond in his lifetime produced a respectable and respected body of writing on history, philosophy, and literature. The duke of Buckingham introduced him to London's intellectual elite with whom he would discuss music, literature, philosophy. "Old Evremond [*sic*] would talk forever," says Spence — deism and atheism with Hobbes, Epicureanism with Waller and Cowley, the stage with Sedley and Howard and perhaps Dryden. Of Saint-Evremond, Dryden was later to write in a preface to a miscellaneous collection of Saint-Evremond's essays in English translation (1692): "There is not only a justness* in his conceptions, which is the foundation of good writing, but also a purity of language and a beautiful turn of words, so little understood by modern writers."

Notwithstanding this rather full intellectual and social life, Saint-Evremond moped. Then in 1675, Hortense Mancini, now the duchesse Mazarin, hove on the scene. Engaging in what seems to have been the main physical exercise of a number of seventeenth-century French ladies, she was fleeing from her crazed husband and had made for Charles II of England. Charles set her up in a house hard by the duck pond of

* Exactness or precision.

which Saint-Evremond was the nominal keeper. A comparison of the royal pensions accorded the mistress and the philosopher shows that at £4000 per year (perhaps $200,000), Hortense was approximately thirteen times more favored of the king than Saint-Evremond.

In 1675, Saint-Evremond was fifty-nine, the duchesse Mazarin probably thirty-five (although some biographers say twenty-nine), and Ninon fifty-two. It is probably just as well that Ninon and Saint-Evremond were in different cities, for Ninon might have been tempted to fight for Saint-Evremond as she had four years earlier fought for Charles de Sévigné. Saint-Evremond and the duchesse Mazarin became very intimate, although whether in the physical realm he got much more than an occasional peck on the cheek is highly doubtful. But whatever their physical relationship, Hortense filled an aching void. She did for him what Ninon had done earlier — provide a salon over which he could preside and where he could set the tone — relaxed, elegant, distinguished.

At the duchesse Mazarin's salon in London, the fare was very similar to Ninon's in Paris. "All manner of subjects were discussed . . ." reports Des Maizeaux. "Philosophy, History, Pieces of Wit, Gallantry, Plays, Authors, ancient and modern, the niceties of the French tongue." The duchess, although intelligent and well tutored, had little of Saint-Evremond's and Ninon's depth or sensitivity, except in music. A significant difference between Ninon's and the duchess's salon was the hectic gambling at the latter. Poor Saint-Evremond lost consistently to Hortense, who appears to have had not too much conscience. Like Ninon, Hortense had a passion for cleanliness, although evidently exaggerated, for it seemed to irk Saint-

Evremond, whereas there is no similar mention vis-à-vis Ninon.
Saint-Evremond himself had become slovenly as he aged. A
ditty went:

> Old Evremond renowned for Wit and Dirt
> Wou'd change his living oftener than his Shirt,
> Roar with the rakes of state a month, then come
> To starve another in his hole at home.

"I defy Dulcinea," * wrote Ninon to Saint-Evremond much
later in 1687, "to remember her knight [Saint-Evremond] with
more joy than I do . . ." Ninon is referring to the duchesse
Mazarin when she mentions Dulcinea, which was Saint-
Evremond's nickname for the duchess. By this time Ninon no
longer had to fear the competition of the duchess, who had
been brought low by the death of Charles II in 1685. Evidently
his successor, James II, did not feel any quasi-levirate obligation
either to assume or look after his brother's mistress, for he
stopped her pension. The duchess, now forty-seven, was probably more an object of pity than love. Thus Ninon could afford
to be playful and relaxed in her letter.

Saint-Evremond, too, was in desperate straits, for James had
stopped his pension also. Louis XIV, called the God-given, certainly did not temper injustice with mercy in his long exile of
Saint-Evremond, who had loyally fought for him during the
Fronde. He once again petitioned Louis for pardon and was
once again refused. His income was proably now no more than
the 600 livres ($1200 to $3000) he received from his French
source. Through it all he retained his sense of humor and his
Epicurean belief in the efficacy of reason. Earlier he had

---

* Dulcinea was Don Quixote's beloved. Saint-Evremond often signed himself the
Knight of the Sorrowful Countenance (Don Quixote).

written Ninon: "A little reason will make us taste the good things as deliciously as possible and cause us to adjust to the bad things as patiently as possible."

In 1689, a turn came. Saint-Evremond's friend, William of Orange, succeeded the deposed James II on the throne. Not long after, Des Maizeaux tells us, "he [William III] gave him [Saint-Evremond] tangible marks of his favor." He even gave back to Hortense one-half of her old pension — £2000 per year (perhaps $100,000). Furthermore, Louis XIV at last pardoned Saint-Evremond. But Saint-Evremond declined Louis's offer permitting him to return — ostensibly on the grounds of advanced age (seventy-three) and health. The more likely reasons are: he was sensitive about the large wen on his forehead to which his English friends had become accustomed; he felt much more secure, both economically and personally, under his old friend, William III, than under his old enemy, Louis XIV; Saint-Evremond preferred the political climate in England, now a constitutional monarchy, to that of France under an absolute king.

Ninon was of course grieved at Saint-Evremond's decision not to return to France, but her reproach was of the mildest. Nor does she let pride prevent her from opening her heart. The following letter to Saint-Evremond is also notable in that it contains Ninon's frequently quoted saying: "The joy of a spirit is the measure of its power." In this short sentence is the essence of her philosophy.

I was all alone in my room, tired out with reading, when someone told me: "There is a gentleman here who comes from Monsieur de Saint-Evremond." You may imagine how easy I found it to shake off all my former weariness!

I had the pleasure of speaking about you and I learned about things which letters never say — your perfect health and occupations. The joy of a spirit is the measure of its power . . . I could have wished to have spent the rest of my life with you and had you thought as I do, you would now be here. However, it is very pleasant to remember those whom we have loved . . .

There is a hiatus in the correspondence for a few years. How many letters were lost we cannot even guess. The next one, quoted immediately below, of 1696, seems almost to answer the touching one quoted above, which may have been written as late as 1694.

*From Saint-Evremond to Ninon*

I have received the second letter you wrote me . . . everything conspires to make me yearn for the happy times which I have passed in your company and to wish futilely to see you once again. I don't have the strength to transport myself to France, and you have attractions there which don't allow you to come to England . . . England has its charms, and I would be an ingrate were I not to admit that I have found it engaging.

I have learned, with much pleasure, that Monsieur the comte de Gramont has recovered his former health and has become devout. Up to now I have crudely contented myself with being a good plain honest man, but now I needs must do more, and I only await your example to become devout . . .

What I find most unfortunate at my age is that hope is gone — that hope which is the gentlest of the passions and which contributes most to make us live agreeably. What pains me the most is the despair of ever seeing you again. I needs must content myself with writing in order to maintain a friendship which has stood the test of time, of far removed places and the customary coldness of old age. This last word relates to me alone; nature will commence through you to demonstrate that it is possible not to age . . ."

Saint-Evremond knew he was not taking much of a chance when he told Ninon he was only waiting for her to become religious for him to follow. The subject of religion fascinated him. A year later he was on the same theme.

> . . . If they had told me that you were become devout, I could have believed it. That would be moving from a human passion to the love of God and would give the soul something to occupy itself with. But not to love at all, that is a kind of annihilation which just does not go with your heart . . .

Elsewhere Saint-Evremond wrote, "Devoutness is the last of our loves* . . . one turns to God in order to seek a change, to form in one's soul new desires, and make it feel the agitations of a budding passion. Devoutness will sometimes bring back to an old woman the delicacy of feeling and the tenderness of heart which the very youngest may not know in marriage or in a threadbare love affair."

We can see by the next letter in the series (1697) that there are gaps in the correspondence again. Ninon's is obviously answering a letter which is lost.

> I learn with pleasure that my soul is dearer to you than my body, and that your good sense guides you always to what is best. As a matter of fact, my body is no longer worthy of attention . . .
>
> I have recently heard of a certain Prologue† set to music which

---

* A favorite topic of Saint-Evremond's. He used this identical expression at least twice.
† Written by Saint-Evremond.

I should very much like to see performed in Paris. The beauty*
who is the subject of it would excite the envy of every woman in
the audience . . .

Now that our kings are friends, shouldn't you take a trip here?
For me this would be the greatest blessing of the peace.†

The letters are a little like a ballet with the principals execut-
ing their pas de deux with infinite grace but little passion. Saint-
Evremond did not or could not make the suggested trip, but he
wrote Ninon in 1698 that he was asking a handsome young
man, whom he felt she would find pleasing, to visit her. The
youth was the twenty-eight-year-old duke of St. Albans
(Charles II's natural son by Nell Gwynn), who had been sent
to France to congratulate Louis XIV on the marriage of his
grandson.

I take a lively pleasure in young people — handsome and bloom-
ing — who are capable of touching my old heart. As there has
always been much similarity in our tastes, fancies, and sentiments,
I trust you will not be displeased to receive a young cavalier who
has a way with the ladies: he is the duke of Saint-Albans and I
have asked him, as much for his own sake as yours, to visit
you . . .

Let me know how our old friend, Monsieur de Gourville, is.
I suppose his affairs go well; if he is sick, I am sorry.

My particular friend, Dr. Morelli, is accompanying my lady the
countess of Sandwich, who is going to France for her health. The
late earl of Rochester, father of my Lady Sandwich, had more wit
than any man in England; my Lady Sandwich has even more

---

* The duchesse Mazarin.
† Allusion to Treaty of Ryswick in September 1697, ending the war between England and France.

than her father; she is as generous as she is witty, and as amiable as she is witty and generous . . .

Pray try to get some wine from Monsieur de Gourville for me; I lodge with Monsieur de l'Hermitage, one of his relatives — a most honorable gentleman who has taken refuge in England because of his religion. It angers me that the conscience of the French Catholics could not suffer him to live in Paris, or that the delicacy of his own conscience made him leave. He certainly deserves the approbation of his cousin [Gourville].

Gourville is mentioned frequently in the correspondence. He had prospered mightily since the days, three and one-half decades before, when he had warned Saint-Evremond of his [Saint-Evremond's] impending arrest and shortly after had had to flee himself, leaving one-half his money securely with the reliable Ninon, the other half catastrophically with the false prelate. Gourville had been pardoned and was now loaded with honors. At his château he lived in grand style. He would send his old and often needy friend, Saint-Evremond, choice wines, perhaps from his own vineyards. In return, Saint-Evremond sent tea to their mutual friend Ninon, whom Gourville had practically canonized after the incident of the casket which she had so faithfully safeguarded. Evidently when Gourville's Huguenot cousin, de l'Hermitage, was forced to flee France after the Revocation of the Edict of Nantes, Saint-Evremond took him in. He comments that it is better to convert than flee — one is not offending God. Is he not God of both religions?

Ninon had no interest in meeting the young, handsome duke of St. Albans, but Saint-Evremond pleased her greatly by directing the countess of Sandwich to her. Fortunately the next letter in the series is extant, for Ninon is obviously answering Saint-Evremond's — a bit testily at first.

> What makes you think that the sight of a young man would give me pleasure? Your senses deceive you as to those of others. I have forgotten everything except my friends . . . My porter said I wasn't in and took your letter which has given me as much joy as any I have ever received from you.
>
> How you hanker after good wine, and how sad I am not to be able to report back success! Monsieur de l'Hermitage could tell you, just as well as I, that Monsieur de Gourville does not leave his bedroom, that he is pretty much indifferent about all manner of tastes, a good friend always, but one from whom his friends wouldn't think of asking a favor, for fear of bothering him. That said, if by some hint, which I do not foresee, I can use my skill in the matter of the wine, have no doubt that I will . . .
>
> They told me that Monsieur Dubois would go [to London]; he is a shrewd little man who will please you, I think.

Ninon was fairly shrewd herself. The "shrewd little man" was a cardinal and prime minister of France when he died twenty-five years later. She continues:

> I have twenty of your letters in my hands; people read them with admiration. You can see that good taste is not a thing of the past in France . . .

As there remain only eleven letters altogether from Saint-Evremond to Ninon, even including those going all the way back to 1669, we can see how many were lost when Ninon said she had twenty in her hands — presumably many of them of recent vintage. In 1698, she seems to have been rather ill and hears from Saint-Evremond's lady friend, the duchesse Mazarin. They are now too old to be rivals — if they ever were.

*From Ninon to Saint-Evremond* 1698

. . . I have had ample cause for gratitude to the world and to my friends during my illness but I have felt nothing more touching than this mark of goodwill.* Do the necessary, since it's wholly on your account it was bestowed . . .

How I envy those who go to England, and what pleasure it would be to dine once more with you! Isn't it almost gross to mention dinner? The mind has great advantages over the body; however the body often furnishes little treats . . . which offer the mind relief from sad thoughts. You have often laughed at mine; I have banished them all. There is no longer time for them when one has reached the terminal period of one's life. We must content ourselves with each day as we live it. Day to day desires, whatever you may say of them, are just as much to be prized as long range ones; they are much more sure of realization. There's a pretty moral for you; keep well — that's all that counts.

In another letter Ninon points out that at a certain stage in life we come to value a good stomach more than a clear mind. Saint-Evremond replies:

At eighty-eight † I eat oysters every morning; I dine well and sup not badly . . .

When I was young I admired only the things of the mind, being less interested in the things of the body than I should have been; today I redress the wrong as much as I can . . . You have done differently. You had some regard for the body in your youth; now you pay attention to nothing but the mind. I'm not so sure you are right in esteeming it so highly. One reads practically nothing worthwhile remembering; one hears practically nothing worthwhile listening to. However miserable are the

* The letter from the duchesse Mazarin.
† Saint-Evremond was actually eighty-two.

senses at my age, yet the impressions that agreeable objects make on them affect me more pleasurably [than things of the mind] and we are very wrong to want to mortify them.

The dialogue across the Channel continues — sweet, sad, and low-keyed. In 1699 Ninon writes:

We are to merit the praises of posterity by the duration of our life and our friendship. I believe I'll live as long as you. I am weary of always doing the same thing and I praise the Swiss who threw himself in the river for that reason. My friends take me up on this score and assure me life is good as long as one is at peace and the mind is healthy. Vigor of body fills us with other thoughts and one would prefer its vigor to that of the mind. But all is useless when one cannot change things; it is well to banish thoughts which serve no useful purpose.

It gives me much happiness to know that my Lady Sandwich found me pleasing. I did not think that in my declining years I could be a fit companion for a woman of her age.* She has more wit than all the women of France, and more true merit. She is leaving us; it is an occasion for regret for all who know her, and for me particularly. If you had been here, we'd have had some repasts worthy of the old days. Love me always.

All who return from England speak of the beauty of Madame the duchesse Mazarin. You have so endeared Madame Mazarin to me that I cannot hear her spoken of without pleasure. Goodbye, monsieur, but why isn't it hello? We must not die without seeing each other.

Ninon was either ill-informed about the duchesse Mazarin or more likely was going through the steps of the gracious ballet which required one to pay compliments. At fifty-nine, the duchess was no longer a beauty and, in desperately trying reju-

---

* Lady Sandwich was twenty-five.

venation nostrums, she brought about her early death. Some hold she committed suicide when she saw herself losing out in a competition for the same man with her daughter. Saint-Evremond was desolate. His one intimate relationship in England was gone. As soon as Ninon heard of the duchess's death, she hastened to write Saint-Evremond in July 1699 with her usual simplicity and honesty. (It is here she composed her oft quoted: "I hold those wise who know how to be happy.")

What a loss you have sustained, monsieur! * Were we not to be lost some day ourselves, it is impossible we should ever be comforted. I condole with you utterly. You have just lost a delightful relationship which was your prop in a foreign country. Those who live long must expect to see their friends die. Your mind, your philosophy, will come to your aid and support you. I have felt this death as if I had had the honor of knowing Madame Mazarin. She thought of me in my sufferings; I was touched by this goodness, and what she meant to you endeared her to me.

There is no remedy for this, nor is there any against that which happens to our poor bodies. Take care of yours.

Your friends are delighted to see you so hale and wise, for I hold those wise who know how to be happy. A thousand thanks for the tea you sent me . . .

You will soon have my Lady Sandwich† with you again; we see her depart with much regret. I hope her return will afford you some consolation. I don't know English ways; this lady has been very French here.

Adieu a thousand times, monsieur. If we could think with

---

* "Madame Mazarin died this morning at 8 o'clock. It is what we must all do, the later the better" — Lord Jersey to Mathew Prior, British ambassador to Versailles. Whitehall, June 22, 1699.

† The Francophile Lady Sandwich had recovered from serious illness in Paris. Lord Jersey to Mathew Prior, June 16, 1699: "Pray persuade her to come home . . . I promised her to talk of Paris to her, and I shall very faithfully keep my word . . ."

Madame de Chevreuse, who believed she was going to be able to chat with all her friends in the other world, it would be a sweet thought indeed.

Ninon, aged seventy-six, would have given much to believe in an afterworld, but she could not, despite the strenuous efforts of Jesuits and Jansenists to convert her. The approach of death did not alter her firm beliefs. Foxhole conversions were not for her — or Saint-Evremond. They stoutly refused to allow fear to impose what their reason had always rejected. The realization by both — that they would never meet again in this world or in the next of which they denied the existence — weighed heavily upon them. The melancholy days were come.

The opening line of Ninon's next letter no doubt bolsters the view of those who hold that Ninon was still having love affairs. "Profitless desires" may well have a suggestion of the physical, but if it has, the definite implication is that the desire was not indulged. Again the letter which Ninon is answering is lost. It might have shed light.

1699

Your letter has filled me with profitless desires of which I considered myself no longer capable. "The days pass," as that good man Des Yveteaux used to say, "in ignorance and indolence, and these days destroy us and make us lose the things to which we are attached . . ." Formerly you used to say that I would die of nothing but reflections; I try not to engage in them any more and to forget on the morrow the time which I live today . . .

One clings to a wretched body the way one does to an agreeable one . . . A good appetite is something I still enjoy. Would to God I could pit my stomach against yours and speak of all the characters we have known, the remembrance of whom rejoices me more than the presence of the crowd of people whom I see. Although it may be good to see this crowd, there is no rapport . . . What a comparison — this present age with the one we have seen! . . .

If his next letter is a true indicator, Saint-Evremond seems to have recovered much of his old exuberance within a few months of the duchesse Mazarin's death. The last years of the duchess's life were miserable. She was still crippled by debts, owing Saint-Evremond 400 guineas (about $21,000) at the time of her death — a sum he could ill afford to write off. Far removed from her place as the cynosure of two reigns previous, she had grown careless of her manners and appearance, had taken to drink. She was a ruin and not even a magnificent one. No doubt Saint-Evremond had tried not to see this, but the contrast between the derelict duchesse Mazarin and the ever-dignified, ever-fastidious Ninon, still sought out by the outstanding people of the day — young and old — must have been striking. At eighty-three he still is in top form as he pens Ninon one of his best letters.

1699

The last letter which I received from Mademoiselle de Lenclos always seems to me the best, and this is not because the sense of the present pleasure prevails over the remembrance of the past. The true reason is that your mind grows stronger every day. If your body is like your mind, I shall hold up but badly my end of the battle of stomachs of which you speak. I was willing to make a trial of my appetite against that of my Lady Sandwich at a great repast at my Lord Jersey's; I was not worsted.

All the world acknowledges my Lady Sandwich's wit, and I am convinced of her good taste by the extraordinary esteem she has for you. She did not outdo me in praising you, no more than in appetite. You are of all countries, as much esteemed in London as in Paris. You are of all times, and when I cite you as doing honor to *my* time, the young folks claim you for *their* time. Thus there you are — mistress of the present and of the past; may you also extend your power over the future! Not that it is reputation I have in view — yours is already assured for all time. I hold another thing more essential: it is life, of which eight days are worth more than eight centuries of glory after death . . .

No one puts a greater value on youth than I, and now that I have only the remembrance of it, I follow your example and adjust to the present as well as I can. Would to God Madame Mazarin had been of your opinion! She'd be living still, but she must needs have died the greatest beauty* in the world . . .

Live! Life is good when it is without pain.

Sainte-Beuve refers to the "naturalness, originality, and simplicity" of Ninon's letters. The last of her letters to Saint-Evremond which is preserved is happily one of her best. It incorporates some of Ninon's philosophy, illustrates well her economy of language and clear-sightedness. It contains her famous "It is not enough to be wise, one must be engaging" — a maxim which sums up as well as anything the secret of French feminine charm.

1699

Wit is very dangerous in friendship. Your letter would have spoiled anyone else but me. I know your vivid and astonishing imagination and was therefore forced to recall that Lucian has written in praise of even a fly . . . Would to God you really believed all you said about me! I could then dispense with all the

---

* Allusion to the use by the duchess of harmful cosmetics which allegedly caused her death.

countries.* Furthermore, it is to you that all the glory belongs.

What a masterpiece your last letter is! It has been the subject of all the conversations in my chamber for the last month. You return to youth; you do well to love it. Philosophy goes well with a sprightly wit. It is not enough to be wise, one must be engaging. I see well that you will always be pleasing so long as you continue to think as you do now.

Few people resist the years; I trust that I am not yet completely overwhelmed by them. I could wish with you that Madame Mazarin had regarded life in itself without always thinking of her face which would ever have been lovely, even when good sense would have taken the place of glamour.

My Lady Sandwich will always conserve the vigor of her wit even when she loses her youth — or so I think. Adieu, monsieur. When you see my lady the countess of Sandwich, make sure she remembers me: I'd be much troubled to be forgotten by her.

Ninon shows her usual perceptiveness in predicting the indestructibility of the young countess of Sandwich's charm. Pope and Lord Chesterfield were later to attest to it. Chesterfield was to tell his son that an indispensable part of his education was to come from his attendance at the countess's famous salon in Paris, which she later established when Ninon was just a memory — but evidently a fondly cherished memory. Bret, writing in 1751, finds himself at a loss for words in trying to communicate the countess's regard for the octogenarian she had known in her twenties:

It would only attenuate the idea which madame the countess of Sandwich conserves of her old friend were I to try to paint it in

---

* Allusion to previous letter from Saint-Evremond where he says, "You are of all countries."

these Memoirs. It is enough to say that forty-six years have in no wise diminished her sorrow, and that the name of Mademoiselle de Lanclos awakes in her heart every day the sentiments of esteem and admiration which she conceived for her at the end of the last century.

It should not be thought that during the last two decades of her life Ninon was doing little but waiting for letters from Saint-Evremond and writing him of her longing and of the friends of their youth. She was reading that old Stoic, Seneca, who counseled resignation, and was keeping herself young by entertaining la bonne compagnie — well-bred, intelligent, interesting people. Again and again the phrase *la bonne compagnie* crops up in the contemporary and later descriptions of Ninon's salon. Sainte-Beuve refers to Ninon's salon as "a school of politeness and honor." Ninon taught not just grace and ease, but something basic — considerateness and the art of being obliging without obsequiousness. This refinement of spirit a seventeenth-century contemporary likened to the spirit of charity. The twentieth-century critic Monsieur Georges Mongrédien calls it "the religion of honor, the last and most disinterested of the religions of an aristocracy." It was Ninon's religion.

The phenomenal element in Ninon's life was unquestionably her ability to attract and hold the cream of French society when she was in her late seventies and in her eighties. "To eighty-seven," * writes the marquis de La Fare, "she was still sought after by the best company of her time." Another contemporary,

---

* La Fare was stretching it a little. Ninon was eighty-two or at most eighty-five when she died.

and former pupil, the marquis de Dangeau, writes in his *Journal:* "Though she was very old, she had conserved so much wit and reason that the best company used to assemble every day at her house." She would chide, with an ease born of self-confidence, her old benefactor Bonrepaus for not calling on her. ". . . I was a little put out," Ninon wrote him in 1690, "to learn that you had visited Mademoiselle de Scudéry* without coming here. When you are doing the old folks of the quarter, I see who gets the preference . . . Let me know when you want me to attend you here or elsewhere." Ninon had never forgotten the interest Bonrepaus had taken in the welfare of her son, the chevalier de La Boissière. The same year Ninon read a proclamation:

> Louis, by the grace of God, king of France and of Navarre, to all present and future, greetings. Our dear and well-loved Louis de Mornay, marquis de Villarceaux, professing the Catholic . . . religion, has very humbly demonstrated to Us that during his marriage, he had been intimate with Anne Lenclos, from which issued Louis-François, called La Boissière, their natural child, whom they have raised . . . in the practice of virtues and exercises of war for many years; that he has given proof of his valor and of his affection for our service, that he has merited the commission of captain of one of our vessels . . . to expunge a stain on his person . . . We have, by these presents . . . the said Louis-François de Mornay de La Boissière legitimized . . .
>
> Signed, LOUIS.

Ninon and the century grew old together. The leaves rained down in all seasons of the year in the 1690s. One year after La Boissière's legitimization, she heard with a pang that his father

* The famous novelist, Madeleine de Scudéry, lived near Ninon in the Marais. She was at least thirteen years older than Ninon.

Villarceaux, the only lover she had accorded more than three months, was gone. The year 1693 carried off two of her best friends — the fragile, easily hurt Madame de La Sablière, and the delicate, ever faithful Charleval.

*From Ninon to Saint-Evremond*

Monsieur de Charleval has just died, and I am so grieved that I seek to console myself in the thought that you will share the sorrow with me. I used to see him every day; his mind had all the charms of youth and his heart all the goodness and tenderness one desires in true friends. We often used to speak of you and all the originals [characters] of our time. His life and mine which I lead at present were full of rapport. A loss like this is worse than dying yourself.

Send me news of yourself. I interest myself in your life in London just as if you were here; old friends have charms that one never appreciates as much as when one is bereaved.

These years were not, however, one long period of mourning. Ninon knew well how to make the best of things and that lamentation and self-pity would avail nothing and merely alienate her company. She seems never to have lost her power to charm and attract people. A letter in 1693 from an old friend, the abbé de Tréville (one of her many friends whom we have not met — we cannot meet them all), illustrates the exceptionally intimate relationship which it was evidently Ninon's peculiar genius to be able to establish. Tréville had been one of Louis XIV's bosom friends of his youth and was extremely highly regarded.

. . . In truth I know not how to write any more except to you . . . For three months we have had an Irish doctor here. What goes on between him and his patient is more ridiculous than all that Molière ever put on stage, but I have nobody to laugh with, and you are the only one I want to talk to.

Adieu, mademoiselle, preserve for me the honor of your friendship.

In 1694, Madame Cornuel, Ninon's chief rival as a wit, passed on. A poet wrote Madame Cornuel's epitaph, ending up by bestowing on Ninon a high accolade:

> Finally, to make you in a few words
> Understand her* merit —
> She had the esteem of Lanclos.

But that same year Ninon's circle, which was fast being depleted of old friends, received new blood when two young abbés, Gédoyn and Fraguier, left the Jesuits and came to pay Ninon court. They had left a religious order for a salon which made of order a religion. Later Fraguier wrote:

> I knew Mademoiselle de Lanclos the last thirteen or fourteen years of her life . . . She had a mind and manners which excelled all others in attractiveness; and her probity was so pure that the mixture of charm and virtue made her a prodigy. If she had spent her life in the most important offices of state, she would not have had an old age more honorable, more respected than that which succeeded a life full of gallantry and love . . . It was her destiny to attract the most distinguished people of the Court and town . . . One would never have forgiven oneself for having hurt her in the slightest.
>
> There was a natural rapport, an intimate affection among all who beheld her . . . Her conversation was easy and light. The contrary wounded her, but she did not show it; she only revealed herself to her intimates. She perceived the good in the midst of a

* Madame Cornuel's.

thousand faults and cherished it. She had the confidence of all the world — in great matters as well as small.

All that she thought was well thought out. All that she said was well said. And all that she did was well done. Her house was the rendezvous of honorable people. And Mademoiselle de Lanclos, superior in some ways to the greatest geniuses, was always the most revered of all.

In 1695, Ninon's former foe, Madame de Sévigné, reported to her daughter, Madame de Grignan: "Women are now seeking out Mademoiselle de Lanclos the way men did in other days." And again: "Corbinelli tells me of the marvelous company of men he finds at Mademoiselle de Lanclos's." Ninon's health was getting frailer. She mentions it to Bonrepaus but still has the spirit to add that she will go out to dine with him "if the spices are spared." Her health caused concern to Madame de Sévigné's relative, Monsieur de Coulanges, who on February 3, 1696, writes to Madame de Sévigné, "Our lovable Lenclos has a cold which likes me not; one sees nothing but colds in town . . ." And again on February 19: ". . . Our poor Lenclos also has a low, slow fever, with a little heightening in the evening, and a sore throat which worries her friends." Later that year, Monsieur de Coulanges was unexpectedly mourning Madame de Sévigné, who died of smallpox while nursing her daughter through a long illness. Doubtless, Ninon was glad that long before Madame de Sévigné's death, the celebrated letter writer had forgiven her for filching her husband and son.

But Ninon's heart seemed almost perpetually sore now as tie after tie with a happier past dissolved. In 1696, La Bruyère, the famed satiric author of *Les Caractères,* died — not before paying Ninon one of her greatest tributes: "A beautiful woman who has all the qualities of an honnête homme is the most delicious of all. In her [Ninon] one finds all the merit of both sexes." Sixteen ninety-six also claimed the once robust Miossens. It pained her that such incomparable vigor was now stilled. She and Saint-Evremond were "writing the epitaph of the world" all right, as she had said they would some eight years earlier.

Death took a holiday in 1697, but Ninon was saddened to note that the stunningly liberal effort of the Jesuits to effect a rapprochement between Catholicism and Confucianism had been condemned by the theologians at the Sorbonne. Shades of the valorous struggle of Molière against obscurantism! She resolved to draw the matter of the criticism of the Jesuits' ecumenicity to the attention of Fontenelle. He must carry on the struggle against bigotry. She was getting very tired.

Paris was becoming cleaner. In 1697, an ordinance had been passed prohibiting the nocturnal practice of throwing out of windows all manner of filth — dirty water, urine, and excrement. Ninon heard with mild amusement the stories of the difficulty (and the peril) the police experienced in catching offenders. In 1698, Ninon's sailor son, La Boissière, age forty-five, married a Creole from Martinique, Marguerite de Cacqueray de Valmenière. It is not known if Ninon attended the wedding. Certainly if it took place in some naval port, Ninon was absent, for she was not going out much anymore in Paris, let alone traveling. "It falls to me alone," she had written Bonrepaus, "not to be able to nor want to change either friends or place." On fine days she would warm herself in the sunny gardens of the nearby Place Royale and feed the birds, whose descendants are there to this day. Perhaps Saint-Evremond was similarly watching his ducks in St. James Park in London. Ninon was still sending him messages. The following in 1700 is probably to Bonrepaus in London.

> . . . Since you have been good enough to tell Monsieur de Saint-Evremond the kind things you write me, I would lose much by substituting my pen for you. I would prefer that he be a bit hoodwinked.* You have seen the state of my body which is neither healthy nor sick. The spirit is almost the same but the friendship I have for him never changes . . .

From her window Ninon watched workmen going up and down the streets suspending lanterns from the facades of the houses; they were raised and lowered with the aid of a rope and pulley. It would be safer to walk at night but that would be for others, as Ninon now kept her house after dark.

In 1701, Ninon was jolted by the death of her old friend Madeleine de Scudéry, age ninety-four. Ninon had been seeking more and more comfort in the austere Seneca who taught acceptance of life *and* death. "To be no more and never to have been, are they not the same thing?" asked the Stoic. "Neither one nor the other is yours for the asking . . . If you could extend life, to what point would you extend it? Why these tears, these desires? . . . All is ordered inexorably . . . You will go the way of all things . . . There is no road which does not end."

Ninon seemed to get a kind of cold comfort out of this; not so Saint-Evremond. Alarmed by Ninon's immersion in Seneca, he had written, "You give an attractiveness to Seneca which he is not usually accorded." Elsewhere Saint-Evremond wrote,

---

* About her signs of old age, perhaps.

"His type of virtue frightens me, and after its contemplation the least wicked would abandon himself to voluptuousness . . . He speaks so much of death and leaves us with such black thoughts that I do all I can not to remember a word he says." Saint-Evremond added he would prefer Ninon devout to the "stiff and dry wisdom of Stoicism."

Ninon did not become devout. There is little evidence she did anything more than was necessary to secure herself Christian burial. Ninon had seen what had happened to Molière when he died. She left fifty francs ($100 to $250) to the priest who heard her confession "to say fifty masses for the repose of my soul," and the will started out in standard form — "In the name of the Father, the Son, and the Holy Ghost . . ."

In 1703, it was Saint-Evremond's turn. He never wavered in his anticlericalism, refusing the ministrations of a priest to the last. He even managed a little humor near the end. The priest was urging him "to reconcile himself" — with the Church, of course. To which the old man replied, "Willingly, reconcile me again, I pray you, with my appetite." His death cast a pall over Ninon. She could never reconcile herself to the fact that this light, which had guided her all through her life, was extinguished. She would read and reread his letter to her of 1685: "At my age, one hour of life well lived is to me more important than concern about a middling reputation." She knew by heart his ". . . life, of which eight days are worth more than eight centuries of glory after death." Ninon could not be comforted.

Saint-Evremond had few material things to leave. "I leave to the Executor [Lord Galway] the care of burying my body without Pomp . . . I bequeath to the poor French Refugees*

* Protestants who had fled France after the Revocation of the Edict of Nantes.

the sum of Twenty Pounds Sterling [$1000 approximately]. I also bequeath to the poor Roman Catholicks, or of any other Religion, the like sum of Twenty Pounds Sterling." * When Ninon made her will about a year later, she too forbade pomp. "For my burial, ten crowns [$60 to $150] in order that it be the simplest possible."

Saint-Evremond's instructions to be buried without pomp were carried out, but the English were more concerned about his reputation than he. He lies in Westminster Abbey, in the hallowed Poets' Corner, in the midst of the tombs of Chaucer, Spenser, and Cowley.

The same year that Saint-Evremond died, Gourville, about two years younger than Ninon, also breathed his last. Again Ninon knew acute grief. There were now none of her old friends left — except Madame de Maintenon, and she was as good as lost in the gloomy grandeur of Versailles. Ninon knew it was getting time to go. She put her affairs in order. "I give to Monsieur de Gourville, nephew of the late Monsieur de Gourville, for the obligations I have to his uncle, my house . . . and because I have always and personally loved him." Ninon was ever grateful to Gourville the elder for the opportunity he had given her, some forty years earlier, to be of service to him by holding safe his casket of gold crowns when he had been forced to flee. She provided liberally for her servants: 3000 francs ($6000 to $15,000) to her valet La Pierre, 2000 francs to his sister, her chambermaid, 200 francs to Catherine, the cook. "I forgot to say that I forbid La Pierre and his sister to go into mourning; if I wanted that, I would leave money for it . . ." She left 16,000 francs ($32,000 to $80,000) to the abbé de Tria-

* Translation by Des Maizeaux.

non-Lagrange to dispose of according to instructions not specified in the will. There is little doubt that this bequest was
for her son La Boissière. She also left substantial gifts of money
to her mother's relatives, as well as dresses and skirts, once
again requesting that the beneficiaries not put on mourning
"for the little legacy I have left them."

The notary Arouet, Ninon's executor, was Voltaire's father
— Arouet being almost an anagram of Voltaire. Ninon had
heard of the young Voltaire's precocity from her admirer, the
abbé de Châteauneuf. The will is dated December 19, 1704.
The following year the abbé de Châteauneuf who, Voltaire
states, was a great friend of his mother's, brought Voltaire, aged
eleven, to see Ninon, still as mentally alert as ever. "At last,"
Voltaire tells us, as if he had been trying to visit Ninon for
years, "they thought it good to take me to her house. The abbé
had the run of it." Writing to a member of the French Academy in 1752 he says:

> I reply to all your questions. The majority of the anecdotes
> about Mademoiselle de Lanclos are true, but many are false. The
> article in her will of which you speak is not fiction; she left me
> 2000 francs* [$4000 to $10,000]. I was a child; I had done some bad
> verses which they said were good for my age. The abbé de Châ-
> teauneuf . . . had brought me to her, and I had pleased her —
> how I don't know . . .
>
> She urged me to do some verses; better she should have urged
> me not to . . . The career of Ninon, who didn't do any verses†
> and who enjoyed and gave much pleasure, is certainly preferable
> to mine."

* Ninon's will says 1000 francs
† Hardly any.

The dramatic confrontation — the wrinkled, bespectacled Ninon encouraging the little Voltaire to write poetry, while the awe-struck child kept silent, taking everything in — is probably the last recorded incident in her life. On October 17, 1705, Ninon died. The abbé de Châteauneuf composed her epitaph:

> There is nothing which death does not conquer,
> Ninon, who for nearly a century, served love
> Has at last finished her days.
> She was both the honor and the shame of her century.
>   Fickle in love
> Delicate in her pleasures,
> To her friends, faithful and wise
> To her lovers, tender and volatile.
>
>     .     .     .     .     .     .     .     .
>
>   In life she had great faith,
> But, leaving nothing to chance,
> She had no belief in an afterworld.

Ninon was buried in the church of Saint Paul. It was destroyed in the Revolution. What became of her physical remains is uncertain, although they may still lie in the basement of the razed church beneath the pavement. But France and some other European countries have never lost sight of her image. Unlike many other famous people who die, are forgotten, and are then resurrected, she never seems to have gone into total eclipse. Saint-Simon tells us, "L'Enclos lived much beyond eighty, always healthy, visited, respected . . . Her death made news." From then on interest in her, if anything, grew. The public must have been very curious about her because there followed a flood of reminiscences, several by abbés for whom Ninon evidently exercised a special attraction. The abbés Châteauneuf, Fraguier, Gédoyn, and D'Olivet all penned paeans. "The most proper mothers," recalled D'Olivet, "maneuvered to gain admission for their sons . . . into this amiable society [Ninon's], which they regarded as the center of good company."

In 1751, a clergyman wrote to Voltaire asking information about Ninon. "I am very glad, monsieur," replied Voltaire, "that a minister of the Holy Gospel desires news of a priestess of Venus. I have not the honor of being of your religion . . . but I have let the holy time of Easter slip by before replying to your questions, assuming that you would not have wanted to read my letter during Holy Week." Then follows a short biography of Ninon occupying several pages. The letter concludes: "I hear that they have just published two new *Memoirs* on the life of this philosopher [Ninon]. If this vogue continues, there will soon be as many histories of Ninon as of Louis XIV . . . Say with me a little *de profundis* for her. I have the honor to be . . ."

Some twenty years later a minor literary controversy arose. A Russian, Count Schouwalof, wrote such a good "Letter to Ninon" (in verse) that Frederick the Great of Prussia was sure that Voltaire was playing another of his tricks — attributing his own writings to somebody else.

*From Frederick to Voltaire (at Ferney)*

Potsdam, July 30, 1774.
. . . We have received here the verses of a so-called Russian to Ninon de Lanclos . . . All that comes from the factory of the patriarch of Ferney [Voltaire].

It took more than one letter from Voltaire to convince the king, who several times wrote back he still strongly suspected

Voltaire had a hand in the poem. A member of the Academy did too.

Voltaire's contemporary, and pet aversion, Rousseau, did not by any means have unqualified admiration for Ninon.

"Why," Rousseau demands, "do you say that modesty makes women false? Those that shed it most, are they nevertheless more genuine than others? Far from it; they are a thousand times more false . . . I know only of Mademoiselle de Lenclos whom one can cite as a known exception to these remarks. Moreover Mademoiselle de Lenclos was considered a prodigy.

"In her contempt for the virtues of her sex, she had, they say, preserved those of ours; they vaunt her sincerity, her uprightness, her dependability in business matters, her fidelity in friendship; finally to put the finishing touches on the portrait of her glory, they say she made herself a man. Very good. But with all her lofty reputation, I wouldn't have wanted this man either for my friend or my mistress."

Fear and lack of self-confidence may explain Rousseau's rejection of Ninon as both mistress and friend. The neurotic, sickly Rousseau was no Lothario; as a lover, he might easily have been frightened by a person of Ninon's erotic power. With his perverseness and persecution complex, he would likely have been uncomfortable with Ninon even as a friend. He may have realized that she would probably not have put up with his petulant thin-skinnedness. It is notable that the main woman in his life, with whom he lived for years, was an unlettered, unattractive drudge with whom he could feel superior and whom he often treated like a dog. If he had behaved himself, Ninon would probably have welcomed him to her salon — as she did all men of intellect who had manners. But the very thought that Ninon would not have considered him as a lover may have so riled Rousseau that he seems to have felt he must get even with her by banishing her utterly.

A list of the tributes to Ninon would fill chapters. Interest in her spread far beyond the confines of France — Holland, Prussia, Russia, England. "Old Lady Sandwich," wrote the English letter writer, antiquarian, and novelist, Horace Walpole, on July 26, 1757, "has died at Paris and milord has given me the portrait she had of Ninon de Lenclos . . ." Walpole had a famous printing press at Strawberry Hill and itched to get his hands on Ninon's letters to Lady Sandwich. In September 1757, he wrote Lady Hervey in French, beseeching her help:

> . . . In brief, madame, I am in that critical pass of either losing the portrait of Mademoiselle de Lenclos, or having both that portrait and her letters to Lady Sandwich . . . Think how proud I'd be to print at Strawberry Hill the original letters of Ninon! . . . A cause like ours would transmit, I should think, ardor to Lady Strafford herself. If she would help us to regain *Notre-Dame-des-Amours,* I shall add saint Raoul * to my calendar.

The canonization of Ninon was on its way. She would have smiled at *"Notre-Dame-des-Amours."* Walpole never got the letters; they are lost. Ninon was probably at her best in them — writing animatedly in her late seventies to the stimulating Lady Sandwich, one-third her age.

Just as Ninon had at times during her life been outrageously persecuted, so after her death was she the object of extravagant adulation. Louis XV's queen, Marie Leckzinska, no femme fatale, was finding the competition of the royal mistresses very

---

* Favorite cat of Lady Strafford's.

tough. She seems to have wanted to communicate with, perhaps consult oracularly, the legendary epitome of feminine allure.

"The queen," writes the marquis d'Argenson in 1751, "is falling into a superstitious devoutness. At all times she goes to see the Beautiful Darling: it is a skull. She claims to have that of Mademoiselle Ninon Lenclos. Several ladies of the Court who pretend to devoutness have similar skulls at their homes. They dress them with ribbons and coifs, they light them with lanterns, and they remain a half hour in meditation before them."

Saint Ninon! Voltaire could have dispensed with his *de profundis*. Adulation was mixed with superstition, adulation was mixed with vulgarity. Ninon's appeal seems to have had a broad spectrum as we may see in the following popular poem of the early eighteenth century.

> After having lived 100 years
> Here lies the famous Ninon
> Who has placed herself, despite her c . . .*
> In the ranks of illustrious men.

The tributes continue right down to our time. In *Le Deuxième Sexe,* Simone de Beauvoir has written:

The Frenchwoman whose independence seems to me the most like that of a man is perhaps Ninon de Lenclos, seventeenth-century woman of wit and beauty. Paradoxically, those women who exploit their femininity to the limit create for themselves a situation almost equivalent to that of a man . . . Not only do they make their own living like men, but they exist in a circle almost

---

* The dots are in the original.

exclusively masculine; free in behavior and conversation, they can attain — like Ninon de Lenclos — to the rarest intellectual liberty. The most distinguished are often surrounded by writers and artists who are bored by "good" women.

Emile Magne states that no woman ever received so much notice from so many illustrious pens as Ninon. He might have added "and un-illustrious." She has been celebrated in poetry, plays, operas, operettas, spurious letters, novels, biographies, articles — of very uneven quality. She appears as the subject, or victim, of at least twenty-three theatrical pieces with names such as *Molière chez Ninon,* 1788; *Ninon de Lenclos et le prisonnier masqué,* 1806; *Le Fils de Ninon,* 1834; *Nanon, Ninon and Maintenon, ou les trois boudoirs,* 1844; *Un duel chez Ninon,* 1849; *Un soir chez Ninon,* 1911. Her name appears between that of Francis Bacon and Pascal in M. Lincoln Shuster's collection — *The World's Great Letters,* 1940. Until but recently the movies seem mercifully to have left her alone. But in 1964 a film, *Cyrano et D'Artagnan,* has both of those superb swordsmen engage Ninon and Marion de l'Orme in an amorous duel. Not satisfied with this exercise in unbridled imagination, the plot adds to Ninon's roster of lovers — as if there were not enough already — none other than Descartes, the author, *inter alia,* of *Discours de la méthode (Treatise on Method).* After Descartes leaves, the inquisitive Marion, in a line worthy of Ninon, asks, *"Et sa méthode?"* (And his technique?) Of course the incident is purest fiction. It is doubtful whether Ninon ever knew Descartes even socially, let alone in the biblical sense. Besides, she was a loyal devotee of Gassendi, Descartes's arch philosophical foe. Ninon might have betrayed a lover, but never a philosophy.

Sainte-Beuve, it will be recalled, writing in mid-nineteenth

century, asserted that Ninon was no less than one of the historic
links between the emancipated thinkers of the sixteenth and
eighteenth centuries. He goes on to pay tribute to her
uniqueness, not, however, without an accompanying Victorian
wag of the finger:

> And now, when one has spoken of Ninon with fairness, with
> charm, and without making too much of the scandalous . . . and
> of the distressing in the wildness of her early years, we must never
> forget that such a destiny, unique and singular, does not happen
> twice, that it depends on an incomparable good fortune, aided by
> a genius for altogether special conduct, and that any woman, who,
> following her [Ninon's] example would try to treat love cavalierly
> and at the same time consider friendship as sacred, would run the
> great risk of falling by the wayside . . .

This tribute, coming from such an Olympian critic, would
no doubt have pleased Ninon. But there are strong grounds for
suspecting that, given her basic simplicity, she never set her
sights to walk upon the stage of history. Ninon, whom some
insist on calling a courtesan, never went lusting after fame, fortune, or false gods. There was nothing emptier, she had written the marquis de Lassay in the twilight of her life, than "the
buckler of Achilles, the baton of a marshal of France, or the
crozier of a bishop." Her aims were much more modest, but
focused on what she regarded as of fundamental moral importance.

Ninon used to reread Saint-Evremond's letters. The last
(preserved) letter, that of January 1, 1700, went:

> . . . You say you are old with all the graceful humor and wit of
> young people. I have a curiosity that you might be able to sat-
> isfy: when you remember your youth, does not the remembrance

of the past give you certain ideas as far removed from the languor of indolence as from the storms of passion? Do you not feel in your heart a secret opposition to the tranquillity that you imagine you have given to your mind?

> . . . May the generous Fates above
> Grant you thirty years of Love
> And of Philosophy.*

That is what I wish you this first day of the year, the day when those who have nothing to give, send wishes instead of gifts.

The Fates granted her five years, not thirty. Ninon was evidently clear enough the night of her death to have composed a poem:

> I put your consolations by,
> And care not for the hopes you give;
> Since I am old enough to die,
> Why should I longer wish to live? †

From her valedictory poem it is clear that to the extent that anyone can ever be ready, Ninon was ready to accept the inevitable. What disease she died of is unknown. Nor is there any evidence of a deathbed conversion. Ninon, apparently unafraid, remained an esprit fort to the end. Saint-Evremond, her teacher and true love, would have approved. Equally unrecorded is whether Ninon, along with the duchesse de Chevreuse, realized her hope of conversing with her friends in an afterworld.

The tradition says that Ninon's passing was gentle — just a sleep and a forgetting.

* Translation from *Daughters of Eve*, by Gamaliel Bradford.
† Translation of John Hayward in *Letters of Saint-Evremond*.

# Bibliography

Adam, Antoine. *Histoire de la littérature française au XVII^e siècle.* Vols. 2, 3, 4. Paris: 1957.

———. *Les Libertins au 17^e siècle.* Paris: 1964.

Arnaud, Lella. *Ninon de Lenclos.* Paris: 1958.

Auger, Louis-Simon, ed. *Lettres de Madame de Maintenon.* Paris: 1815.

Austin, Cecil. *The Immortal Ninon.* London: 1927.

Baumal, Francis. *Le Féminisme au temps de Molière.* Paris: 1923.

Blondel, Jacques François. *Architecture françoise.* Paris: 1752.

Boudhors, Charles H. *Revue d'histoire littéraire de la France.* Vol. 33. Paris: 1926.

Bradford, Gamaliel. *Daughters of Eve.* New York: 1930.

Brantôme, seigneur de. *Vies des dames galantes.* Paris: 1857.

Bret, Antoine. *Mémoires sur la vie de Mademoiselle de Lenclos.* Amsterdam: 1755.

Breton, Guy. *Histoire d'amour de l'histoire de France.* Vols. 3, 4. Paris: 1957.

Bussy-Rabutin. *Histoire amoureuse des Gaules.* 3 vols. Paris: 1856.

Capefigue, M. *Ninon de Lenclos et les précieuses de la Place Royale.* Paris: 1864.

Chasles, Emile. "Ninon de Lenclos." *Les Emaux de Petitot.* Paris: 1862.

Châteauneuf, abbé de. *Dialogue sur la musique des Anciens.* Paris: 1725.

Colombey, Emile. *Ruelles, salons et cabarets.* Paris: 1858.

———. *Correspondance authentique de Ninon de Lenclos.* Paris: 1886.

Creuzé de Lesser, C. C. Auguste. *Ninon de Lenclos ou l'epicuréisme.* Paris: 1800.

Day, Lillian. *Ninon.* New York: 1957.

Derys, Gaston. *L'Ami de Ninon de Lenclos.* Paris: 1910.

Diderot, Denis. *L'Encyclopédie.* Paris: 1755.

Douxmenil. *Mémoires pour servir á l'histoire de la vie de Mademoiselle de Lenclos.* Edited by G. M. Napy. Paris: 1908.

Dulong, Claude. "Ninon de Lenclos et ses amis." *Revue de Paris.* Paris: 1964.

Durant, Will and Ariel. *The Age of Reason Begins.* New York: 1960.

——. *The Age of Louis XIV.* New York: 1963.

Dyssord, Jacques. *Ninon de Lenclos: courtisane et honnête homme.* Paris: 1936.

Endore, Guy. *Voltaire, Voltaire.* New York: 1961.

Epton, Nina. *Love and the French.* New York: 1959.

Estey, Norbert. *All My Sins.* New York: 1954.

Ferval, Claude. *Ninon et son cortège.* Paris: 1925.

Frégault, Guy. *François Bigot.* Montreal: 1948.

Gaiffe, Félix. *L'Envers du Grand Siècle.* Paris: 1924.

Galopin, Arnould. *Ninon de Lenclos.* Paris: 1911.

Gédoyn, abbé. *Oeuvres diverses.* Paris: 1745.

Girard, Charles. "Ninon de Lenclos" (extrait de *L'Histoire de Saint-Evremond*). Paris: 1865.

Girardet, Philippe. *Le Destin passionné de Ninon de L'Enclos.* Paris: 1959.

Gobineau, Marcel. *Ninon de Lanclos.* Paris: 1957.

Gondoin, Jules. "Education amoureuse: Ninon de Lenclos et le marquis Charles de Sévigné." *La Nouvelle Revue* 161 (1939): 87–100.

Goudal, Jean. *Ninon de Lanclos.* Paris: 1937.

Gourmont, Rémy de. *Promenades littéraires.* 3d ed. Paris: 1906.

Hall, Geoffrey F. *Moths Around the Flame.* London: 1935.

Hayes, Helen Kendrick. *The Real Ninon de l'Enclos.* London: 1908.

Hazard, Paul. *The European Mind.* London: 1953.

Hillairet, Jacques. *Evocations du vieux Paris.* Paris: 1953–1958.

Houssaye, Arsène. Preface to *La Cour de Ninon*, by Emile Colombey. Paris: 1858.

Humphreys, Arthur L. *Ninon de Lenclos*. London: 1904.

Jacob, Paul L. *Marion de Lorme et Ninon de Lenclos*. Paris: 1859.

*Journal du voyage de deux jeunes Hollandais à Paris en 1656–1658*. Paris: 1899.

Lachèvre, Frédéric. *Les Derniers Libertins*. Paris: 1924.

Lannau, Rolland A. *Les Grandes Amoureuses au couvent*. Paris: 1862.

Lanson, Gustave and Tuffrau, Paul. *Histoire de la littérature française*. Paris: 1931.

Lenotre, G. "Un Peintre de nu." *Le Temps* (May 9, 1925).

Le Roux de Lincy, Antoine-Jean-Victor. *Les Femmes célèbres de l'ancienne France*. Paris: 1847–1858.

Lewis, H. W. *The Sunset of the Splendid Century*. London: 1954.

*L'Intermédiaire des chercheurs et curieux* 88: (April 20–30, 1925): 330, 435, 436; 89 (1926): cols 666, 725–26.

Loménie de Brienne, Louis-Henri. *Mémoires*. Paris: 1916.

Loomis, Stanley. *Du Barry*. New York: 1959.

Magne, Emile. *Madame de La Suze et la société précieuse*. Paris: 1908.

——. *Le Plaisant Abbé de Boisrobert*. Paris: 1909.

——. *Madame de Châtillon*. Paris: 1910.

——. *Une Amie inconnu de Molière*. Paris: 1922.

——. *La Vie quotidienne au temps de Louis XIII*. Paris: 1942.

——. *Ninon de Lanclos*. Paris: 1948.

Maurois, André. *A History of France*. Translated by Henry L. Binsse. New York: 1960.

Michaud, Louis Gabriel. *Biographie universelle ancienne et moderne*. Paris: 1811–1862.

Mirecourt, Eugène de. *Confessions de Ninon de Lenclos*. Paris: 1864.

Mitford, Nancy. *Voltaire in Love*. London: 1957.

——. "Rooms for Improvement." *Horizon* (November 1961).

Mongrédien, Georges. *Marion de Lorme à la Place Royale — Oeuvres Libres*. Paris: 1921.

——. *Libertins et amoureuses*. Paris: 1929.

————. *La Vie quotidienne sous Louis XIV.* Paris: 1948.

————. *La Vie de société au XVII^e et XVIII^e siècles.* Paris: 1950.

Motteville, Madame de. *Mémoires.* Paris: 1855.

Nolhac, Pierre de. *Quelques portraits féminins.* Extraits des oeuvres de Sainte-Beuve.

Nyabongo, Virginia Simmons. "Madame de Maintenon and Her Contribution to Education." *French Review* (January 1949).

Perrens, F.-T. *Les Libertins en France au 17^e.* Paris: 1896.

Pintard, René. *Le Libertinage érudit dans la première moitié du XVII^e siècle.* Paris: 1943.

Quatemère de Roissy. *Histoire de Ninon de Lenclos.* Paris: 1824.

Reynier, Gustav. *La Femme au 17^e siècle.* Paris: 1929.

Roux, Amédée. *Les Emaux de Petitot.* Paris: 1862.

Rowsell, Mary C. *Ninon de L'Enclos and Her Century.* London: 1910.

Sackville-West, Victoria. *Daughter of France.* London: 1959.

Sainte-Beuve, Charles Augustin. *Oeuvres II, Portraits littéraires.* Paris: 1844.

————. *Causeries de lundi.* Translated by E. J. Techmann. Paris: 1849.

————. *Nouveaux lundis.* Paris: 1863.

Saint-Evremond, Charles de Marguetel de Saint Denis, seigneur de. *Oeuvres Choisies.* Paris: 1881.

————. *Letters of Saint-Evremond.* Translated by John Hayward. London: 1930.

Saint-Simon. *Mémoires.* Paris: 1897.

————. *Saint-Simon at Versailles.* Translated and selected by Lucy Norton. New York: 1958.

Sanders, Joan. *La Petite: Louise de la Vallière.* Boston: 1959.

Sévigné, Madame de. *Lettres.* Paris: 1818.

————. *The Best Letters of Madame de Sévigné.* Translated anonymously. Edited with Introduction by Edward P. Anderson. Chicago: 1904.

Somaize, Antoine Baudeau, sieur de. *Le Grand Dictionnaire des précieuses.* Paris: 1661.

Spink, John Stephenson. *French Free-Thought from Gassendi to Voltaire.* London: 1960.

Steegmuller, Francis. *The Grand Mademoiselle.* New York: 1956.

Tallemant des Réaux. *Historiettes.* Paris: 1854.

————. *Love-Tales from Tallemant.* Translated anonymously. London: 1925.

Tinan, Jean de. *Exemple de Ninon de Lenclos amoureuse.* Paris: 1898.

Touchard-Lafosse, Georges. *The Triumph of Madame de Maintenon.* The Rollicking Chronicles, vols. 2–4. Translated by Henry C. Sneyd London: 1928–33.

Voltaire. "Lettre sur Mademoiselle de Lenclos." *Oeuvres.* Paris: 1829–40.

Wakeman, Henry O. *The Ascendancy of France 1598–1715.* London: 1959.

Walckenaer, Monsieur le Baron. *Mémoires de Madame de Sévigné.* Paris: 1842.

Weyl, Fernand [Nozière, Fernand]. "La Vie amoureuse de Ninon de Lenclos." *Leurs Amours.* Paris: 1928.

Wrangel, Fredrik Ulrik. *Première Visite de Christine de Suède à la cour de France 1656.* Paris: 1930.

# Index